Airport

In recent years, the airport sector has moved from an industry characterised by public sector ownership and national requirements into a new era of airport management, which is beginning to be dominated by the private sector and international players. Airports are now complex enterprises that require a wide range of business competencies and skills to meet the needs of their users, just as with any other industry. Moreover, deregulation of air transport markets has made the airport sector much more competitive and given airports greater incentives to develop innovative, proactive and aggressive marketing strategies so that they can reap the benefits of these developments. New types of airline business model, such as low cost carriers, have emerged through deregulation; in many cases these require airport marketers to adopt a completely different approach and have encouraged a further deviation from past practice. The travelling public is also becoming more experienced, and is generally placing greater demands on the airport operator to deliver a quality product at a time when more stringent controls, especially as regards security, have been introduced.

This book fills an important need for an up-to-date, accessible and in-depth textbook that introduces students and practitioners to the principles and practice of airport marketing, as well as the major changes and future marketing challenges facing the airport sector. It applies principles of marketing to the airport industry, and examines airport marketing and its environment, how to define and measure the market for airport services, airport marketing planning and individual elements of the airport marketing mix (product, price, promotion and distribution). The book integrates key elements of marketing theory with airport marketing in practice. Each chapter contains extensive industry examples from different types of airport around the world to build on the theoretical base of the subject and show real-life applications.

The dynamic nature of the airport industry requires students and practitioners to have a thorough contemporary appreciation of airport marketing issues and challenges. This comprehensive and accessible textbook, written by two airport marketing experts, satisfies this need and is essential reading for air transport students and future managers.

Nigel Halpern is Associate Professor at Molde University College. Nigel is also Senior Research Scientist with Molde Research Institute and Visiting Research Fellow with the Centre for Tourism Research at the University of Westminster. He was previously Principal Lecturer and Subject Group Director in Aviation at the Centre for Civil Aviation, London Metropolitan University. Nigel currently teaches and conducts research and consultancy in transport and tourism, focusing largely on airport marketing.

Anne Graham is Reader in Air Transport and Tourism at the University of Westminster, having previously worked in air transport consultancy. She is Editor-in-chief of the *Journal of Air Transport Management* and the author of *Managing Airports*. She has been involved in air transport teaching, research and consultancy for over 25 years.

Airport Marketing

Nigel Halpern and Anne Graham

Routledge
Taylor & Francis Group

LONDON AND NEW YORK

First published 2013
by Routledge
2 Park Square, Milton Park, Abingdon, Oxon OX14 4RN

Simultaneously published in the USA and Canada
by Routledge
711 Third Avenue, New York, NY 10017

Routledge is an imprint of the Taylor & Francis Group, an informa business

British Library Cataloguing in Publication Data
A catalogue record for this book is available from the British Library

Library of Congress Cataloging in Publication Data
Halpern, Nigel.
    Airport marketing / Nigel Halpern, Anne Graham.
        pages cm
    Includes bibliographical references and index.
    1. Airports—Economic aspects. 2. Airports—Management.
    3. Aeronautics, Commercial—Economic aspects. I. Graham, Anne. II. Title.
    HE9797.4.E3H35 2013
    387.7'360688—dc23   2012046166

ISBN: 978-0-415-52938-9 (hbk)
ISBN: 978-0-415-52939-6 (pbk)
ISBN: 978-0-203-11790-3 (ebk)

Typeset in Sabon and Frutiger
by Keystroke, Station Road, Codsall, Wolverhampton

MIX
Paper from
responsible sources
FSC® C013056
www.fsc.org

Printed and bound in Great Britain by
TJ International Ltd, Padstow, Cornwall

Contents

List of figures vii
List of tables ix
Preface xi
Acknowledgements xiii
List of abbreviations xv

1 Introduction   **1**

    1.1   Evolution of airport marketing 1
    1.2   Approach to airport marketing in this book 7
          References 11

2 The airport marketing environment   **13**

    2.1   Introduction to the airport marketing environment 13
    2.2   The airport's microenvironment 15
    2.3   The airport's macroenvironment 24
          References 42

3 The market for airport services   **45**

    3.1   The airport's customers 45
    3.2   Airport market segmentation 52
          References 61

4 Airport marketing research   **63**

    4.1   Definition and the role of marketing research 63
    4.2   The nature of airport marketing research 65
    4.3   The ASD process 66
    4.4   Secondary research 71
    4.5   Primary research 79
          References 87

5 Airport marketing planning   **88**

    5.1   Introduction to the marketing planning process 88
    5.2   The airport marketing planning process 89

Contents

| | 5.3 | Example airport marketing programmes | 115 |
| | | References | 115 |

6 | **The airport product** | | **117** |

	6.1	Definition of the airport product	117
	6.2	Features of the airport product and its controllability	120
	6.3	The airport brand	125
	6.4	Evaluating the product on offer	130
	6.5	Planning airport products	133
		References	140

7 | **Airport pricing** | | **142** |

	7.1	Factors that can affect airport pricing decisions	142
	7.2	Sources of airport cost and revenue	144
	7.3	Types of airport user charge	147
	7.4	Economic regulatory environment	156
	7.5	Incentive mechanisms	159
		References	167

8 | **Promotion of airports** | | **169** |

	8.1	The promotional mix	169
	8.2	The changing communications landscape	186
	8.3	Integrated and effective marketing communications	188
		References	190

9 | **Airport distribution** | | **193** |

	9.1	Introduction to airport distribution	193
	9.2	Evolution of airport distribution	195
	9.3	Approaches to airport distribution	195
	9.4	CRM	209
		References	217

Index | | | **219** |

Figures

1.1   Change in marketing staff at selected UK regional airports, 1991–1997   5
1.2   Methods used by airports to market themselves to airlines   6
1.3   Marketing expenditure at US large hub airports, 2011   7
2.1   The marketing environment   14
2.2   Organisational chart for Copenhagen Airports   15
2.3   Organisational chart for Dallas/Fort Worth International Airport   16
2.4   Organisational chart for CAG   17
2.5   Organisational chart for Dubai Airports   18
2.6   International airport passengers at African airports by month,
        2010–2012   25
2.7   Scheduled RPKs by alliance, 2011   30
2.8   RPKs by airline type, 2003 and 2011   31
2.9   Economic growth and airport passenger demand, 1996–2011   32
2.10 Forecast growth rates of GDP, RPKs and RTKs by region, 2011–2031   33
2.11 Share of airport passengers by global regions, 2009 and 2029   34
2.12 Jet kerosene price and fuel as a proportion of total airline operating
        cost, 2002–2012   35
3.1   Accompanying visitors at Los Angeles International Airport by purpose
        of trip and type of passenger, 2006   47
3.2   Key positioning strategies for airports in Europe   60
4.1   Stages in the ASD process   67
4.2   UK CAA passenger survey for London Heathrow Airport   74
4.3   Types of survey performed in the last five years at US airports   81
4.4   London City Airport Budapest questionnaire   82
5.1   Main stages in the marketing planning process   88
5.2   Portfolio analysis models   92
6.1   The airport product for airlines   118
6.2   The airport product for passengers   119
6.3   Homepage of Turin Airport   123
6.4   Homepage of Gold Coast Airport   124
6.5   Airport logos   128
6.6   Importance–performance grid   132
6.7   The passenger experience at the airport   133
6.8   LCC product preferences   136

6.9 Advert for family-orientated product features at London Heathrow
     Airport   138
7.1 Factors affecting airport pricing decisions   143
7.2 Total airport revenue by region and source, 2010   146
7.3 Worldwide airport revenue by item, 2010   146
7.4 Main mechanisms for regulating airport charges   157
8.1 The promotional mix   170
8.2 Castellón Airport sponsorship of Villarreal Football Club   170
8.3 Fort Smith Regional Airport 'Simply Fly Fort Smith' campaign   171
8.4 Promotional leaflet used by Pajala-Ylläs Airport   172
8.5 Airport banners on anna.aero, October 2012   174
8.6 Swedavia World Routes advertisement   176
8.7 Singapore Changi Airport '2x7%' campaign   178
8.8 Prince George Airport advertisement for Facebook   181
8.9 Social media used by airports worldwide, as of year-end 2010   183
8.10 'Check-In to Great Deals at DFW Airport' social media campaign   184
8.11 London Heathrow Airport advertising campaigns, summer 2011   187
9.1 Distribution structure of an airport   194
9.2 Freedoms and possible restrictions of Council Directive 96/97/EC 201
9.3 Ground handling market at airports in Europe, 1996 and 2010   202
9.4 Frankfurt Hahn Airport's homepage   209
9.5 Comarch's CRM suite for airports   210
9.6 FlyDBQ Rewards programme   213
9.7 Bristol Airport Rewards   214
9.8 RIX Club   214
9.9 iPhone screenshots for myLJLA   216

Tables

1.1 Expenditure by US commercial service airports on marketing, advertising
    and promotions, 2011   6
1.2 Characteristics of a service and implications for airport marketing   7
2.1 Suppliers of airport services at Humberside Airport and East Midlands
    Airport, 2011   19
2.2 Stakeholders at Amsterdam Schiphol Airport, 2012   23
2.3 Stakeholders at London Heathrow Airport, 2012   23
2.4 Examples of airport privatisations   27
2.5 Use of self-service, mobile and social network services by airports in
    Europe, 2011   38
2.6 British social attitudes survey, 2003–2011   40
2.7 Factors likely to influence future scenarios for aviation in the UK   41
3.1 Airport information provided on The Route Shop and Routes Online
    websites for potential airlines   49
3.2 Factors influencing cargo operators' choice of airport   49
3.3 Reasons for passenger airport choice at UK airports (% respondents),
    2011   51
3.4 Reasons for passenger airport choice at Washington Airports
    (% respondents), 2009   51
3.5 Segmentation variables for key airport customers   53
3.6 Factors influencing LCCs' choice of airport   54
3.7 Passenger segmentation variables related to trip characteristics at
    Frankfurt Airport, 2011   57
3.8 Passenger segmentation variables related to trip characteristics at
    Athens International Airport, 2010   58
3.9 Passenger lifestyle segmentation based on demographic variables at
    Dallas/Fort Worth International Airport, 2009   59
3.10 Passenger segmentation related to shopping behaviour at selected
    European airports   59
4.1 Typical information provided by airport marketers for airlines at ASD
    meetings   70
4.2 Examples of types of data obtained from BSP sources used by Nice Côte
    d'Azur Airport to support its ASD activities in 2012   72

4.3	Examples of traffic data used by Nice Côte d'Azur Airport to support its ASD activities in 2012	73
4.4	Most popular airport survey methods	86
5.1	Sydney Airport's corporate intentions	90
5.2	Substitution possibilities at a number of airports in Australia	94
5.3	SWOT analysis for Muskoka Airport	98
5.4	SWOT analysis for Cardiff International Airport	99
5.5	Most common SWOT factors cited by British Columbia's northern airports	100
5.6	Example airport marketing objectives	102
5.7	Selection of agreements made between airports during 2012	104
5.8	Example marketing programme for an airport	110
5.9	Example marketing programme for an airport	112
6.1	Categories of brand names	126
6.2	Proportion of airports in each region that use each name category	129
6.3	Example MCTs at airports, September 2012	135
7.1	Worldwide airport operating costs by item (2010) and area (2009)	145
7.2	Proportion of non-aeronautical revenue at airports worldwide by source (%), 2010	147
7.3	Cost-based principles for determining airport charges	148
7.4	Malaysia Airports PSC, 2012	149
7.5	Nairobi Jomo Kenyatta International Airport landing and take-off charges, 2012	150
7.6	BSCA landing charge discounts (scheduled or charter flights), 2012	151
7.7	Macau International Airport aircraft parking fees, 2012	151
7.8	Tallinn Airport ground handling charges, 2012	153
7.9	Agreement between Ryanair and BSCA	160
7.10	Summary of EC guidelines on airport start-up aid	161
7.11	Example airport incentive schemes offering discounts, as of 2012	163
7.12	Phoenix Sky Harbor International Airport marketing support, 2012	165
8.1	Categories of social media used by airports	182
8.2	Summary of promotional tools	185
9.1	Levels of congestion at airports	198
9.2	Role of airports in slot allocation	199
9.3	Key attributes of successful concession programmes	204
9.4	Main features of Airport U	215

Preface

The idea of writing this book came up during a meeting in London a few years ago. We were due to discuss a different airport-related project but the need for a comprehensive and up-to-date book on airport marketing arose and it was not long before we had put pen to paper. We have both developed a passionate interest in airport marketing during the last 20 years or so; something that has surprised friends and family, who are quick to ask, 'Do airports do any marketing?' This book provides a resounding 'yes' in answer, demonstrating how marketing has become an important business discipline for airports during the last few decades. We have tried to produce a book that applies principles of marketing to the airport industry, integrating key elements of marketing theory with airport marketing in practice. We hope that after reading it you will also share our passionate interest in airport marketing, and agree that marketing has become a vital tool for airports seeking to create value for their customers and to build strong relationships.

31 October 2012

Nigel Halpern
Molde University College, Norway

Anne Graham
University of Westminster, UK

Acknowledgements

Writing a book of this nature is not possible without the support and cooperation of a range of people. We would like to thank the publisher, Routledge – and in particular Emma Travis, Carol Barber, Philippa Mullins and Lindsey Hall – for showing a keen interest in our proposed book and for their patience, support and encouragement along the way.

We would like to thank the many students and practitioners we have encountered over the years, who have introduced us to the fascinating world of airports and have contributed to our knowledge and understanding of airports and airport marketing. We would also like to thank the many airports, airport authorities, advertising agencies, and aviation industry agencies and associations that have responded with interest and enthusiasm to our requests for information, and have provided kind permission to reproduce images of their work, many of which are included in this book. These include: Airport U, Billund Airport, Changi Airport Group, Christchurch International Airport Limited, Cologne Bonn Airport, Dallas/Fort Worth International Airport, Doncaster Sheffield Airport, Dubuque Regional Airport, Fort Smith Regional Airport, Frankfurt Hahn Airport, Gold Coast Airport, Liverpool John Lennon Airport, London City Airport, London Heathrow Airport, Malta International Airport, Marseille Provence Airport, masius, Moroch, Pajala-Ylläs Airport, Prince George Airport, Queensland Airports Limited, SAGAT, Subside Sports, Swedavia, TAV Airports Holding Company, TAV Monastir, Tornedalenmedia, Turin Airport, Vincent Lopresti, Wellington Airport and Wichita Airport Authority. We would also like to thank Rafael Echevarne of ACI World, who helped with the proposal for this book, and the UK Civil Aviation Authority (CAA) for kindly agreeing for their passenger survey to be reproduced. Further details about the survey can be sought from the UK CAA, Aviation Intelligence, http://www.caa.co.uk, Tel: +44 20 7453 6280/6277.

Last but not least, we would like to thank family and friends for their support and understanding, and for putting up with the disruption to their lives while we have been writing this book; in particular, Anne-Merete, Leo, Felix, Ian, Lorna, Callum and Ewan.

Abbreviations

4 Cs	Customer, cost, communication, convenience
4 Ps	Product, price, promotion, place
7 Ps	Product, price, promotion, place, physical evidence, processes, people
AAAE	American Association of Airport Executives
A-CDM	Airport-collaborative decision-making
ACI	Airports Council International
AdP	Aéroports de Paris
AEA	Association of European Airlines
AENA	Spanish Airports and Air Navigation
AMA	American Marketing Association
ANOVA	Analysis of variance
AOPA	Aircraft Owners and Pilots Association
APD	Air passenger duty
ARI	Aer Rianta International
ASA	Air service agreement
ASD	Air service development
ASEAN	Association of Southeast Asian Nations
ASQ	Airport service quality
ATM	Air traffic management
B2B	Business-to-business
B2C	Business-to-consumer
BCG	Boston Consulting Group
BOT	Build–operate–transfer
BRIC	Brazil, Russia, India and China
BSCA	Brussels South Charleroi Airport
BSP	Billing and settlement plan
BTS	US Bureau of Transportation Statistics
CAA	Civil Aviation Authority
CAG	Changi Airport Group
CAR	Irish Commission for Aviation Regulation
CC	Competition Commission
CFI	European Court of First Instance
CHF	Swiss Franc
CIM	Chartered Institute of Marketing

List of abbreviations

CIPR	Chartered Institute of Public Relations
CRM	Customer relationship management
CUSS	Common-use self-service
CUTE	Common user terminal equipment
DAA	Dublin Airport Authority
EC	European Commission
ELFAA	European Low Fares Airline Association
EU	European Union
EUR	European Euro
F&B	Food and beverage
FAA	US Federal Aviation Administration
FIDS	Flight information display screens
GBP	British Pound
GDP	Gross domestic product
GE	General Electric
GIP	Global Infrastructure Partners
HDR	High Density Traffic Airports Rule
IATA	International Air Transport Association
ICAO	International Civil Aviation Organisation
ICE	Institution of Civil Engineers
IMF	International Monetary Fund
KLIA	Kuala Lumpur International Airport
LAGs	Liquids, aerosols and gels
LCC	Low cost carrier
LCCT	Low Cost Carrier Terminal
LVL	Latvian Lat
LVNL	Air traffic control in the Netherlands (Luchtverkeersleiding Nederland)
MCT	Minimum connect time
MIDT	Market information data tapes
MII	Majority-in-interest
MOP	Macau Pataca
MoU	Memorandum of understanding
MTOW	Maximum take-off weight
MYR	Malaysian Ringgit
NAS	Canadian National Airports System
NGO	Non-governmental organisation
NOK	Norwegian Kroner
NZD	New Zealand Dollar
OAG	Official Airline Guide
O–D	Origin–destination
OECD	Organisation for Economic Co-operation and Development
PDA	Personal digital assistant
PEST	Political, economic, socio-cultural, technological
PESTE	Political and legal, economic, socio-cultural, technological, environmental
PESTEL	Political, economic, socio-cultural, technological, environmental, legal

PFC   Passenger facility charge
PPP   Public–private partnership
PRM   Person with reduced mobility
PSC   Passenger service charge
QSI   Quality service index
RDF   Route development fund
RFID   Radio-frequency identification
RFP   Request for proposals
RPK   Revenue passenger kilometre
RTK   Revenue tonne kilometre
SMART   Specific, measurable, achievable, relevant and time-orientated
SWOT   Strengths, weaknesses, opportunities and threats
TAV   Tepe and Akfen Airports Group
THB   Thai Baht
TKP   Tonne kilometre performed
TSA   Transportation Security Administration
UK   United Kingdom
UNWTO   United Nations World Tourism Organization
US   United States of America
USD   United States Dollar
VFR   Visiting friends and relatives
WLU   Work load unit
WTO   World Trade Organization

Chapter 1

Introduction

This chapter provides an introduction both to the book and to the subject of airport marketing. It consists of two main sections. The first considers how airport marketing has evolved, including the forces that have influenced change, how airport marketing has emerged within the context of the marketing era, and the growth and cost of airport marketing. The second section outlines the approach to airport marketing taken by this book, including how definitions of marketing can be applied to airports and the implications of service industry marketing, and concludes with an overview of the book's structure.

1.1 Evolution of airport marketing

1.1.1 Forces that have influenced change

Until the 1980s airports generally adopted a passive approach to marketing. The view from many in industry, even until fairly recently, was that airports were natural monopolies and were not in a position to influence the decisions of their target markets through marketing. This traditional view has been challenged during the past few decades. For instance, Tretheway (1998) asks whether airport marketing is an oxymoron – a contradiction in terms like the phrases 'jumbo shrimp', 'accurate estimate' and 'American English'. Fortunately for this book, Tretheway answers in the negative, suggesting that a large proportion of products and services at most airports are subject to competition, and that airport marketing decisions can help to build relationships that have a profound impact on airport customers. Tretheway accentuates these opinions in later articles (e.g. see Tretheway and Kincaid, 2010). More recently, Thelle *et al.* (2012) provide comprehensive evidence of airport competition, and the growing role and importance of airport marketing in Europe.

Airport competition has been encouraged by a number of factors, many of which are examined in more detail in Chapter 2. Demand for air transport, measured in revenue passenger kilometres (RPKs), is characterised by long-term growth: it has doubled every 15 years since the 1970s, and is forecast to double again in the next 15 years. Over three billion passengers travelled by air in 2011; this is expected to grow by 4.7 per cent each year during the next 20 years to over 7.5 billion passengers by 2031. In addition, 22 million tonnes of cargo was transported by air in 2011. Cargo demand, measured in revenue tonne kilometres (RTKs), is expected to grow at an even faster rate than passenger demand: by 4.9 per cent each year over the same period (Airbus, 2012).

In combination with long-term growth, air transport markets have become increasingly deregulated. This process began in the US domestic market in 1978, followed by the liberalisation of a number of international routes to and from the US, such as the so-called 'open market' agreements signed by the US and the Netherlands, Belgium, Germany, Singapore, Thailand, Korea and the Philippines between 1978 and 1980. Similar agreements were made in Europe during the 1980s, such as those signed by the UK with the Netherlands, Ireland and Singapore from 1984 (Doganis, 2010).

Many domestic markets are now fully deregulated. For example, Chile, New Zealand and Canada deregulated during the 1980s, while Australia, India, Venezuela, Peru, South Africa, Mexico, Argentina, Malaysia, Thailand, Kenya, Brazil and countries in Europe deregulated during the 1990s (Williams, 2002). The European air transport market was the first international market to be deregulated and this was achieved through three packages of liberalisation introduced in 1987, 1990 and between 1993 and 1997. Each package reduced restrictions on the setting of fares, frequency and capacity, market access, and the ownership and control of airlines. The EU has since negotiated a number of so-called 'open skies' agreements with other countries, such as with the US in 2008. An Association of Southeast Asian Nations (ASEAN) open skies agreement between ten Southeast Asian countries is due to be completed by 2015.

Prior to deregulation each country tightly regulated its own domestic market, while international regulation was based on bilateral air service agreements (ASAs) between governments; these set fares, frequencies, capacities and market access. Many international routes are still based on bilateral ASAs, but the restrictions traded by them are generally not as strict as they have been in the past. One of the main consequences of deregulation has been that airlines are now more footloose. They are freer to choose where they fly to and from, and generally set fares, frequencies, capacities and routes according to commercial considerations. This has provided airports not only with increased opportunities to attract new routes through marketing but also with challenges associated with retaining existing routes. For example, 2500 new intra-European routes were created in 2011 while 2000 were closed. This has resulted in a net increase of 500 new routes but also in a high degree of churn on existing routes (Thelle et al., 2012).

New types of airline business model, such as low cost carriers (LCCs), have emerged through deregulation. These have provided further opportunities for airports, in many cases requiring airport marketers to adopt a completely different approach and encouraging a further deviation from past practice (e.g. see Barrett, 2004). The travelling public is also becoming more experienced and less loyal, enjoying a greater choice of airports and air services, and generally placing greater demands on airports to deliver a quality product at a time when more stringent controls are being implemented, especially with regard to security.

As airports grow, they are able to exploit opportunities to develop commercial activities and increasingly seek to do so in order to diversify their business. This means that airport marketing often extends to a much wider range of customers, targeting not only airlines and passengers but also workers at an airport: so-called 'farewellers and weepers', 'meeters and greeters' and the general public, providers of aviation services (e.g. ground handling and catering companies), providers of commercial passenger services (e.g. retail, food and beverage, car parking and car rental companies), buyers (e.g. of airport advertising, real estate, or airport consultancy services), and suppliers (e.g. construction and engineering companies).

Airport marketing is also considered increasingly important because of the impact an airport can have on the economic and social development of the surrounding area. For this reason, airport marketing undertaken by both publicly owned and privately owned airports may often have wider objectives rather than just to enhance the well-being of the airport operator. Collaboration with stakeholders such as local businesses, tourism and regional development agencies is more common-place at airports than with many other industries because of the wider implications of traffic growth.

Changes in the airport business environment have given airports a greater incentive to develop innovative, proactive and aggressive approaches to marketing. This has been encouraged further by recent transformations in the way airports are owned and operated. In many countries the sector has moved from an industry characterised by public sector ownership and national requirements into a new era of airport management, where larger airports have become major international companies that tend to be owned and operated by the private sector. The first major airport privatisation of the British Airports Authority (BAA) in the UK took place in 1987, and the trend for airport privatisation has continued. Many smaller airports are still publicly owned and may even be operated on a not-for-profit basis, such as the National Airports System (NAS) airports in Canada, but a growing number are operated as commercial entities. This is especially the case in Europe, where over 20 per cent of airports are already privatised or are operated as public–private partnerships, while 74 per cent of publicly owned airports are operated as corporatised entities, abiding by commercial and fiscal discipline like any other competitive business, according to data from Airports Council International (ACI) (ACI Europe, 2010).

1.1.2 Airport marketing and the marketing era

Parallels can be drawn to some extent between how marketing has evolved as a concept and how airport marketing has evolved in practice. Theory suggests that companies operated in a production-orientated era until the 1950s, with a focus on means of production and an assumption that consumer needs and wants do not change quickly. This was followed by the sales-orientated era between the 1950s and 1960s, when companies would focus on promoting an existing product or service without really determining what consumers need and want.

Many airports were developed for military rather than civilian purposes, especially around the time of the Second World War. Transferring them to civilian use, governments decided which airlines would operate between which airports under the system of government ownership and control mentioned earlier in this chapter. Main airports were often developed as status symbols – the objective being to make the country look strong and powerful – but the airports were not necessarily customer-orientated or profitable. This did not matter, since they were government owned and did not have private shareholders seeking a return on their investment. Other regional and local airports also tended to be publicly owned, often by local authorities that were proud and protective of their airport, especially given that it provided the region with opportunities for connectivity. Many were created for regional development purposes, in schemes driven by (over)ambitious local politicians. This still occurs today. For instance, 24 regional airports were built during Spain's boom years, often as 'monuments to the vanity and hubris of local bigwigs' (Jones, 2012). Several have since closed as a result of too little traffic, such as Central Ciudad Real Airport, which closed in 2012 after just three years of operation. Others have never even seen a plane or passenger, such as Castellón Airport, which was completed in 2011 and has remained empty ever since.

In addition to being developed for political as opposed to market-orientated objectives, the vast majority of airports – irrespective of size or ownership – have traditionally focused on operational capabilities needed for safe and efficient movement of aircraft, people and cargo. They have not concentrated on the pre-determined needs and wants of customers, nor operated as commercial enterprises with a focus on marketing.

The literature suggests that we are now in a marketing-orientated era that emerged in the 1970s, characterised by companies that are focused on developing products and services that meet customer needs and wants. Despite examples to the contrary, such as Spain's ghost airports (which are reminiscent of the sales-orientated era), there is evidence of this marketing-orientated era at airports, although it appeared here slightly later than the 1970s as a result of significant widespread changes not really taking place in the industry until the 1980s.

It is, however, important to note that companies did not just start marketing as the marketing-orientated era emerged. Marketing has existed in some form or another for a long time, albeit in what might be considered a pre-modern form of marketing. Early evidence of this is the barter trade in ancient Egypt, Songhai and Ghana, where exchanges added value for both parties; as Baker points out, 'the enigma of marketing is that it is one of man's oldest activities and yet it is regarded as the most recent of business disciplines' (Baker, 1976: ix). This is also the case with airports. By virtue of the desire of governments to develop them as status symbols, as well as the glamour associated with air travel since its inception, airports have always been marketed in some way or another, although the marketing activities were certainly not as targeted, customer-orientated and varied as they are today. Some of the earliest examples of airport marketing activities can be seen on the internet, including many vintage posters. One example, showing an airplane and a seaplane, was created by Harry Herzog for the Works Progress Administration Federal Art Project in New York City in about 1937 to promote New York's municipal airports (Floyd Bennett Field, North Beach Airport, and East River Seaplane bases on Wall Street and 31st Street).

Contemporary approaches to marketing have also evolved, such as relationship marketing (focusing on building good customer relations and retaining customers through loyalty), industrial marketing (focusing on building and maintaining good relations with other businesses and organisations), social marketing (focusing on marketing activities that benefit and do not harm society), e-marketing (internet-based marketing), and more recently social media marketing. As this book will demonstrate, there is evidence to suggest that airports have embraced the full range of contemporary approaches to marketing: for example, by introducing airport loyalty schemes, collaboration with local stakeholders, sponsoring local community events and activities, and using the internet as a platform for various marketing activities including social media marketing. Darwin International Airport ran a social media marketing campaign on Facebook in 2012, using a poster of the airport and its modern jet aircraft with the words 'Like Us' coming from the contrail of an old biplane. This provides an interesting contrast to the earlier example of the poster used to promote New York's municipal airports. Instead of pushing general messages to a general audience, Darwin International Airport's campaign encouraged people to join the airport on Facebook so that they can connect, communicate and interact with each other.

1.1.3 Growth and cost of airport marketing

It is not easy to quantify the growth in airport marketing. There tends to be a lack of historical data from which trends can be derived, while current data, such as on airport marketing budgets and activities, is often commercially sensitive. Publicly available data often lacks transparency because marketing costs are rarely separated from other costs, such as those for sales and administration. Similarly, employees with responsibility for marketing may not be employed or work specifically in marketing but in other areas: for example, with a local authority, corporate head office, or another department in the airport, such as sales, administration or public relations. At smaller airports, it may be the airport manager who has responsibility for marketing, along with a wide range of other duties.

There have been some attempts to quantify the growth in airport marketing. Humphreys (1999) investigated the number of marketing staff employed at a selection of regional airports in the UK between 1991 and 1997. The number grew at each airport, and the ratio of marketing staff to passengers also increased at seven of the nine airports (see Figure 1.1).

Thelle et al. (2012) provide further evidence from a number of airports. For example, marketing staff numbers at Copenhagen Airport increased from two full-time employees in 2000

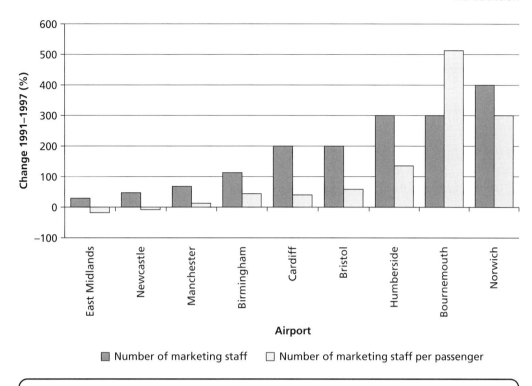

Figure 1.1 Change in marketing staff at selected UK regional airports, 1991–1997
Data source: Humphreys (1999)

to four in 2005 and eight in 2012, while expenditure on sales, marketing and administration at Zurich Airport increased from CHF 17.6 million in 1999 to CHF 39.1 million in 2011. ASM (2009) surveyed more than 100 airports of all sizes and all over the world. One aspect of the survey was to investigate what methods airports use when marketing to airlines. The survey found that 94 per cent of airports actively market themselves to airlines; this was consistent across all airport sizes and regions. Methods involving face-to-face contact are most commonly used, including attending airline and airport route development conventions/trade shows, and meeting with airlines in their offices or at the airport (see Figure 1.2).

As Chapter 7 will show, sales and marketing (including personnel costs) contributes 4.5 per cent of total airport operating costs (ACI, 2010). Evidence of actual expenditure on marketing is available for US airports from the US Federal Aviation Administration (FAA), and shows that 480 commercial service airports in the US spent USD 116.6 million on marketing, advertising and promotions (excluding personnel costs) in 2011 (FAA, 2012). This only amounts to less than 1 per cent of total operating costs, but equates to an average expenditure per airport of USD 242,925. Large differences exist between different categories of airport; actual expenditure per airport is higher for larger airports, but the proportion of expenditure to total operating costs is higher for smaller airports (see Table 1.1). Large differences also exist between airports within the same category (e.g. see Figure 1.3).

Along with increased industry activity in this area, there is also a growing interest in airport marketing as a field of academic study. Kramer *et al.* (2010) provide a marketing guidebook for

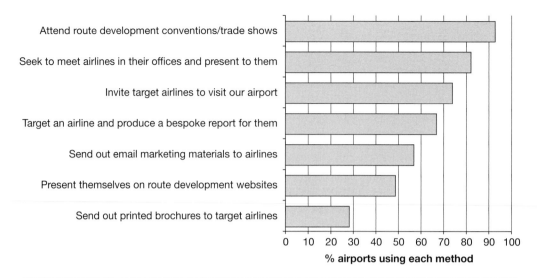

Attend route development conventions/trade shows

Seek to meet airlines in their offices and present to them

Invite target airlines to visit our airport

Target an airline and produce a bespoke report for them

Send out email marketing materials to airlines

Present themselves on route development websites

Send out printed brochures to target airlines

0 10 20 30 40 50 60 70 80 90 100

% airports using each method

Figure 1.2 Methods used by airports to market themselves to airlines
Data source: ASM (2009)

Table 1.1 Expenditure by US commercial service airports on marketing, advertising and promotions, 2011

Category of airport	No. of airports	Expenditure			
		Total operating (USD)	*Marketing (USD)*	*Average (USD)*	*% marketing to total operating*
Large hub	29	10,403,242,360	49,069,876	1,692,065	0.5
Medium hub	36	3,154,690,244	23,552,944	654,248	0.8
Small hub	72	1,687,050,994	27,092,698	376,288	1.6
Non-hub	343	1,345,407,988	16,888,514	49,238	1.3
Total	480	16,590,391,586	116,604,032	242,925	0.7

Data source: FAA (2012)

Note: marketing includes expenditure on marketing, advertising and promotions (not including personnel costs).

small airports, Jarach (2005) examines the new management vision of airport marketing, and a growing number of book chapters and journal articles consider general approaches to airport marketing (e.g. see Tretheway, 1998; Graham, 2008; Halpern, 2010a; 2010b; Tretheway and Kincaid, 2010). There are also a growing number of articles examining specific elements of airport

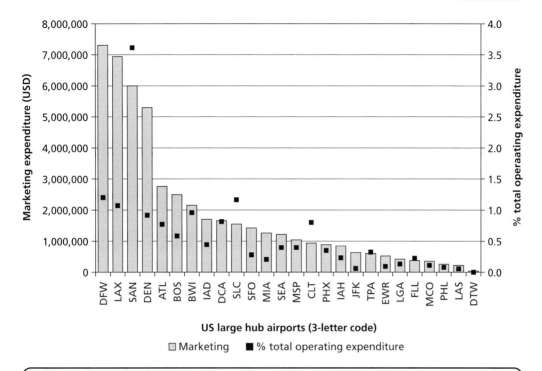

Figure 1.3 Marketing expenditure at US large hub airports, 2011

Data source: FAA (2012)

Note: three large hub airports (HNL, ORD and MDW) are not included, because marketing expenditure was recorded as USD 0 for these three airports. Marketing includes expenditure on marketing, advertising and promotions (not including personnel costs).

marketing, such as branding (e.g. see Halpern and Regmi, 2011) and price incentives (e.g. see Fichert and Klophaus, 2011).

1.2 Approach to airport marketing in this book

Despite the growing interest from both academia and industry, there is still a need for an up-to-date, accessible and in-depth textbook that introduces students and practitioners to the principles and practice of airport marketing, as well as the major changes and future marketing challenges facing the airport sector. This book attempts to fill that gap. It applies principles of marketing to the airport industry, integrating key elements of marketing theory with airport marketing in practice. As such, it is important to start by defining marketing within an airport context.

1.2.1 Defining marketing within an airport context

The Chartered Institute of Marketing (CIM) and the American Marketing Association (AMA) are two of the world's most influential marketing bodies. CIM (2009: 2) defines marketing as 'the management process responsible for identifying, anticipating and satisfying customer requirements profitably', while AMA (2012) defines it as 'the activity, set of institutions, and processes for creating, communicating, delivering, and exchanging offerings that have value for customers, clients, partners, and society at large'. Both stress that marketing is a process that has objectives and outcomes. The CIM definition places emphasis on three key stages in the process: identification of customer requirements, a more long-term objective to anticipate those requirements and a more short-term objective to satisfy those requirements. AMA has a similar view, highlighting the need to create, communicate, deliver and exchange offerings that have value. In the CIM definition profitability is an outcome of the marketing process, while the AMA definition emphasises the exchange of offerings that have value. The latter is a broader outcome that may still involve profit but can also include non-monetary values. This is more relevant for airports because although profit may be an important outcome – especially for those that are operated as commercial entities – airports also seek to exchange offerings of value that are not profit-related, particularly in the case of publicly owned and not-for-profit airports.

The AMA definition also emphasises the range of markets that may be targeted, including customers (end-user recipients of airport products and services) but also clients, partners and society at large. This is again relevant to airports that have both end-user customers (airlines, passengers and cargo) and a diverse range of other customers for whom they need to create, communicate, deliver and exchange offerings of value. The CIM definition does not specifically refer to types of target market, perhaps taking the view that all those mentioned in the AMA definition may be considered to be customers. We take that view in this book, using 'customers' as a generic term for end-users as well as other target markets, such as clients, partners and society at large. The range of airport customers is examined in more detail in Chapter 3.

A third definition worth mentioning is from well-known marketing academics Armstrong and Kotler (2007: 5–6). They define marketing as 'the social process by which individuals and organisations obtain what they need and want through creating and exchanging value with others'. They go on to say that marketing is 'the process by which companies create value for customers and build strong customer relationships in order to capture value from customers in return'. The latter definition recognises the importance of long-term relationships with customers; this is particularly relevant to airports, especially given their reliance on repeat business (e.g. from airlines, passengers and cargo companies), but also because of their composite nature and the impact they have on their surrounding area.

1.2.2 Service industry marketing

Airports are essentially providers of a service, and marketing plays a different role in service companies than in companies dealing purely with goods, where operational parts of the organisation deal with production and the marketing department deals largely with selling. This approach does not work with services such as airports, in which production and consumption often occur simultaneously and through interaction between the organisation, other stakeholders and suppliers, and the end-user. Staff responsible for marketing in a service company must therefore develop and maintain much closer and more wide-ranging relationships than is typical in many goods companies because of the inseparable nature of the different aspects of the service.

Like goods, airports are physical objects that can be seen, touched, heard and smelt; as discussed in Chapter 6, they offer tangible product features, such as the infrastructure and facilities they provide for the end-user (e.g. a slot for take-off and landing or a car parking space). However, unlike goods, there is generally no exchange of permanent ownership for physical components of an airport when customers pay to use it, meaning that it is important for airports to reinforce brand identity and encourage loyalty through marketing. In addition, customers paying to use an airport are often paying for service features that are intangible. Airport marketing therefore needs to develop tangible cues that provide evidence of the benefits available, such as signals of service quality that customers may then associate with the airport. Heterogeneity of airport services can cause a problem here because service features such as service quality may vary depending on when, where and how they are delivered, and by whom. Airports therefore need to invest in recruitment and training, and from a marketing perspective it is important to measure and manage the performance of service features.

Finally, services tend to be perishable: they cannot be stored for later sale or use. This is the case for most airport products and services, which means that airports are not able to create inventories, and may face problems in matching demand with supply. Using market research to anticipate and plan for future demand is important, and airports can also use individual elements of their marketing mix to influence and respond to changes in supply and demand, such as using

Table 1.2 Characteristics of a service and implications for airport marketing

Service characteristic	Implications for airport marketing
Inseparable The airport product is generally produced and consumed simultaneously, often through interaction between the airport, other service providers and the end-user.	Important for airports to develop and maintain close relationships because interaction determines the service outcome.
No transfer of ownership Airport customers do not generally gain personal or unlimited access to the products and services they pay for.	Important for airports to reinforce brand identity and encourage loyalty.
Intangible Airport products and services generally have no substance; they cannot be seen, tasted or touched.	Important for airports to develop tangible cues that provide evidence of the benefits available (e.g. levels of service quality).
Heterogeneous The quality of airport products and services generally varies depending on when, where and how they are provided, and by whom.	Important for airports to invest in quality control (e.g. staff training and management systems).
Perishable Airport products and services generally cannot be stored for later sale or use.	Important for airports to anticipate and plan for future demand and use elements of their marketing mix to influence and respond to changes in supply and demand.

Source: compiled by the authors

differential pricing (e.g. incentives to stimulate demand during quiet periods), reservation systems (e.g. for car parking and slot allocation), and procedures for managing fluctuations in demand (e.g. contracting third party service providers, sharing capacity with other service providers, and using flexible, part-time staffing during busy periods). A summary of service characteristics and their implications for airport marketing is provided in Table 1.2.

1.2.3 How this book is structured

This book takes a systematic approach to the subject of airport marketing. It consists of nine chapters representing different but very much related and interlinked stages in the marketing process; as such, there is some degree of overlap between chapters. In addition, chapters are not restricted to examining only pure airport marketing issues. Where relevant, wider issues that have implications for marketing, such as the regulation of airport user charges, slot allocation mechanisms and approaches to concession contracting are also discussed. Similarly, airport marketing is often assumed to be focused only on promotional activities; hence the small number of staff often employed in marketing-dedicated functions at airports. However, this book provides a much wider perspective on airport marketing, reflected by the scope of the nine chapters.

Chapter 2 considers the airport marketing environment, which consists of two main elements: the microenvironment – this refers to internal forces within the company and industry that affect a company's ability to serve its customers; and the macroenvironment – this refers to wider societal forces that affect the microenvironment, such as politics and legislation, the economy, culture and society, technology and environmental issues.

Chapters 3 and 4 investigate how to define and measure the market for airport services. In particular, Chapter 3 examines the market for airport services, including the range of airport customers and their behaviour, and airport market segmentation, while Chapter 4 assesses how airports can use marketing research as a function for linking customers to the marketer, including the role of marketing research and research methodologies that can be used by airports. Chapter 4 also explores airports' use of marketing research, giving special attention to the air service development (ASD) process.

Chapter 5 provides a strategic, long-term perspective by examining airport marketing planning; a systematic process through which airports can anticipate how best to exploit their future business environment. The chapter introduces the marketing planning process, including its role and importance for airports, and focuses on individual elements of the process, including corporate intentions, situation analysis, marketing decisions and implementation.

Chapters 6 to 9 provide an operational, short-term perspective by exploring the airport marketing mix: a tactical toolkit that can be controlled and used by airports to exploit market trends and to position their products and services in the marketplace. Individual elements of the marketing mix are widely known as the '4 Ps' first introduced by McCarthy (1960). These include product (the product or service produced), price (the amount charged for the product or service), promotion (the methods used to market the product or service), and place (the distribution channels used to sell the product or service).

The 4 Ps have been reinvented on a number of occasions. For instance, they have been extended to the 7 Ps in order to include three service-orientated elements: physical evidence, processes and people. More recently, Lauterborn (1990) has suggested that the 4 Ps should be replaced with the 4 Cs in order to reflect a more customer-orientated philosophy, whereby product becomes customer needs and wants, price becomes cost to the user, promotion becomes communication, and place becomes convenience. Despite the range of philosophies, the fundamental principles are the same: individual elements of the marketing mix are combined to generate the optimal desired response from target markets. The traditional 4 Ps provide a sufficient framework for this book.

Chapter 6 defines the airport product, exploring its main product and service features and the amount of control an airport operator has over them. The nature and use of branding by airports is also discussed. The chapter concludes by assessing how the product can be evaluated and planned to meet the needs and expectations of airport customers.

Chapter 7 examines factors that can affect airport pricing decisions before considering the cost and revenue structure of airports, types of airport charges, economic regulation of airport charges, and incentive mechanisms used by airports.

Chapter 8 explores the range of marketing communications tools used by airports (known collectively as the promotional mix) and the advantages and disadvantages of each tool. The chapter also addresses the changing landscape for marketing communications, and factors that airports subsequently need to consider when developing an integrated and effective approach to marketing communications.

Chapter 9 investigates how approaches to airport distribution have evolved, especially in terms of the way airports conduct business with their target markets. The chapter also discusses how airports use customer relationship management (CRM) as a means for managing their interactions with customers.

References

ACI (2010) *Airport Economics Survey 2010*, Montreal: ACI.

ACI Europe (2010) *The Ownership of Europe's Airports*, Brussels: ACI Europe.

Airbus (2012) *Global Market Forecast 2012–2031*, Toulouse: Airbus.

AMA (2012) *Definition of marketing*, Chicago: AMA. Online. Available at: http://www.marketingpower.com/AboutAMA/Pages/DefinitionofMarketing.aspx (accessed 6 October 2012).

Armstrong, G. and Kotler, P. (2007) *Marketing: An Introduction*, 8th edn, Upper Saddle River: Pearson Education.

ASM (2009) Industry Trends and Climate Survey: Interim Research Results, Live Webinar, July 2009.

Baker, M.J. (1976) *Marketing: Theory and Practice*, 1st edn, Oxford: Macmillan.

Barrett, S.D. (2004) 'How do the demands for airport services differ between full-service carriers and low cost carriers?', *Journal of Air Transport Management*, 10(1); 33–9.

CIM (2009) *Marketing and the 7Ps: A Brief Summary of Marketing and How it Works*, Maidenhead: CIM.

Doganis, R. (2010) *Flying Off Course: Airline Economics and Marketing*, 4th edn, Abingdon: Routledge.

FAA (2012) *FAA operating and financial summary report 127*. Online. Available at: http://cats.airports.faa.gov/Reports/reports.cfm?AirportID=2597&Year=2011 (accessed 20 October 2012).

Fichert, F. and Klophaus, R. (2011) 'Incentive schemes on airport charges – theoretical analysis and empirical evidence from German airports', *Journal of Air Transport Management*, 1(1); 71–9.

Graham, A. (2008) *Managing Airports: An International Perspective*, 3rd edn, Oxford: Butterworth-Heinemann.

Halpern, N. (2010a) 'The marketing of small regional airports', in G. Williams and S. Bråthen (eds) *Air Transport Provision in Remoter Regions*, Farnham: Ashgate.

Halpern, N. (2010b) 'Marketing innovations: sources, capabilities and consequences at airports in Europe's peripheral areas', *Journal of Air Transport Management*, 16(2); 52–8.

Halpern, N. and Regmi, U.K. (2011) 'What's in a name? Analysis of airport brand names and slogans', *Journal of Airport Management*, 6(1); 63–79.

Humphreys, I. (1999) 'Privatisation and commercialisation: changes in UK airport ownership patterns', *Journal of Transport Geography*, 7(2); 121–34.

Jarach, D. (2005) *Airport Marketing: Strategies to Cope with the New Millennium Environment*, Farnham: Ashgate.

Jones, D. (2012) 'The price of financial folly: As airports and luxury flats stand empty as monuments to Spain's overspending, miners' protest over subsidy cuts ends in bloody clashes', *Mail Online* 12 July 2012, London: Associated Newspapers. Online. Available at: http://www.dailymail.co.uk/news/article-2172339/Airports-seen-plane-ghost-towns-luxury-flats-The-hubris-Spains-descent-anarchy.html (accessed 20 October 2012).

Kramer, L., Fowler, P., Hazel, R., Ureksoy, M. and Harig, G. (2010) *ACRP Report 28: Marketing Guidebook for Small Airports*, Washington, DC: Transportation Research Board.

Lauterborn, B. (1990) 'New marketing litany: four Ps passé: C-words take over', *Advertising Age*, 61(41); 26–7.

McCarthy, J. (1960) *Basic Marketing: A Managerial Approach*, Irwin: Homewood.

Thelle, M.H., Pedersen, T.T. and Harhoff, F. (2012) *Airport Competition in Europe*, Copenhagen: Copenhagen Economics.

Tretheway, M.W. (1998) 'Airport marketing: an oxymoron?' in G.F. Butler and M.R. Keller (eds) *Handbook of Airline Marketing*, New York: McGraw Hill.

Tretheway, M. and Kincaid, I. (2010) 'Competition between airports: occurrence and strategy' in P. Forsyth, D. Gillen, J. Müller and H-M. Niemeier (eds) *Airport Competition: The European Experience*, Farnham: Ashgate.

Williams, G. (2002) *Airline Deregulation's Mixed Legacy*, Farnham: Ashgate.

Chapter 2

The airport marketing environment

This chapter examines the environment in which airport marketing operates. It consists of three main sections. The first provides an introduction to the airport marketing environment, including the two main elements – the microenvironment and macroenvironment – and their role and importance for airport marketing. The next two sections examine each of these environments in detail.

2.1 Introduction to the airport marketing environment

Airport marketing activities cannot be considered in isolation. Every airport operates within a marketing environment that plays a key role in influencing the airport's marketing strategy and planning decisions. It provides both opportunities and threats for airports and is constantly changing, often with dramatic and unpredictable consequences. It is therefore essential for airport marketers to fully develop their marketing research skills and techniques to ensure that a thorough and reliable knowledge and understanding of their unique marketing environment is gained.

There are a number of ways that the marketing environment can be assessed. Cooper *et al.* (2008) identify four different levels. Level one is 'the organisation': marketing functions need to be well organised, well-resourced and integrated with other organisational functions. Next is level two, 'company markets', which includes all the markets for the products and services being offered. Level three is 'organisational stakeholders'; this includes all interest groups that affect the decision-making of the organisation, such as shareholders, competitors, customers, employees, unions, the government, suppliers, debtors, banks and the local community. Finally there is level four, 'the wider environment', which covers factors outside the direct control of the organisation.

A closely related alternative view involves dividing the marketing environment between the micro- (or internal) and macro- (or external) environments (Kotler *et al.*, 2008). A similar approach is taken in this chapter (see Figure 2.1). The microenvironment consists of factors and forces close to the organisation that have a direct effect on its ability to serve its customers and on its marketing strategy. These consist of the organisation or company itself, suppliers, marketing intermediaries, customers, competitors and stakeholders. By contrast, the macroenvironment consists of factors and forces that belong to the broader society, affecting all organisations operating in a particular market. These factors influence the microenvironment, and hence the marketing activities undertaken.

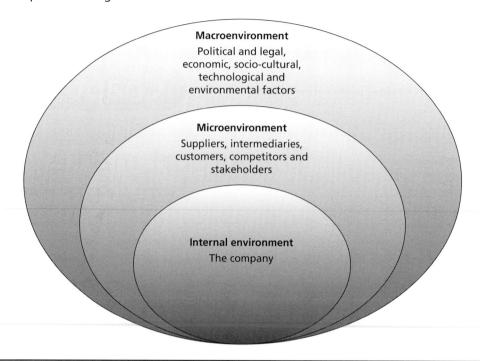

Figure 2.1 The marketing environment
Source: compiled by the authors

There are a number of ways of categorising such factors, such as with a PEST (political, economic, socio-cultural, and technological) analysis, or an extended PESTEL (political, economic, socio-cultural, technological, environmental and legal) analysis or some similar grouping (Dibb *et al.*, 2006; Pride and Ferrell, 2008). The categories may well not be mutually exclusive, with some issues coming under more than one heading. For this chapter a PESTE (political and legal, economic, socio-cultural, technological and environmental) approach has been adopted, similar to that of Shaw (2011), who argues that in the aviation industry most quasi-legal issues are better dealt with under the political heading. Irrespective of the mnemonic chosen, the key aim is to assess all the external forces that influence the organisation.

Knowledge of the micro- and macroenvironments is vital for undertaking the situation analysis that is a key stage of the airport marketing planning process, as discussed in Chapter 5. In particular, an in-depth understanding of the nature of suppliers, customers, competitors and PESTE factors is crucial in order to carry out an effective external marketing audit. Since it is constantly changing, research into the marketing environment must be continually updated to ensure that such changes are reflected in the analysis, and that realistic opportunities and threats are identified. The microenvironment contains many controllable factors that a company can have some influence over. Many of the macroenvironmental factors are less controllable, although in some instances there may be scope for organisations to exert influence to encourage change; for instance, by lobbying government or running media campaigns.

2.2 The airport's microenvironment

2.2.1 The company

The company aspect of the microenvironment refers to all the internal functions of the organisation. Each of these will influence marketing decisions. Marketers must work closely with top management associated with all these activities and ensure that their marketing plans are consistent with overall corporate intentions and with the strategies of all the other departments. Most importantly, the marketing function of any organisation must be seen as an integral activity by all to ensure success.

There is considerable variation in the organisational structures of airports and in the location of marketing activities within these structures. For example, at Copenhagen Airports, Marketing and Sales is one of the six main departments, the others being External Relations, Human Resources, Operations, Assets and Technology, and Finance and Business Support (see Figure 2.2). However, many marketing decisions have implications for other departments such as Human Resources and Finance. Similarly, at Dallas/Fort Worth International Airport there are six main departments: namely Finance and Information Technology Services, Administration and Diversity, Operations, Revenue Management, Marketing and Terminal Management, and Government and Stakeholder Affairs (see Figure 2.3). The main functions of marketing, customer service and ASD are covered under Marketing and Terminal Management but again there need to be close links to other areas such as finance, human resources, commercial revenue and stakeholders' affairs, which are the responsibility of other departments. At many airports there is a distinction between the marketing of the aeronautical and non-aeronautical areas but there clearly needs to be close communication and coordination between these two activities. For example, at Kansai International Airport there is both an Aviation Sales and Marketing Department and a Terminal Sales and Marketing Department.

Elsewhere there may not be a dedicated marketing department. For example, Changi Airport Group (CAG) has five main departments: Airport Management, Air Hub Development, Commercial, Corporate and Finance, as well as Changi Airports International, which is a wholly

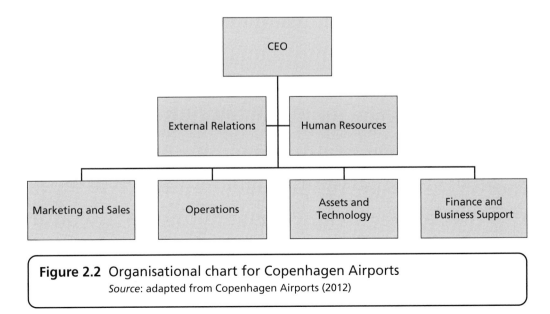

Figure 2.2 Organisational chart for Copenhagen Airports
Source: adapted from Copenhagen Airports (2012)

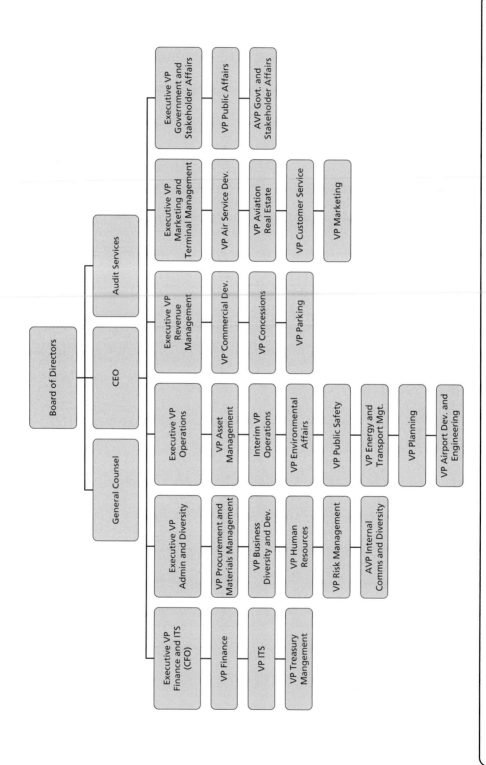

Figure 2.3 Organisational chart for Dallas/Fort Worth International Airport

Source: adapted from Dallas/Fort Worth International Airport (2012)

owned subsidiary and both an investor in and manager of a number of other airports (see Figure 2.4). Marketing activities are primarily split between Air Hub Development, which promotes passenger and cargo traffic, markets the Changi Airport brand and undertakes market research, and Airport Management, which is responsible for marketing facilities to passengers. In addition, the Commercial department focuses on maximising commercial revenue streams and so is strongly influenced by marketing strategies, especially those directed at the passenger. At Dubai Airports, marketing is the responsibility of the Strategy and Development department, the other departments being Dubai Air Navigation Systems, Commercial, Operations, Group Services (including Finance and Quality Assurance) and Human Resources and Development (see Figure 2.5). These are just a few examples of the many varied organisational structures that exist. However, irrespective of the specific structure, it is essential for airport marketers to work closely with the other departments and functions as these will have major impacts on their ability to successfully deliver their marketing strategies and plans.

2.2.2 Suppliers

Suppliers provide the organisation with the goods and services it needs to create its products. In the manufacturing industry, this is relatively straightforward as it will relate to materials that are needed in the manufacturing process. Poorer quality or more expensive materials will have a direct impact on the final product and its price, and hence affect its attractiveness to target markets. Similarly, any delay in supplying the materials will have a bearing on the organisation's ability to satisfy demand for its goods in a timely manner. Thus it is very important for organisations to develop strong and effective relationships with their suppliers.

The situation is more complex for the airport industry because it offers a composite of many products and services such as air traffic control, security, ground handling and retail (the airport product is discussed in detail in Chapter 6). Each element is reliant on a different subset of suppliers. In addition, the airport operator may choose to outsource many of the services that it provides; in effect such outsourced service providers in turn become suppliers themselves to the

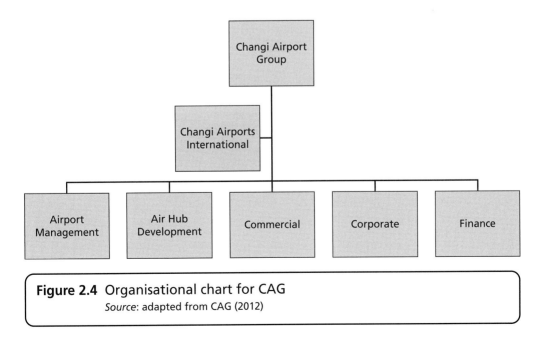

Figure 2.4 Organisational chart for CAG
Source: adapted from CAG (2012)

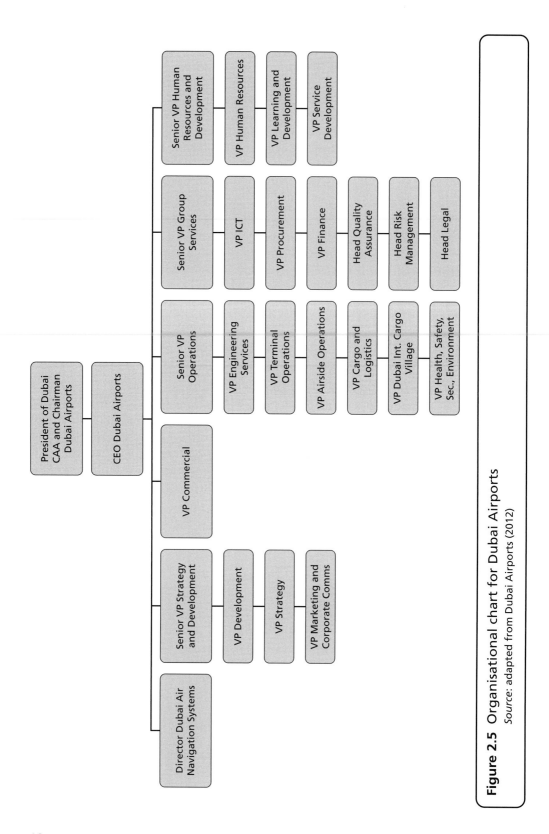

Figure 2.5 Organisational chart for Dubai Airports
Source: adapted from Dubai Airports (2012)

Table 2.1 Suppliers of airport services at Humberside Airport and East Midlands Airport, 2011

Airport service	Humberside Airport	East Midlands Airport
Passenger search	In-house	Outsourced
Hold baggage	In-house	Outsourced
Access control	In-house	Outsourced
Trolley circulation	In-house	In-house
Fire service	In-house	In-house
Air traffic control	In-house	In-house
Car park operations	In-house	Outsourced
Direct retailing	Concession	Concession
Cleaning	In-house	Outsourced
Passenger handling	In-house	Outsourced
Baggage handling	In-house	Outsourced
Freight handling	In-house	Outsourced
Fuel supply	In-house	Outsourced

Source: adapted from LeighFisher (2011)

airport operator. The way such outsourced services are provided, and whether there are competing firms, will have an impact on the price and quality of service. Thus decisions relating to the choice of supplier will affect not only the airport's finances but also its ability to effectively satisfy the needs of its target markets. However, in some cases such as with the provision of immigration, customs and maybe security services, the airport operator will have no choice but to accept the government agency (which is responsible for this activity) as their sole supplier.

Table 2.1 illustrates that even for two airports in the same country (the UK) there can be considerable variation in the supply of individual airport services and processes. At Humberside Airport nearly all services are provided in-house, while the majority are outsourced at East Midlands Airport. It is therefore important for marketers to be aware of supplier developments at two levels: firstly related to suppliers of the airport operator's own activities and secondly related to the outsourced services at the airport.

2.2.3 Marketing intermediaries

In general, marketing intermediaries are firms that help organisations promote, sell and distribute their products to customers. With manufacturing companies, physical distribution intermediaries that stock and move goods can be important. This is not relevant to airports because of the fixed location of their product, although travel agents that sell the airline product, which in part is made up of a specific airport's services, can indirectly be considered distribution intermediaries. There are also financial intermediaries such as banks and credit companies, which help with the buying and selling of products. These include insurance companies used to insure against the risks associated with an organisation's activity. The traditional public sector ownership of airports meant that there used to be more limited scope for using different financial intermediaries, while state ownership also usually reduced the perceived risks of operation. However, in today's world of greater private sector involvement in airports and high public sector debt, the situation is rather different.

There are also marketing service agencies, which include intermediaries such as market research companies, advertising agencies, media and marketing consultancy firms. As with other industry sectors, airports vary in their use of such intermediaries. Some operators, such as London Heathrow Airport with their market research activity, take the view that the requirement for specialist airport knowledge, together with other factors such as irregular hours and security checks, makes it more worthwhile to have their own market research team (this is discussed in Chapter 4). Organisations such as anna.aero and Routes, discussed in Chapter 8, are examples of intermediaries that help promote the airport product to airlines, while intermediaries involved specifically in the airport distribution process are discussed in Chapter 9. Airport marketers need to ensure that they are familiar with all the intermediaries they could potentially use and are able to evaluate the potential benefits and drawbacks of using them.

2.2.4 Customers

Customers are individuals or firms that buy the goods and services an organisation produces: satisfying their needs and requirements is vital for the success of any organisation. In general terms there are usually five different customer markets: individuals, businesses that use the goods and services for their own product, resellers (such as certain intermediaries), governments that use the goods and services for public services, and international consumers that could include any of the previous customer groups if they are from another country.

Again, the airport industry is rather unusual when this concept is applied to the sector. The two main customers are often defined as airlines (which pay airports directly for rights to use their products and services), and passengers (who use airport products and services but do not pay airports directly). Most airports tend to define both airlines and passengers as key customers, whereas some airlines consider passengers as solely their customers, and themselves as the main customers of airports. With leisure or holiday travel, it may well be the tour operator rather than the airline that is the core business customer. Travel agents could be characterised as resellers. As Chapter 9 demonstrates, there is more of a grey area with other businesses such as ground handlers, retail concessionaires and freight forwarders. These use parts of the airport product (and pay for it through concession fees or rents) to sell their own individual services and so could be defined as customers. However, they also contribute to the airport operator's overall product and so could alternatively be described as suppliers. The same reasoning could be applied to businesses that are developed on airport land beyond the terminal as a consequence of an airport operator's strategy to develop an airport city or aerotropolis (see Chapter 6).

In addition to passengers, there will be other individuals that can be considered airport customers. These include those who see off or meet the passenger. There may also be aviation enthusiasts who will come to the airport because of this interest and other visitors with a desire to use the commercial or meeting facilities. Staff employed in any of the organisations at the airport may also use the airport facilities and so again in a broad sense can be defined as airport customers. Hence a typical airport serves a significant number of different customer markets. The global nature of the air transport industry means that many of these markets are international by nature. Each of these markets has its own specific characteristics, needs and requirements, which will be discussed in more detail in Chapter 3.

2.2.5 Competitors

Competitors can be simply defined as other organisations that create and market products that are similar to, or can be substituted for, the products on offer from the organisation whose marketing environment is under consideration. All potential competitors must be continually monitored to assess their relative strengths and weaknesses, and to determine how to gain a competitive edge over them. Trends such as globalisation and lower barriers to entry may lead to more new entrants to the market and a greater threat of substitute products; these need to be taken into account.

Airport competition is a complex area, and for each airport the number and nature of the competitors will depend on numerous factors (Forsyth *et al.*, 2010). Clearly, location is a key determinant, but as with other organisations the range and quality of facilities and services on offer and the price paid will also play important roles. The passenger market is particularly complicated to consider because passenger choice of airport will be largely determined by the nature of the airlines which serve the airport, in terms of the fares, destinations and services on offer. Hence airport competition here will be closely linked to the amount of airline competition that exists (Graham, 2006).

If an airport is located on a small island or in a remote region, it may have very few direct competitors. Likewise, airports that have a high concentration of both short-haul and long-haul services, which are likely to appeal most to legacy scheduled carriers with networked services, may have quite a limited number of competitor airports. This is unless the airport is competing as a hub by providing good flight connectivity and efficient passenger transfers. For example, in Europe airports such as Amsterdam Schiphol, Frankfurt and Paris Charles de Gaulle have traditionally been viewed as competitors for transfer passengers; now Istanbul Ataturk Airport is also developing its role as a hub in this region. These hub airports have been joined by a growing number in Asia such as Beijing Capital International Airport, Hong Kong International Airport, Incheon International Airport, Suvarnabhumi Airport, Kuala Lumpur International Airport (KLIA) and Singapore Changi Airport. Competing hubs do not even need to be in the same region, a notable example being Dubai International Airport, which competes with some of these Asian airports for transfer traffic between Europe and Oceania.

If airports are physically close, their catchment areas may overlap, especially for short-haul traffic, so airports may have a number of direct competitors for such traffic. This is less common for long-haul services as a result of tighter traffic rights restrictions in bilateral ASAs, and since competing long-haul services tend to be less viable because of the thinner nature of the traffic. Regional airports often have overlapping catchment areas that may continually expand or contract, depending on the nature of air services and surface links on offer at neighbouring airports (see Chapter 4 for a discussion about catchment areas).

There are some major urban areas or cities where more than one airport serves the local population. Notable examples are the European cities of London and Paris, and the American cities of New York and Washington. San Francisco and Moscow are also served by multiple airports. Sometimes the airports may be under the same ownership, as with Aéroports de Paris (AdP), which owns Paris Charles de Gaulle, Paris Orly and Paris Le Bourget airports, and the Port Authority of New York and New Jersey, which owns John F. Kennedy International, LaGuardia and Newark Liberty International airports. Such common ownership may reduce the amount of potential competition between the airports. In the UK, the airport company formerly called BAA used to own three London airports (Heathrow, Stansted and Gatwick) and three Scottish airports (Edinburgh, Glasgow and Aberdeen) but a recent review by the Competition Commission (CC) concluded that this common ownership inhibited competition and hence required BAA to sell Gatwick, Stansted and Edinburgh or Glasgow (see UK CC, 2009). Gatwick, Stansted and Edinburgh have already been sold.

There is also the situation where there may be a secondary airport competing with a major airport within a common catchment area. This is often the case with secondary airports that serve LCCs such as Brussels South Charleroi Airport (BSCA), Paris Beauvais Airport and Frankfurt Hahn Airport. However, there are other types of alternative secondary airport, such as London City Airport, that compete while offering a product designed for the business market rather than for LCCs.

Finally, there are a few cases when an airport can compete with other airports that do not share a catchment area or serve common transfer traffic. For instance, an airport may compete to be a base for a LCC, especially in Europe where there are a number of pan-European carriers now (e.g. easyJet, Ryanair and Norwegian). In this situation, LCCs will be less influenced by the proximity in location and more concerned about the operating environment and costs. Likewise, freight forwarding companies will often decide which airport to use based on cost, schedule and handling factors rather than the specific location of the airport, particularly in Europe where most long-haul cargo is trucked on arrival to its final destination. Elsewhere – for example, in North America – airports may compete as embarkation points for cruise holidays.

In a broader sense airport competitors do not necessarily have to be other airports. For instance, competition may come from other modes of transport, most notably high speed rail (as is the case in some European regions and in countries such as Japan), or from video-conferencing facilities. In terms of commercial facilities for passengers, there may be a whole range of competitors including airlines, downtown tax free shopping, discount stores and internet retailing. In summary, identifying potential competitors in all areas of operation is very important for airport marketers, particularly as these competitors provide crucial input to the external audit for marketing planning, which is discussed in Chapter 5.

2.2.6 Stakeholders

Stakeholders or publics are groups with an interest in (either actual or potential), or an effect on, an organisation's ability to successfully implement their marketing strategy. In general, these groups can be classified as financial (e.g. banks, investors), governmental (e.g. government departments, agencies), media-related (e.g. newspapers, television), citizen-action focused (e.g. consumer organisations, pressure groups), local (e.g. resident and community groups) and internal (e.g. employees, managers) (Kotler et al., 2008). The financial stakeholders will influence the organisation's ability to generate investment funds, while government stakeholders will play a key role in defining an organisation's operating and business environment through their policy initiatives and legislation. Media attention can have either a positive or negative impact on an organisation and so needs to be managed carefully. Organisations also have to take account of other stakeholders such as citizen-action and local resident groups that will have views and attitudes towards the products on offer and associated marketing activities. Similarly, internal stakeholders need to be effectively communicated with to ensure that they are adequately informed and motivated to successfully perform their individual roles.

The airport industry is no different: an airport operator has many stakeholders it needs to engage with and keep well informed. Jarach (2005) divides these into four main areas: citizens, public stakeholders, logistic stakeholders and support stakeholders. At large airports, each of these areas may include many different subgroups. For instance, Tables 2.2 and 2.3 illustrate how Amsterdam Schiphol Airport and London Heathrow Airport classify their key stakeholders, and while there are some differences in detail, there are also a number of common features, as would be expected. Each major airport stakeholder group will have different expectations: for instance, customers seeking quality, efficient operations and value; employees seeking security, fair pay and job satisfaction; governments seeking economic development for the region or

Table 2.2 Stakeholders at Amsterdam Schiphol Airport, 2012

Stakeholder group	Stakeholders
Customers	Includes passengers and visitors, concessionaires, tenants, airlines and handling agents.
Sector partners	Includes airlines, handling agents, aviation industry and air traffic control in the Netherlands (Luchtverkeersleiding Nederland, LVNL).
Partners	Includes shareholders, financial parties, subcontractors, suppliers, and knowledge and research institutions.
Society	Includes local residents, interested parties, non-governmental organisations (NGOs) and associations.
Government authorities	Includes European, central and local government.
Employees	Includes Schiphol Group employees and trade unions.

Source: adapted from Schiphol Group (2012)

Table 2.3 Stakeholders at London Heathrow Airport, 2012

Stakeholder group	Stakeholders
Aviation industry	Includes airports, airlines, aircraft and engine manufacturers and air navigation service providers (such as National Air Traffic Services: NATS).
Customers	Includes passengers, airlines, retailers and other tenants.
Employees	Includes staff that work for the airport, Heathrow Express and other businesses.
Government	The government plays an important role in shaping the business through legislation and policy setting.
Local communities	Includes those people affected by airport operations, including those employed at the airport.
NGOs	Includes community groups and national organisations often taking a particular interest in environmental issues.
Regulators	Includes the UK CAA and the UK CC.
Suppliers	Includes companies that supply goods and services needed to operate the airport.

Source: adapted from BAA (2012)

country and taxation revenue; and local communities and society seeking preservation of the environment and of their quality of life. Quite clearly, these interests will not always align, as with the trade-offs associated with benefits gained from customers in constructing a new runway against the added environmental nuisance and disruption for the local communities. It is therefore important for airport marketers to fully understand the interests of these different groups and to establish, alongside management from other relevant departments, effective dialogue and cooperation with them all, so that both issues of mutual attention and conflicts of interest can be addressed.

2.3 The airport's macroenvironment

2.3.1 Political and legal factors

These include all government policies and associated regulations, conventions and laws. Consideration of these involves an assessment of general issues such as political stability, ideology and motivation, as well as specific policies that directly affect the organisation. The policies may place constraints on the operating environment of the organisation; protect customers, employees and other stakeholders; and open up new business opportunities.

There are many political and legal factors for the airport industry, but it is difficult to view these in isolation from other parts of the aviation industry, such as airlines and air traffic control, because of the close interrelationships between these sectors. In addition, aviation's international nature means that most governments do not have total freedom to initiate policies that are fully independent of those of other countries. Many decisions related to aviation are determined at a global level through the International Civil Aviation Organisation (ICAO), which is an agency of the United Nations and has around 190 countries as members. Many policies have emerged as a consequence of the Chicago Convention of 1944, which established an international regulatory air transport system to deal with the many aspects of aviation. There are also likely to be regional influences that airport marketers need to consider: for instance, the European Commission (EC) has been playing an increasingly active role in aviation policies and regulation in Europe.

2.3.1.1 The global political situation

The general political environment continues to be unstable in certain regions of the world; as a result, there is an ongoing threat of terrorist attacks, war or internal conflict. This has an impact on both the demand and supply of airport services and has created a more volatile or uncertain operating environment. This may cause airlines to reduce, suspend or withdraw services as demand falls because of safety and security concerns. The impacts can potentially be widespread, such as after 9/11 when global airport passenger traffic declined by 2.6 per cent in 2001 and again by 0.4 per cent in 2002. For North America, the impact was greater, with corresponding drops in passenger numbers of 6.3 and 2.7 per cent. Other events – for example, the attacks at the Luxor Temple in Egypt in 1997 and the Kuta nightclub in Bali in 2002, which both reduced visitor numbers by around 20 per cent in the following year – may have more localised effects but nevertheless will result in major challenges for the airports concerned (Graham, 2008a). In such cases, effective crisis and recovery management must be a key element of marketing strategies of all sectors of the travel industry, including airports. A more recent event is the political unrest in North Africa, known as the Arab Spring of 2011, which resulted in substantial declines in international passenger numbers in Africa for most months in 2011 as tourists shifted their holidays to different destinations (see Figure 2.6).

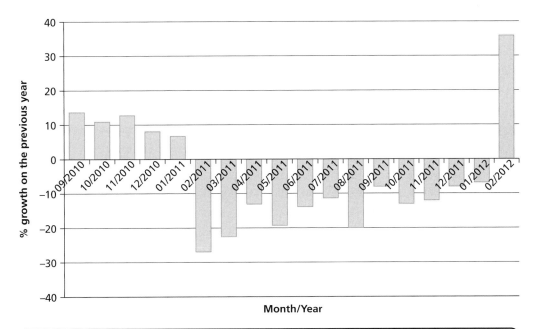

Figure 2.6 International airport passengers at African airports by month, 2010–2012

Data source: compiled by authors from ACI data

The impact of such developments can also mean that passengers become subject to more rigid security and immigration procedures that can cause disruption to journeys and affect the passenger experience, increasing the hassle factor associated with passing through an airport. In the US, security services were totally reorganised after 9/11 with the establishment of the Transportation Security Administration (TSA), which consequently had far-reaching impacts on airport costs, passenger travel habits and flow patterns through the terminal (Aaronson, 2005; Raffel and Ramsay, 2011). Recent examples when more stringent security regulations have been introduced have come after the attempted shoe bomb in December 2001, after the liquid explosives scare in August 2006 and the attempted underwear bomb of December 2011. Such responses have tended to be reactive, adding new security measures after each occurrence. For example, as a consequence of the liquid explosives scare, only a limited amount of liquids, aerosols and gels (LAGs) can now be taken on board as hand luggage and must be in a see-through plastic bag. Similarly, the attempted underwear bomb has encouraged greater use of full body scans to detect such bombs, although this remains a controversial development because of privacy and health concerns.

All these changes can clearly have marketing implications, especially in terms of how passengers perceive air travel and their airport experience, and their ability to fully take advantage of the commercial facilities at the airport. Future developments to streamline some of the processes and make them less onerous and intrusive will very much depend on enhancing the ties between government agencies, airports and airlines to ensure more harmonisation and better sharing of intelligence information, together with developing more efficient detection processes, especially with the use of advanced technology and biometrics. Indeed the International Air Transport Association (IATA) has a vision for the 'checkpoint of the future'. This will involve three different levels of security, for 'known traveller', 'normal', and 'enhanced security' passengers, based on a biometric identifier in the passport or other travel document that triggers the results of a risk assessment conducted on previously held passenger information (IATA, 2012a).

2.3.1.2 Airport ownership and privatisation

As discussed in Chapter 1, the airport industry has come a long way from being viewed as purely a state-owned public utility, dependent on public finances to serve the needs of airlines. Worldwide, many airports have loosened their ties with government, have adopted more business-like management philosophies, and are now viewed as commercial enterprises rather than public infrastructure. This has required a shift in government thinking concerning its involvement with airports. In some cases to fulfil certain objectives, such as raising additional capital funds or improving efficiency, governments have gone one stage further by privatising their airports (Graham, 2011a).

The first major privatisation occurred in the UK in 1987 with BAA; since then a number of other countries, in both developed and developing regions, have seen it become an increasingly important trend. A 2007 study of 459 airports worldwide showed that 24 per cent of airports were either partially or fully under private ownership (ICAO, 2008). In 2008, it was found that 13 per cent of airports in Europe were owned by public–private shareholders and 9 per cent were fully privatised: in total, airports with some kind of private involvement handled nearly half of all European passenger traffic (ACI Europe, 2010). In developing countries, or low/middle income countries as defined by the World Bank, there has been private participation in airports in 48 different countries (World Bank, 2011).

Airport privatisation is actually a very broad term that covers a range of different alternatives (Graham, 2008b). In all cases there is a transfer of management to the private sector and there may also be a transfer of ownership. A partial or total share flotation has been used at some airports, but has not been a popular model in recent years. More common options now are a trade sale, when some or the entire airport is sold to a trade partner or consortium of investors, or a concession agreement, when the airport will be operated by a partially or totally private consortium for a fixed period of time – typically between 20 to 30 years. Similar to the concession model is project finance privatisation such as a build–operate–transfer (BOT) project, which requires investment in a major large piece of infrastructure such as a new airport or terminal (see Table 2.4).

The amount of influence a government can exert over an airport is clearly dependent on the type of ownership that exists. For many countries, the transfer to the private sector of airports considered to be strategic and vital national or regional assets with both economic benefits and environmental costs to the communities they serve is a politically sensitive policy. So a substantial number of airports choose to remain under public ownership and opt to benefit from private management expertise and funding through concession or BOT models and public–private partnerships (PPPs). By contrast, little state control will remain after an airport has been floated on the stock market or privatised with a trade sale. However, even in these cases, governments may decide to maintain control by only partially selling the airport: this has also been a popular option with many airports.

Private and public sector owners are likely to have different objectives and priorities that may affect all areas of operation, including marketing. In particular, through their ownership of airports, governments may support airline services because of the broader catalytic impacts, such as an increase in inbound tourism or the encouragement of inward investment that such services may bring to the surrounding region. This may result in direct internal marketing support and airline incentives but such policies have proved controversial in some cases, especially in Europe, where it has been argued that they could be viewed as state aid to airlines, which is illegal

Table 2.4 Examples of airport privatisations

Type of privatisation			
Share flotation	*Trade sale*	*Concession*	*Project finance/BOT*
BAA	Liverpool	Barranquilla	Athens
Vienna	East Midlands	Caratagena	Terminal 4, John F.
Copenhagen	Birmingham	La Paz	Kennedy International
Rome	Naples	Santa Cruz	International Airport
Ljubljana	Brisbane	Cochabamba	Ankara
Auckland	Melbourne	Luton	Hyderabad
Malaysia Airports	Sydney	Argentinean airports	Bangalore
Beijing	Dusseldorf	Montevideo	Tirana
Zurich	South Africa	San Jose	Larnaca
Florence	Wellington	Cali	Paphos
Frankfurt	Hamburg	Lima	Varna
Hainan Meilan	Malta	Montega Bay	Burgas
Airports of Thailand	Brussels	Delhi/Mumbai	Amman
Venice	Budapest	Antayla	Tbilisi
Paris	Kosice	Male	Batumi
Pisa	Leeds Bradford	Pristina	Monastir
	Xi'an	St Petersburg	Enfidha
	BSCA	Zagreb	Izmir
			Medinah

Source: compiled by the authors from various sources

Note: the table only shows the first privatisation; in a few cases a different model now exists

(Echevarne, 2008). As discussed in Chapter 7, there was a test case concerning BSCA: this resulted in EU guidelines on start-up aid to airlines from airports being agreed (these are currently in the process of being revised). Elsewhere, if government links through ownership have been severed with privatisation, such support may come from external public bodies such as regional development agencies or tourism authorities. The route development fund (RDF) in the UK was a good example of this (Smyth *et al.*, 2012). RDFs are discussed in more detail in Chapter 7. Whether the airport is in public or private hands will also have an impact on how it is viewed by the local community, and hence will influence other marketing activities such as public relations.

Privatisation of airports has also opened the door for the emergence of multi-airport international companies (Forsyth *et al.*, 2011). Some of these are well-established airport operators, such as Fraport, AdP, Zurich Airport, CAG and Malaysia Airports that have expanded beyond previously well-defined national barriers. However, there are also other operators, originally from other sectors such as property, utility, infrastructure and construction that saw some potential synergies with airport operations. These include Ferrovial, Vinci, Hocthief, Peel Holdings, GMR and GVK. Financial investors, such as investment banks, pension funds and private equity funds, have also become directly involved with running airports, as in the case of Global Infrastructure

Partners (GIP), which manages London City, London Gatwick and Edinburgh airports. Clearly, the type of organisation that owns the airport will have a significant impact on all operations, from its mission and vision established by top managers and downwards through the organisation, including its marketing function. It is also different managing a group of airports compared to being focused on just one. From a marketing viewpoint such airport groups may be able to benefit from shared knowledge and expertise and economies of scale with certain activities. However, the promotion of a common brand, which is typical of so many other multi-national companies, is not a usual feature of such companies (branding is discussed in Chapter 6).

2.3.1.3 Airport regulation

It is often feared when airports have been privatised that they will abuse their market power and will not always operate with the interests of the airport users in mind, raising charges, reducing the quality of service and under-investing in facilities. This has frequently resulted in formal economic regulation being introduced at the same time as privatisation. Although such prescribed systems are not solely limited to privatised airports, it is generally more common to find less formal processes just requiring government approval of charges at state-controlled airports. Clearly, the system of economic regulation a government adopts will have a major influence on how the airport prices its products, the amount of control exerted by the regulator, and the type of relationship that can be developed between the airport operator and its customers. In addition, airport operators need to comply with the worldwide charging principles established by ICAO, and if based in Europe will also be subject to the EC directive on airport charges. These are explained in detail in Chapter 7, which looks at pricing.

If the regulatory system introduces some control on prices, there is often a concern that this will consequently provide a strong incentive for airports to cut service levels in pursuit of cost-saving measures. For this reason, under some regulatory regimes there is a condition that service quality should be monitored, and in some cases rebates to airlines are allowable if certain targets are not achieved. In Australia, satisfaction ratings by passengers and survey feedback from airlines and agencies at the airports are monitored. At other airports, such as the London airports of Heathrow, Gatwick and Stansted, the airports of AdP, Dublin Airport, Delhi's Indira Gandhi International Airport, and Mumbai's Chatrapati Shivaji International Airport, service targets are set. For example, at the London airports these are based on an aerodrome congestion delay measure, a group of objective operational measures and some scores from passenger feedback surveys (Chapter 4 provides a discussion on how airport service quality is measured). Rebates for poor performance and bonuses for good service are linked to these.

In addition to government policies related to security, ownership and price control at airports, there are many others – established at a global, regional or national level – that need to be taken into account by airport marketers. These cover diverse areas such as safety, persons with reduced mobility (PRMs) and consumer protection. Airports are also subject to an increasing number of environmental regulations. In Europe, there is also the directive on access to the ground handling market at community airports, which was introduced in 1996 to ensure that such activities were offered on a fully competitive basis. It had as its aim the end of all ground handling monopolies and duopolies within the EU by opening up the market to third party handlers, recognising the right of airlines to self-handle and guaranteeing at least some choice for airlines in the provision of ground handling services (the ground handling market is discussed in more detail in Chapter 9). The EC is now planning to introduce new regulation in this area, to provide for greater choice and to reinforce stable employment conditions, as part of its airport package reforms proposed in 2011 (see EC, 2011). This clearly has marketing implications, as it will have an impact on the airport product which is on offer to its customers.

One of the most basic obstacles to airport competition is the shortage of airport slots (which is discussed in more detail in Chapter 9). The EC's 1993 regulation on common rules for the allocation of slots at community airports (further amended in 2004) gave a legal basis in Europe to the voluntary IATA scheduling committee rules; these are used virtually everywhere (except the United States) where demand for slots exceeds supply. The most important of these rules is 'grandfather rights', which gives any airline that operated a slot in the previous season the right to operate it again, as long as 80 per cent of the flights are actually operated: the so-called 'use it or lose it' rule. Although this system provides a relatively stable environment for allocating slots, it is not the most effective in managing their scarcity or in encouraging competition. Hence there has been increasing pressure, particularly in the EU, for slot allocation reform using market mechanisms, and this has also been proposed in the EC's 2011 airport package for secondary trading. For airport marketers, slot reform is an important issue, as it can play a key role in determining an airline's ability to operate from a congested airport.

2.3.1.4 Airline developments

In addition to the political forces that have substantially changed the ownership and regulation of airports, there has been a fundamental transformation of the airline political environment. This has been primarily due to the continuing liberalisation and deregulation of the airline industry, which has moved away from the traditional system of tight regulatory interference of airlines' operations by freeing up constraints in the areas of market entry, capacity and pricing. As mentioned in Chapter 1, this trend started in the US with domestic deregulation in 1978, followed by the liberalisation of a number of US international routes. The movement then spread to other regions such as the EU, with the stepwise implementation of the three liberalisation packages for international routes within Europe between 1987 and 1997. In Asia, the ASEAN open skies agreement between ten Southeast Asian countries is due to be completed by 2015. Domestic markets in other countries such as Canada, Australia, Brazil and India have been deregulated, as have many international routes. Some notable examples include the 2008 EU–US open skies agreement and the subsequent agreement with Canada, but elsewhere many other countries in regions such as Asia, the Middle East and South America have also renegotiated more liberal open market or open skies ASAs (Doganis, 2010).

Liberalisation and deregulation have been demonstrated to encourage growth and to open up many markets to much greater competition. The Indian market is just one of many examples that illustrate this. In 2004 there were three carriers operating 34 weekly frequencies between the UK and India, but in 2006 after liberalisation there were five carriers operating 112 weekly frequencies (UK CAA, 2006). Generally, deregulation has encouraged hub and spoke networks and new international connections from regional airports. Many airports will benefit from a more liberal and competitive environment but it is by no means guaranteed. For example, the relaxation of rules relating to airport use with the 2008 EU–US open skies agreement led to both London Gatwick Airport and Shannon Airport in Ireland losing substantial market share of traffic on the North Atlantic routes (Graham, 2011b).

There have also been major changes in the structure and ownership of the airline industry. Historically, almost all the world's major airlines (like airports) were state-owned, primarily for reasons of prestige, defence and to fulfil wider objectives such as economic development and the growth of tourism. However, in the last two decades or so attitudes have changed significantly and many formerly state-owned airlines have been totally or partially privatised. Fully private airlines now include carriers as diverse as British Airways, Lufthansa, Air Canada, JAL, LAN Chile and Qantas, while a mixed ownership structure exists for many other airlines such as Aer Lingus, SAS, Finnair, Malaysia Airlines, Kenya Airways, Air China, China Southern and China Eastern (Morrell, 2007).

The combined impact of airline deregulation and privatisation has encouraged the development of the global alliances of Star, oneworld and SkyTeam, which now account for 60 per cent of all scheduled RPKs (see Figure 2.7). The more liberal environment and more uncertain market conditions have also encouraged joint ventures on North Atlantic and Pacific routes, and airline mergers and acquisitions such as Air France/KLM, British Airways/Iberia, LAN Chile/TAM, Avianca/TACA and Luftansa's purchase of other airlines such as Brussels Airlines, eurowings and Austrian. This is in addition to domestic mergers such as Air India/Indian Airlines, Alitalia/Air One, Delta/Northwest, Continental/United, Southwest/Air Tran and British Airways/BMI. Such airline consolidation provides both opportunities and threats for airports. Links with alliances may bring access to larger markets and an opportunity to serve more widespread destinations. However, the consolidation process may also bring the realignment of schedules and capacities, and even the dropping of a hub entirely to avoid duplication and to streamline services.

Liberalisation and deregulation have also encouraged the development of the LCC industry, which now has a global traffic share of 17 per cent compared to just 6 per cent in 2003 (see Figure 2.8). In some regions, such as Europe, the market share is much higher. Again, there are numerous examples of LCCs bringing much needed traffic to smaller airports and having other positive impacts such as reducing seasonality and raising the airport's profile. However, a number of these carriers have not survived, including Air Polonia, EUJet, Snowflake, Sterling, Volare, Skybus, and Sky Europe (although this sector is not unique in producing failures). LCCs also tend to be rather footloose in terms of shifting from one airport to another. This has added to the more volatile environment, with various airports seeing dramatic increases in traffic as LCCs launch services, and then sudden decreases if the airline fails or shifts to another airport. In addition, as airline consolidation is now accelerating in both the legacy airline and LCC sectors, many airport marketers have the challenging task of negotiating and satisfying the needs of these ever-changing

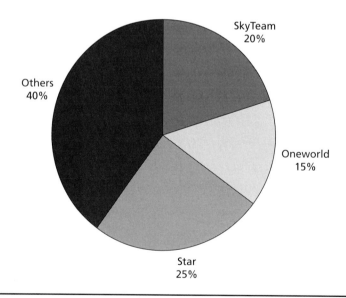

Figure 2.7 Scheduled RPKs by alliance, 2011
Data source: Airline Business (2012)

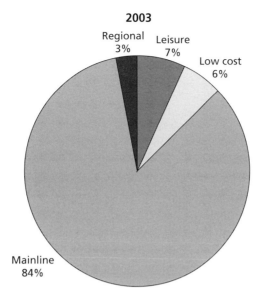

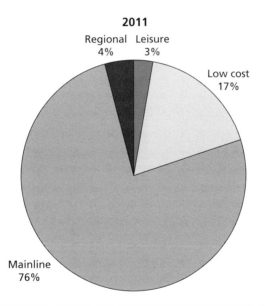

Figure 2.8 RPKs by airline type, 2003 and 2011
Data sources: Pilling (2004); Dunn (2012)

and potentially more dominant customers. New approaches such as long-term contracts between airport operators and LCCs have been adopted in some cases. The evolving airport–airline relationship is examined in more detail in Chapter 3.

2.3.2 Economic factors

Economic factors include both national and global factors that can have a major impact on the demand for the products of an organisation, as well as the way it operates and makes decisions. Some of the most important factors include income growth and distribution, inflation rates, exchange rates, trade patterns and business cycles, buying power and willingness to spend, and levels of employment and taxation.

Demand for aviation services has always very closely followed trends in income growth (Doganis, 2010). Typically, when income or gross domestic product (GDP) rises, passenger and cargo volumes increase; when GDP falls or stagnates, the reverse situation generally occurs. For leisure passengers this will clearly be the result of greater consumer confidence, more disposable income and higher levels of employment when there is economic prosperity. By contrast, when the economy slows down or moves into recession there will be less disposable income, higher unemployment and general insecurity. Likewise, business travel and cargo traffic will mirror the peaks and troughs of business and trade activity, which are closely linked to the economy (Kupfer *et al.*, 2011). Figure 2.9 clearly shows the link between economic growth and passenger demand, particularly when there was relatively healthy growth in the late 1990s and mid-2000s and with the deep recession of 2008 to 2009. There was also a period of uncertainty in 2001 to 2003, both in terms of economic growth and in terms of passenger confidence in the aftermath of 9/11 and ongoing security threats, as discussed earlier in this chapter.

Weak or negative passenger and cargo growth during challenging economic conditions is likely to be a result of airlines flying less full aircraft, reducing frequencies and even suspending some services. This will clearly have an impact on the aeronautical revenues generated by an airport

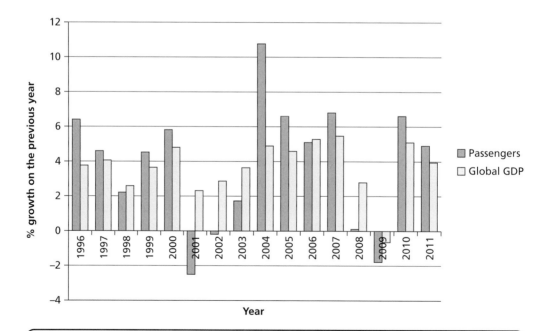

Figure 2.9 Economic growth and airport passenger demand, 1996–2011
Data source: compiled by authors from ACI and International Monetary Fund (IMF) data

operator. However, commercial revenues will also decline, not only because fewer passengers will be flying but also because they are likely to have less money and less confidence in spending on commercial services. It is thus crucial for airport marketers to understand the role played by the health of the economy and the need to work hard to grow or even just maintain traffic levels when the economic and market conditions are poor, perhaps by sharing more of the risk with airlines and other vulnerable customers. For example, Singapore Changi Airport introduced a support scheme for its airlines – its air hub development fund – after 9/11. It then decided to extend this support in 2009 because of the global economic recession, offering a 25 per cent rather than 15 per cent landing fee rebate and a 15 per cent rebate for tenants of offices, airline lounges and warehouse space.

Clearly, economic factors also have major influences on the regional distribution of air traffic. The higher growth predicted for the BRIC countries (Brazil, Russia, India and China) and other emerging nations will lead to increases in passenger and cargo traffic in these regions (Boeing, 2012) (see Figure 2.10). It will mean that the Asia-Pacific region will become the world's largest aviation market in the future, while the Latin American/Caribbean region will have almost a 10 per cent share of the market (see Figure 2.11) (ACI, 2011). New trade links between the emerging economies of Asia and Latin America will also encourage air services directly between these continents, with the decline of the classic model of the developing world almost exclusively supplying goods to the developed world. Indeed, the world region pairs forecast to have the largest average annual growth rates up to 2029 are Asia-Pacific–Latin America/Caribbean (7.8 per cent), Africa–Latin America/Caribbean (7.5 per cent) and Africa–Asia-Pacific (6.9 per cent). Recent examples of new services between these regions include Buenos Aires to Cape Town, Nairobi to Bangkok and Sao Paulo to Guangzhou.

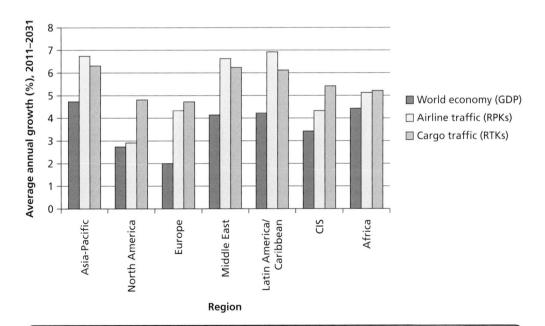

Figure 2.10 Forecast growth rates of GDP, RPKs and RTKs by region, 2011–2031

Data source: Boeing (2012)

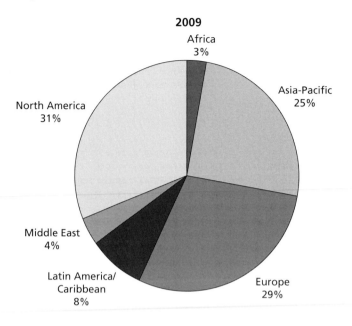

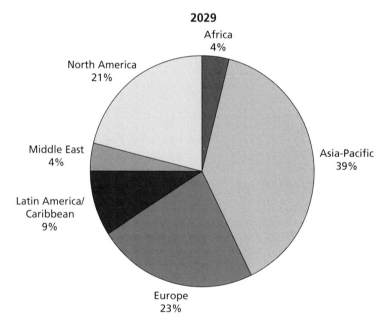

Figure 2.11 Share of airport passengers by global regions, 2009 and 2029
Data source: ACI (2011)

Other important economic influences are cost factors, especially those that will affect an airline's ability to operate efficiently and a passenger's ability to afford to travel. Air fares have fallen significantly as a result of deregulation and liberalisation, in combination with more efficient

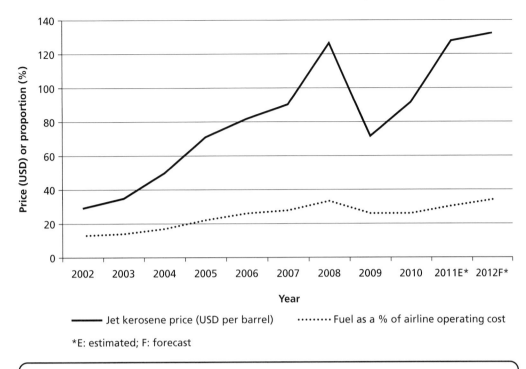

Figure 2.12 Jet kerosene price and fuel as a proportion of total airline operating cost, 2002–2012
Source: IATA (2011; 2012b)

operations. From 1980 to 2010, average worldwide real yields (cents per RPK expressed in USD) more than halved, decreasing 2.4 per cent annually (Airbus, 2011). However, a major uncertainty is the volatile price of fuel, which has generally risen significantly during the last ten years (albeit with a decline in 2009 and 2010) and now accounts for over 30 per cent of airline operating costs compared to just 13 per cent in 2002 (IATA, 2012b) (see Figure 2.12).

Another key cost factor is government passenger or ticket taxes, which are commonly defined as environmental or eco-taxes. These taxes exist in a number of countries such as the UK, Ireland and Germany. Such measures increase the cost of air travel and may have a significant impact on an airport's relative attractiveness. These are highly controversial taxes that have been fiercely debated. While their exact impact on passenger demand is not entirely clear, there is evidence to suggest that they can have a significant bearing on an airport's competitive position if there are alternative airports nearby. When a ticket tax of EUR 11.25 for short-haul travel and EUR 45.00 for long-haul travel was introduced in the Netherlands in July 2008, it was found that some of the traffic shifted to German and Belgian airports: as a result the tax was abolished one year later (Gordijn and Kolkman, 2011). Another example of the potential effect of taxes on airport competition can be found in the UK with air passenger duty (APD). Largely as a result of Continental Airlines threatening to shift its North Atlantic services from Belfast to Dublin in Ireland, where the tax is much lower, it was agreed that passengers would be allowed to pay the smaller short-haul rate on long-haul services from Belfast International Airport to help maintain its competitive position.

2.3.3 Socio-cultural factors

Social factors related to population and demography (such as age, household, education, occupation) and cultural factors (such as attitudes, preferences, values, beliefs, religion and lifestyle) can have many influences on the market potential and customer needs of an organisation, and help to explain trends and fashions. For aviation services these factors, combined with the economic factors previously discussed, will affect the volume and nature of passenger and cargo demand. A key development, for instance, with regard to leisure passenger demand is the growth of the so-called 'grey' or over-55s market. In many developed countries this market segment contains people who not only have the time to travel but are also wealthier, healthier and more experienced travellers than before. In addition, as people live longer and the birth rate falls, in many countries people of this age group will represent an important and growing share of the total population. This development will have a bearing on the types of air service demanded and their timing because these market segments are typically more flexible with travel dates. In turn, this will influence the airport facilities that support these airline services and other airport product and service features such as the retail offer and help for PRMs.

There are numerous other travel trends – especially those related to family structure, life style and life stage – that airports have to take account of, not only because they will affect the volume and nature of airline services but also since they will have an impact on the facilities offered at the airport and the potential for generating commercial income. For instance, in Western economies there is a tendency to have smaller families at an older age and this, combined with an increasing number of couples who are opting to remain childless, means that there are a growing number of young travellers who have fewer income and time constraints than families with children. At the same time, there are also a growing number of single and one-parent family travellers. The nature of business travellers is also changing, with a much wider age range and an increasing share of female passengers (Graham, 2008a). In addition, shifting labour flows in Europe and elsewhere, and a weakening of links related to historic emigration patterns, are causing a shift in the key markets related to visiting friends and relatives (VFR) traffic.

Moreover, passenger travel preferences are changing, particularly with experienced travellers of the more developed world. They are becoming more sophisticated and demanding, which is reflected in the growth in adventure, cultural and special interest holidays and in the demand for new, especially long-haul, destinations. Travellers are also seeking greater flexibility, partly in response to more flexible work patterns, and this has resulted in the growth of trips of different and short lengths rather than the traditional longer holiday break of a week or two. This desire for greater flexibility, coming at the same time as the emergence of the internet as a major travel distribution channel, has meant that the attractiveness of the LCC product is not solely based on low fares. Consequently, and especially in Europe, this has resulted in a significant decline in the package tour holiday product typically offered by charter or leisure airlines. All these shifts in preferences have had a fundamental impact on the airline industry, but again this has spread over to the airport industry as marketers seek to target and satisfy the needs of market segments that have future potential.

As discussed previously, an unstable political environment and a threat of civil unrest and terrorism can have influences on a passenger's ability and motivation to travel. Other shocks or crisis events due to natural disasters, climatic incidents and health concerns can have similar impacts. Recent events include the health scares of SARS and Swine/H1N1 flu, the Indian Ocean tsunami of 2004 and the Japanese earthquake of 2011. Such events tend to have negative effects on the traveller's perceptions of the safety and security of their transport mode and destination, as well as on their overall motivation to travel, and hence influence travel patterns, especially in the short term. In these cases airport marketers need to participate in crisis and recovery initiatives, ideally with other sectors of the tourism industry. For example, in the aftermath of the Japanese earthquake in March 2011, visitor numbers from Singapore declined by 63 per cent between March and May, and passenger movements at Singapore Changi Airport declined by 13 per cent between March and June. As a consequence, the airport launched a three-day 'Enchanting Japan' travel fair at the airport, bringing together various stakeholders in the travel sector to boost consumer confidence and promote tourism to Japan (CAG, 2011).

2.3.4 Technological factors

The technological environment is perhaps the fastest changing feature of the macroenvironment. New technologies and technological advances can create new products and new processes that can benefit customers as well as the organisation providing the product. Technological developments can reduce costs, improve quality and lead to innovation.

Technology has always played a major role in the development of the aviation industry. Advances in aircraft technology and the arrival of new aircraft types have strongly influenced the types of service that airlines offer and the reliability and costs associated with these (Snow, 2011). This in turn has had an impact on the airlines and passengers that can be attracted to certain airports. The supersonic jet Concorde, which was flown on the North Atlantic services of British Airways and Air France between 1976 and 2003, is an obvious example that gave London Heathrow Airport and Paris Charles de Gaulle Airport a distinct advantage for passengers seeking this type of niche service. More generally, the development of longer range aircraft (e.g. the Boeing 777 and the Airbus A330/340) has meant that a number of airports, for instance in Asia, have become more attractive as they can now be served direct from Europe rather than having a technical stop. Some of these technical stop airports have in turn lost out by being bypassed but others, such as Dubai International Airport and Bahrain International Airport, have reinvented themselves as destinations in their own right, or been developed as a cargo base in the case of Anchorage International Airport. The next generation of medium-sized long-haul aircraft, such as the Boeing 787 and the Airbus A350, is likely to open up further opportunities for direct global connections from regional and smaller airports serving longer and thinner routes that previously were not financially viable. This may help charter or leisure operators fly to new long-haul destinations, and indeed the leading UK charter carrier Thomson has ordered eight Boeing 787 aircraft. Likewise, it may help LCCs to develop long-haul services, which to date have been limited and not very successful. Indeed, the LCC Norwegian has recently ordered six Boeing 787s, with the aim of starting long-haul low cost services from Europe to Asia and North America.

Clearly, to take advantage of the opportunities new aircraft types can bring, airports have to ensure that they are ready to cope with the new fleet. The most notable case here is the Airbus A380 aircraft, which requires changes to airport infrastructure (such as reinforcing airfield pavements, extending runway and taxiway widths, and enlarging gate rooms and airbridges) and modifications to other processes (such as check-in, immigration, customs, security and baggage handling) to cope with the larger passenger volumes. An airport may be seriously disadvantaged if it cannot accommodate new aircraft that could be used by its potential airline customers, but it has to weigh this up against the investment costs associated with introducing the new equipment and facilities (Forsyth, 2007).

There are many other technological developments related to airfield and airspace infrastructure that are likely to improve the efficiency of operations, bring down costs in the long run and help to reduce the negative environmental impacts of aviation. As regards overall European air traffic management (ATM), this includes the single European sky project, which is now fully implemented, successor projects such as the SESAR (Single European Sky ATM Research) programme and individual airport initiatives such as airport-collaborative decision-making (A-CDM). This last concept aims to improve airport operations and streamline traffic flows through improved technology that allows the sharing of information in real time. Munich, Brussels and Paris Charles de Gaulle airports were the first to be A-CDM compliant in 2011. Similarly, the NextGen project in the US aims to improve ATM performance. All these developments can enhance the attractiveness of the airport product. However, other technological developments such as high speed rail or video-conferencing may have an opposite effect and so have to be continually monitored.

Within the terminal there are also many opportunities for technological advances (Rose, 2011). Some of these advances will be discussed in more detail in Chapter 9 within the context of CRM. A key area is check-in. In the 1990s self-service kiosks started appearing at airports, installed primarily by airlines for their own use. This was followed by the arrival of common-use self-service (CUSS), with the earliest kiosks being developed at Vancouver International Airport and Narita International Airport in 2002. At around the same time airlines started to encourage internet check-in, providing extra convenience for their passengers and substantially reducing their costs. Mobile check-in is the latest development, which is expected to grow. Some airlines – for example, Ryanair at airports such as London Stansted – no longer provide the option of checking in with a traditional desk. Many of the self-service kiosks can now be used for functions such as flight transfers and for scanning of travel documents such as passports and visas. Currently, 21 per cent of passengers use internet check-in, 19 per cent use self-service kiosks and only 3 per cent use mobile devices. However, these figures are expected to grow to 31, 22 and 15 per cent respectively by 2014, leaving less than one-third using the traditional check-in desk (SITA, 2011a).

Table 2.5 Use of self-service, mobile and social network services by airports in Europe, 2011

	Already used (%)	To be used by 2014 (%)
Self-service		
Kiosk for self-scanning of documents	44	26
Kiosk for flight transfer	24	28
e-gates for check points	9	33
e-gates for self-boarding	3	35
Common bag-drop locations	5	47
Mobile services		
Notification about flight status/delays	48	33
Target passengers with retail promotions	10	60
Navigation to gates/points of interest	5	44
Social network services		
Customer relationship handling	37	35
Flight information and operational updates	36	37
Disruption and emergency updates	26	40

Source: adapted from SITA (2011b)

Technology is increasingly being used for other passenger processes at the airport such as automated e-gates for check points and boarding gates (SITA, 2011b). There are also developments with baggage processing (e.g. self-service bag tagging, self-service bag drop and radio-frequency identification (RFID) for baggage tracking) and paperless and streamlining processes for cargo. For passengers themselves, services on mobile devices and via social networks can be used for customer service as a virtual customer service desk, for informal relationship building, for crisis handing, for corporate communications and to promote commercial services (ACI Europe, 2012). Table 2.5 shows the results of the latest survey of airport IT trends in 2011, which covers two-thirds (by revenue) of the world's top 100 airports. Some of these technologies are not very common at the moment, such as e-gates, common bag drops and some of the mobile services, but by 2014 they are expected to be used by at least one-third of all airports. It is therefore important for airport marketers to be totally familiar with all these new technologies and the benefits they can bring for passengers and other customers.

2.3.5 Environmental factors

Environmental factors have always been a key feature of the marketing macroenvironment but have received a greater profile in recent years as governments and industry have paid more attention to achieving higher levels of environmental sustainability. They include factors such as global warming, pollution control, waste disposal and conservation of energy and other scarce and natural resources.

Most airport operators have always had to address environmental resistance to their activities, primarily because of the noise nuisance and local air pollution created around the airport. This opposition has been very apparent, particularly when proposals have been put forward for expansion plans. In spite of the fact that aircraft models have become significantly quieter and cleaner over the years, the growth in air travel demand, coupled with a greater public voice about environmental issues, has meant that it is important now, more than ever before, for an airport operator to deal effectively with these concerns to ensure the continued well-being of the airport.

Measures airports can use to reduce environmental impacts can have a direct bearing on their attractiveness to airlines, so this needs to be taken into account by airport marketers. For instance, many airports differentiate their charges by noise levels, and an increasing number do this for emissions as well (e.g. London Heathrow, Frankfurt, Zurich, Stockholm Arlanda). The result is that the airports may become expensive for airlines that have older fleets. Airports may also be subject to night time or noise bans or restrictions, often government imposed, which are common practice at airports such as Wellington International, Ronald Reagan Washington National, London Heathrow, Madrid Barajas, Brussels, Frankfurt and Amsterdam Schiphol. These may make the airport less attractive for certain types of airlines, especially cargo operators. For example, DHL shifted its European cargo base from Brussels Airport to Leipzig/Halle Airport because of night time noise limitations at Brussels.

In addition to the environmental impacts caused by aircraft operations, the surface transport to and from the airport will also cause emissions and noise. As a result, a growing number of airports have introduced initiatives to improve public transport use. This may make the airport product more attractive to passengers (e.g. with the building of direct rail links) but could also have a negative effect (e.g. with limits on parking spaces or higher charges). As with other environmental issues, there is a balancing act that needs to be performed for all the different stakeholders of an airport (especially customers versus local residents) and airport marketers must ensure that they take this into consideration.

Historically the environmental issues have been debated primarily at a local level but in recent years a far more wide-reaching concern has risen up the political agenda: that of climate change.

Aviation currently contributes to around 2 to 3 per cent of the world's CO_2 emissions and closer to 4 per cent if non-CO_2 impacts are taken into account (International Transport Forum, 2010; Transport and Environment, 2012). However, while aviation's contribution to greenhouse gas emissions is currently a small part of the total, these emissions are forecast to increase in absolute terms because of traffic growth. In addition, because of improvements being achieved in other sectors, and since there is currently no realistic and commercial alternative to aviation fuel (even though there has been increased experimentation with biofuels), it is expected that aviation will represent a higher share of total emissions in the future. Clearly, this is an issue that needs to be considered by all aviation sectors and not just airports, although action at an airport level to improve local emissions will have a favourable impact.

As global warming concerns escalate, this could potentially have a more fundamental effect on the demand for airline and airport services, as strong moral pressure builds against the taking of air trips, and consumers opt for other modes of transport or not to travel at all. There may also be greater pressure for business travellers to use video-conferencing. Environmental policies at tourist destinations may also influence traveller preferences and holiday choice. Surveys among UK residents illustrate these changing attitudes towards air travel (Department for Transport, 2012) (see Table 2.6). Between 2003 and 2011 the number of respondents agreeing that 'people should be able to travel by plane as much as they like' decreased from 79 to 62 per cent, while

Table 2.6 British social attitudes survey, 2003–2011

	% respondents that agree with each statement, by year of survey								
	2003	2004	2005	2006	2007	2008	2009	2010	2011
People should be able to travel by plane as much as they like.	79	77	70	69	63	66	64	64	62
People should be able to travel by plane as much as they like, even if new terminals or runways are needed to meet the demand.	52	43	43	44	40	42	42	36	37
People should be able to travel by plane as much as they like, even if this harms the environment.	19	15	18	19	19	18	20	18	18
The price of a plane ticket should reflect the environmental damage that flying causes, even if this makes air travel more expensive.	–	–	–	48	49	46	45	42	41

Source: adapted from Department for Transport (2012)

those agreeing with the clause, 'even if it meant having new terminals or runways', decreased from 52 to 37 per cent. A consistent share of only around one-fifth of respondents agreed that people should be free to fly even if this harms the environment. However, in spite of this general increase in concern, a declining number of less than half the respondents (48 per cent in 2006 to 41 per cent in 2011) agreed that 'the price of the plane ticket should reflect the environmental demand that flying causes, even if this makes air travel more expensive'. This demonstrates the dilemma of matching consumers' concern for the environment with their willingness to pay for air travel. Emissions trading has already been introduced in Europe (in 2012), which may increase the cost of travel, especially when combined with passenger taxes such as the APD that have been growing in number.

An airport, just like any other organisation in today's world, is increasingly under pressure to measure its carbon footprint and reduce its own carbon emissions. Swedavia in Sweden became the world's first national airport group to achieve carbon neutrality across its (ten) airports in 2012. Other airports to achieve neutrality include Oslo and Trondheim in Norway, and Malpensa and Linate in Italy. A growing number of airports also belong to ACI Europe's airport carbon accreditation programme; this was launched in 2009 and was subsequently extended to ACI Asia-Pacific members in 2011. As with other industry sectors, airport marketers must recognise the importance of such initiatives and ensure that they are effectively communicated to all stakeholders through public relations and promotional activities.

2.3.6 The PESTE analysis

The PESTE analysis provides a framework for airport marketers to analyse opportunities and threats in their macroenvironment and is an important input for the situation analysis discussed in Chapter 5. The factors will clearly vary in importance depending, for instance, on the location of the airport, the markets the airport serves and the type of services it offers. It is possible to use a PESTE analysis to identify a number of different scenarios that might develop, which can help in guiding the marketing planning process. An interesting example was produced by the UK

Table 2.7 Factors likely to influence future scenarios for aviation in the UK

Main factor	Sub-factors
Political and legal	EU intervention, taxation policy, emissions targets, closure of tax loop-holes.
Economic	Global economic outlook, price of oil, availability of public finance, operational costs, access to credit, growth of Asian economies, airport ownership.
Socio-cultural	Security and safety, ageing population, public attitudes to flying (and influence of the media), immigration, emigration, freedom of movement.
Technological	Alternative fuels, high speed rail technology, video-conferencing.
Environmental	Climate change, air quality, noise pollution, personal carbon accounting, pandemics, congestion.

Source: adapted from ICE (2010)

Institution of Civil Engineers (ICE) when they consulted industry representatives to consider future scenarios for aviation and aviation infrastructure (ICE, 2010). They developed four scenarios: eco-angst (peak oil, economic liberalisation, eco-awareness); laissez-faire (light touch government, regional prosperity, advanced climate change); vortex of despair (political flux, economic malaise, fear) and big stick (interventionist government, economic prosperity in the south east of the UK, carbon rationing). Table 2.7 shows the key factors identified for the analysis, and demonstrates how the PESTE tool can be used.

References

Aaronson, R. (2005) 'Forces driving industry change – impacts for airports strategic scope' in W. Delfmann, H. Baum, S. Auerbach and S. Albers (eds) *Strategic Management in the Aviation Industry*, Aldershot: Ashgate.

ACI (2011) *ACI Global Traffic Forecast 2010–2029*, Montreal: ACI.

ACI Europe (2010) *The Ownership of Europe's Airports*, Brussels: ACI Europe.

ACI Europe (2012) *Digital Report 2012*, Brussels: ACI Europe.

Airbus (2011) *Global Market Forecast 2011–2030*, Toulouse: Airbus.

Airline Business (2012) 'Allied forces', *Airline Business*, September; 28–9.

BAA (2012) *Our stakeholders*, Hounslow: BAA Airports Limited. Online. http://www.baa.com/about-baa/how-we-do-it/our-stakeholders (accessed 15 October 2012).

Boeing (2012) *Current Market Outlook 2012–2031*, Seattle: Boeing.

CAG (2011) *Changi Airport Group launches effort to stimulate Japan travel*, Singapore: CAG. Online. Available at: http://www.changiairport.com/our-business/airport-news/changi-airport-group-launches-effort-to-stimulate-japan-travel (accessed 10 October 2012).

CAG (2012) *What we do*, Singapore: CAG. Online. Available at: http://www.changiairportgroup.com/cag/html/the-group/what-we-do.html (accessed 15 October 2012).

Cooper, C., Fletcher, J., Fyall, A., Gilbert, D. and Wanhill, S. (2008) *Tourism Principles and Practice*, 4th edn, Harrow: Prentice Hall-Pearson Education.

Copenhagen Airports (2012) *Organisation chart for Copenhagen Airports A/S*, Kastrup: Copenhagen Airports. Online. Available at: http://www.cph.dk/CPH/UK/Newsroom/Who+What+and+Where/Key+persons/Organization+Chart.htm (accessed 16 October 2012).

Dallas/Fort Worth International Airport (2012) *Dallas/Fort Worth International Airport organisational chart*, DFW Airport: Dallas/Fort Worth International Airport. Online. Available at: https://www.dfwairport.com/about/pdf/seniorstaff.pdf (accessed 15 October 2012).

Department for Transport (2012) *British Social Attitudes Survey 2011*, London: Department for Transport.

Dibb, S., Simkin, L., Pride, W. and Ferrell, O. (2006) *Marketing: Concepts and Strategies*, 5th European edn, Boston: Houghton Mifflin.

Doganis, R. (2010) *Flying Off Course: Airline Economics and Marketing*, 4th edn, Abingdon: Routledge.

Dubai Airports (2012) *Organisation structure*, Dubai: Dubai Airports. Online. Available at: http://www.dubaiairports.ae/en/about-da/PublishingImages/Org.gif (accessed 15 October 2012).

Dunn, G. (2012) 'Airlines hold up the traffic', *Airline Business*, August; 53.

EC (2011) *Airport Policy in the European Union – Addressing Capacity and Quality to Promote Growth, Connectivity and Sustainable Mobility*, COM(2011) 823 final, Brussels: EC.

Echevarne, R. (2008) 'Impact of attracting low cost carriers' in A. Graham, A. Papatheodorou and P. Forsyth (eds) *Aviation and Tourism: Implications for Leisure Travel*, Aldershot: Ashgate.

Forsyth, P. (2007) 'The impacts of emerging aviation trends on airport infrastructure', *Journal of Air Transport Management*, 13(1); 45–52.

Forsyth, P., Niemeier, H-M. and Wolf, H. (2011) 'Airport alliances and mergers – structural change in the airport industry?', *Journal of Air Transport Management*, 17(1); 49–58.

Forsyth, P., Gillen, D., Mueller, J. and Niemeier, H-M. (eds) (2010) *Airport Competition*, Aldershot: Ashgate.

Gordijn, H. and Kolkman, J. (2011) *Effects of the Air Passenger Tax: Behavioural Responses of Passengers, Airlines and Airports*, EX Den Haag: KiM Netherlands Institute for Transport Policy Analysis.

Graham, A. (2006) 'Competition in airports' in A. Papatheodorou (ed.) *Corporate Rivalry and Market Power*, London: I.B. Tauris.

Graham, A. (2008a) 'Trends and characteristics of leisure travel' in A. Graham, A. Papatheodorou and P. Forsyth (eds) *Aviation and Tourism: Implications for Leisure Travel*, Aldershot: Ashgate.

Graham, A. (2008b) *Managing Airports: An International Perspective*, 3rd edn, Oxford: Butterworth-Heinemann.

Graham, A. (2011a) 'The objectives and outcomes of airport privatisation', *Research in Transportation Business and Management*, 1(1); 3–14.

Graham, A. (2011b) 'The impact of North Atlantic passenger services on airports' in R. Macario and E. Van de Voorde (eds) *Critical Issues in Air Transport Economics and Business*, Abingdon: Routledge.

IATA (2011) *Financial Forecast September 2011*, Montreal: IATA.

IATA (2012a), *Checkpoint of the future*, Montreal: IATA. Online. Available at: http://www.iata.org/whatwedo/security/Pages/checkpoint-future.aspx (accessed 7 January 2013).

IATA (2012b) *Financial Forecast September 2012*, Montreal: IATA.

ICAO (2008) *Ownership, Organisation and Regulatory Practices of Airports and Air Navigation Services Providers 2007*, Montreal: ICAO.

ICE (2010) *Aviation 2040: Future Scenarios for Aviation and Airport Infrastructure*, London: ICE.

International Transport Forum (2010) *Reducing Transport Greenhouse Gas Emissions: Trends and Data*, Paris: International Transport Forum.

Jarach, D. (2005) *Airport Marketing: Strategies to Cope with the New Millennium Environment*, Farnham: Ashgate.

Kotler, P., Wong, V., Saunders, J. and Armstrong, G. (2008) *Principles of Marketing*, 5th European edn, Harlow: Prentice Hall-Pearson Education.

Kupfer, F., Meersan, H., Onghena, E. and Van de Voorde, E. (2011) 'World air cargo and merchandise trade' in R. Macario and E. Van de Voorde (eds) *Critical Issues in Air Transport Economics and Business*, Abingdon: Routledge.

LeighFisher (2011) *UK Airport Performance Indicators 2010/2011*, London: LeighFisher.

Morrell, P. (2007) *Airline Finance*, 3rd edn, Farnham: Ashgate.

Pilling, M. (2004) 'Passenger recovery', *Airline Business*, August; 65–6.

Pride, W. and Ferrell, O. (2008) *Marketing*, 14th edn, Boston: Houghton Mifflin Company.

Raffel, R. and Ramsay, J. (2011) 'Aviation security in the United States' in J. O'Connell and G. Williams (eds) *Air Transport in the 21st Century*, Farnham: Ashgate.

Rose, N. (2011) *Navigating the Airport of Tomorrow*, Madrid: Amadeus/Travel Tech Consulting.

Schiphol Group (2012) *Our stakeholders*, Schiphol: Schiphol Group. Online. Available at: http://www.schiphol.nl/SchipholGroup/CorporateResponsibility/OurStakeholders.htm (accessed 15 October 2012).

Shaw, S. (2011) *Airline Marketing and Management*, 7th edn, Farnham: Ashgate.

SITA (2011a) *Airline IT Trends Survey 2011*, Brussels: SITA/Airline Business.

SITA (2011b) *Airport IT Trends Survey 2011*, Brussels: SITA/Airline Business.

Smyth, A., Christodoulou, G., Dennis, N. Al-Azzawi M. and Campbell, J. (2012) 'Is air transport a necessity for social inclusion and economic development?', *Journal of Air Transport Management*, 22(July); 53–9.

Snow, J. (2011) 'Advances in transport aircraft and engines' in J. O'Connell and G. Williams (eds) *Air Transport in the 21st Century*, Farnham: Ashgate.

Transport and Environment (2012) *A New Flightplan: Getting Global Aviation Climate Measures off the Ground: Aviation Conference Background Report*, Brussels: Transport and Environment.

UK CAA (2006) *UK–India Air Services: A Case Study in Liberalisation*, London: UK CAA.

UK CC (2009) *BAA Airports Market Investigation*, London: UK CC.

World Bank (2011) *Private participation in infrastructure database*, Washington, DC: The World Bank Group. Online. Available at: http://ppi.worldbank.org/explore/ppi_exploreSubSector.aspx?SubSectorID=5 (accessed 15 October 2012).

Chapter 3

The market for airport services

This chapter explores the market for airport services and consists of two main sections. The first discusses the range of airport customers (including trade, passengers and others), their behaviour, and the factors affecting their choice of airport. The second section considers airport market segmentation, covering the segmentation process (including the concept of market segmentation and segmentation variables for key airport markets) and strategies for airport market targeting and positioning.

3.1 The airport's customers

The focal point of any marketing system is always the customer, and a thorough understanding of customers is essential for effectively planning the marketing mix at the later stage of the marketing process. Chapter 2 described how customers can be defined as individuals or firms that buy the goods and services an organisation produces, and that satisfying their needs and requirements is vital for the success of any organisation. It discussed how in general terms there are usually five different customer markets: individuals, businesses that use the goods and services for their own product, resellers (such as certain intermediaries), governments that use the goods and services for public services, and international consumers that could include any of the previous customer groups if they are from another country.

3.1.1 The range of airport customers

For airports there are a variety of markets, each containing customers with specific requirements that need to be satisfied with the blend of tangible and intangible product and service features on offer at the airport. These include passengers, airlines, tour operators, travel agents, freight forwarders and visitors. In a broad sense, other businesses such as ground handlers and retail concessionaires use parts of the airport product to sell their own individual services and pay for it through concession fees or rents, and so can also be considered airport customers. Likewise, employees at the airport contribute to the product, but additionally act as customers when commercial facilities such as retail are involved.

Airports' and airlines' views of the importance of these different groups vary. Airports often define both airlines and passengers as key customers, whereas airlines may consider passengers as solely their customers, and themselves as the main customers of the airports. Freathy and

O'Connell (2000) discuss how airlines can be defined as primary customers with passengers as secondary customers, but argue that this distinction is difficult to maintain in practice because the boundaries of responsibility between airport operators and airlines are often obfuscated in the mind of the passenger. Hermann and Hazel (2012) divide airport customers into five groups: airlines, passengers, non-travellers (employees, visitors and retail customers, meeters and greeters, and neighbours), tenants/service providers (retail, car park, ground handling, advertisers), and potential development partners (real estate developers, hospitality, transportation service providers, government). Graham (2008) uses a simpler classification that defines customers as trade, passengers/freight shippers, other individuals, and other organisations. Trade customers include airlines, general aviation, tour operators, travel agents and freight forwarders.

Airlines are clearly the primary drivers of the overall air travel business: unless they provide a suitable product, passengers and freight shippers will not be able to use a certain airport. As shown in Figure 2.8 in Chapter 2, mainline or network carriers accounted for 76 per cent of RPKs globally in 2011. The second largest passenger market is LCCs, representing 17 per cent of RPKs. Then there are regional airlines (with 4 per cent of global RPKs) and charter/leisure airlines (3 per cent). In addition, the tonne kilometres performed (TKPs) of freight and mail cargo markets account for a global market share of 30 and 1 per cent respectively. This traffic is carried by a mixture of passenger and all-cargo airlines and integrated or express carriers. Furthermore, at some airports general aviation may be an important market. This can cover activities such as flight training, police aviation, air ambulance, aerial fire-fighting, surveying and crop spraying, as well as private flying and leisure pursuits such as skydiving, aerobatics and gliding. Another significant area may be private business or corporate aviation.

Other trade customers include tour operators, which have traditionally sold charter airline seats as part of a package tour. Hence, the tour operator may make the decision as to which airports should be served, while the charter airline will pay for, and consume, the airport product. In this respect, tour operators can be considered separate customers from charter airlines, although this is a grey area as many charter airlines and tour operators belonging to large integrated travel companies. Travel agents indirectly sell certain parts of the airport's product by selling airline seats, and so can be defined both as customers and distribution intermediaries. For cargo traffic, there are other intermediaries, such as freight forwarders or global logistics suppliers, which provide the interface between the freight shipper and airline. They will often make decisions regarding which airport to use to transport the cargo.

The end-users – namely the passengers and owners of cargo that is being transported – are another group of customers. Passengers are clearly of key importance to airports, not only because they consume the product the airline provides but also because they are direct customers for airport commercial facilities. Globally, as shown in Figure 2.11 in Chapter 2, the most significant passenger markets are North America, Europe and Asia-Pacific, with the last expected to become more dominant in the future. By contrast to passengers, the end-user in the cargo market rarely comes into contact with the airport itself. Instead, freight shippers tend only to deal with the forwarder or integrator away from the airport.

The 'other individual' customer category includes all individuals who will use some features of the airport product but will not be direct customers of the airlines. This includes employees at the airport who work for the airport operator, airlines, ground handlers, commercial concessionaires and other organisations. These individuals may use airport commercial facilities, primarily because of their convenience, and other facilities such as car parking. As a very broad rule of thumb there will be around 800 to 1,000 employees at an airport per million passengers; they will be potential customers but this can vary considerably depending on the type of airline and passenger and the role of the airport (Graham, 2008). A survey of a US west coast international airports found that 45 per cent of employees used the food and beverage (F&B) facilities daily and 26 per cent used them just weekly. Equivalent figures for retail were 4 and 18 per cent respectively (LeighFisher, 2011).

In addition, there will be the accompanying visitors known as 'farewellers and weepers' or 'well-wishers' and 'meeters and greeters'. These visitors may use the retail and F&B facilities in the terminal and the car parks. The size of this market will depend on the purpose of trip and length of haul of the associated passengers, and will be influenced by other factors such as culture and nationality. International and long-haul flights for passengers travelling for leisure purposes generally attract the most accompanying visitors. Figure 3.1 confirms that it is business passengers and visitors rather than residents who have the smallest number of accompanying visitors at Los Angeles International Airport. There will also be visitors not directly related to air transport activity. For instance, there may be aviation enthusiasts who visit the airport to view aircraft, buy specialist merchandise and perhaps have a tour of the airport. Local residents may also visit the airport to use the retail and F&B facilities, or business men and women may use conference and meeting facilities.

The 'other organisation' customer category includes concessionaires, who typically provide the terminal commercial facilities such as shops and F&B. Organisations such as handling agents can also be considered customers of the airport. These groups contribute to the airport operator's overall product and so are also defined as suppliers. The same reasoning can be applied to organisations that rent space or land from the airport operator both within and outside the terminal, and to businesses that are developed around the airport as a consequence of an airport operator's strategy to establish an airport city or aerotropolis (see Chapter 6).

It is important to acknowledge that some of these different customer groups will inevitably be interdependent. For instance, if the number of airlines serving the airport decreases, this is likely

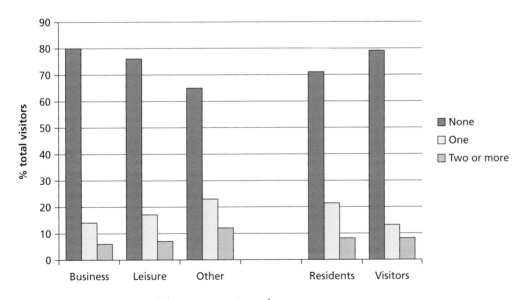

Figure 3.1 Accompanying visitors at Los Angeles International Airport by purpose of trip and type of passenger, 2006
Data source: AMPG (2007)

to reduce the volume of passengers, employees and accompanying visitors, and could ultimately – if the decline is sufficiently large – make the airport less attractive to other customers, such as the providers of commercial facilities. It is also certainly true that the different customer groups, especially the airlines and passengers, will view airports from different perspectives. In most cases, given the competitive nature of the airline industry, the interests of airlines will align quite closely with the interests of passengers. However, this may not always be the case; for instance, with airlines giving too much attention to higher yielding premium passengers, or not supporting expansion plans that might benefit passengers but increase airline competition.

3.1.2 Behaviour of airport customers

Having identified the airport's main customers, it is important to assess their behaviour in relation to the factors that will affect their choice of airport. For each customer, choosing an airport is the result of an amalgam of many complex decision processes. For passenger airlines (and tour operators if relevant), one of the most important factors is the size and nature of the catchment area, especially if point-to-point services are the main focus (Chapter 4 explains how the catchment area is measured). Depending on the type of route being considered, key factors are the business and tourist appeal of the catchment area for incoming passengers, and the characteristics and purchasing power of those residing in the catchment area. The opportunities for carrying cargo (preferably in both directions) on passenger flights need to be considered. If an airline wants to develop or maintain a hub and draw on traffic beyond the immediate catchment area, it will also look for a central geographic location in relation to the markets it wants to serve.

Clearly the airport product has to be able to meet the needs of the airline. There must be sufficient capacity and slots to enable the airline to operate the services they want now and in the future, and other airfield physical capabilities, such as runway length, need to be appropriate. The infrastructure also needs to fit the requirements of the specific airline, such as fast turnarounds for LCCs or reliable transfer facilities for network carriers. Corporate aviation operators will look for a swift, efficient and personalised service for their company executives. Commercial factors to consider include the presence of other airlines and amount of competition that exists at the airport, the fit with the rest of the airline's network, and the potential for its passengers to feed onto other services, or for other services to provide feed for them.

Just as important will be the total visiting costs of operating from the airport. Undoubtedly, the level of aeronautical charges can be crucial here, which is the reason many airports offer pricing discounts and incentives (see Chapter 7). Assistance with related activities such as the funding of market research and promotional campaigns can also be significant. In addition, airline choice will be influenced by other costs such as for handling and refuelling, which the airport operator will generally have less control over. If the airline is planning a significant presence at the airport, or wants to develop the airport as a base, this will involve recruiting local staff and so the cost of labour may be important.

Chapter 8 discusses two key websites that airports use to market themselves to airlines: The Route Shop and Routes Online. Table 3.1 identifies from these websites the main information airport marketers consider it important for airlines to know. This can be broadly categorised into route opportunities, catchment area characteristics, cargo potential, airport facilities, and pricing and marketing support.

With regard to cargo operations, airports need to have strong demand for such services or be centrally located to operate as a cargo hub. Visiting costs can again be very important as cargo traffic can be highly price sensitive and easily shifted from one airport to another by freight forwarders, as long as they can meet the delivery requirements of the shippers. More specific factors will be the ability of the airport to operate at night, and to have quick customs clearance

Table 3.1 Airport information provided on The Route Shop and Routes Online websites for potential airlines

The Route Shop	Routes Online
• New routes and frequency possibilities, and why these routes would work • Marketing and other support • Catchment area • Underserved cargo opportunities and other economic impact factors • Airport facts (geography, infrastructure and operations, important infrastructure developments and/or other news, vital statistics, financials)	• Airline opportunities • Data • Facilities • Catchment area and demographics • Pricing and incentives • Trade • Route development/marketing • Cargo

Sources: The Route Shop (www.therouteshop.com) and Routes Online (www.routesonline.com) websites

times, a good weather record, and convenient road access so that cargo can be efficiently trucked to its final destination. All-cargo flights often use large aircraft that need specialist loading and transfer equipment. In addition, certain types of cargo such as livestock, dangerous or perishable goods may require specialist handling and storage facilities that may not be available at all airports. Gardiner *et al.* (2005a) divide the factors affecting cargo operations into location (geography, local demand, operational availability), airport quality (congestion and delays, user charges, infrastructure, ground access, labour), and third party influences (environmental restrictions, bilateral ASAs, government legislation, freight forwarders, airport marketing). Table 3.2 shows the results of a survey of non-integrated carriers, which were asked to rank the most

Table 3.2 Factors influencing cargo operators' choice of airport

Factor	Rank (1 being most important)
Night operations	1
Minimise overall costs	2
Airport cargo reputation	3
Local origin–destination demand	4
Influence of freight forwarders	5
Airport road access	6
Customs clearance times	7
Financial incentive from the airport	8
Trucking time to main markets	9

Source: adapted from Gardiner *et al.* (2005b)

significant factors that influenced their choice of airport. Night operations were the most important, followed by costs, the airport reputation and local demand. For integrated carriers, factors such as the weather record to ensure high reliability and space to build dedicated facilities needed for such operations may be vital.

Considering passenger choice of airport is more complex. The nature of air services on offer (e.g. in terms of fares, destinations and schedules) – in effect the airline product – will be the crucial factor, as no one will choose to fly from an airport unless it offers the required travel opportunities. The airport can only indirectly influence these factors by marketing to airlines, so in many respects passengers will be more concerned with the flight rather than the airport. They may, for instance, choose to use an airport that would not normally be their preferred choice just to get a cheap airline deal or to gain frequent flyer points. They may also need to travel to airports beyond their local environment to access certain types of flight, such as long-haul services that are not available locally. Each individual will go through a unique and complicated process of analysing many factors in order to make a decision as to which airport to use, and it is essential for airports to try and understand this consumer behaviour.

A key factor that will affect passenger choice will be the airport's proximity and/or ease of access. This will be influenced by the cost and availability of public transport to an airport as well as the cost and convenience of car parking. It may well be that the nearest airport is not the easiest or most convenient for passengers to use. Passenger choice will also be influenced by personal preferences for a certain airport because of factors related to the airport product and the overall experience. For example, in a qualitative study of UK passengers, Sykes and Desai (2009) found that passengers preferred smaller airports because they were less formal, offered better customer care, were less congested, and allowed passengers to feel more in control. Familiarity and reliability were also considered to be important factors, especially for business travellers. Passenger choice may also be influenced by the involvement of third parties or intermediaries such as travel agents or corporate travel offices during their decision process.

Passenger surveys give some insight into reasons for choice of airport. Table 3.3 shows passenger choice factors for seven UK airports: four in London (Heathrow, Gatwick, Stansted and Luton) and three in the regions (Manchester, Birmingham and East Midlands). Location and surface access were the most important factors for all airports, but especially for those in the regions. Routes and frequency factors were much more important at London Heathrow Airport; this reflects its role as the UK's main hub airport, with a higher share of business passengers. By contrast, cost was much more important at London Stansted Airport and London Luton Airport, which are predominantly served by LCCs. This is confirmed by Accent (2011), whose UK survey found that availability of flight was identified as a reason for choice of airport by 63 per cent of business passengers compared to 55 per cent of leisure passengers, while only 23 per cent of business passengers mentioned the cost of the flight in contrast to 35 per cent of leisure travellers. Only 8 to 10 per cent of both groups identified airport facilities as being a significant factor. Similarly, a survey of the three Washington airports (Baltimore Washington International, Dulles International and Reagan National) also demonstrates the importance of accessibility, especially for Reagan National Airport (see Table 3.4). The cost of air travel at Baltimore Washington International Airport, which offers an alternative to Washington and has LCC Southwest as one of its main airlines, is more significant than at the other two Washington airports.

With regard to other individual customers, many are directly linked to the airline or passenger markets and so have no choice but to use a certain airport. This includes employees and accompanying visitors. However, aviation enthusiasts will be attracted to the airport if specific products are provided. Manchester Airport, for example, has its 'runway visitor park'. This includes a tour of Concorde, raised viewing mounds, a children's play area themed on aviation, an aviation shop and an airport orbital cycleway. Similarly, Munich Airport has a visitor park that includes a

Table 3.3 Reasons for passenger airport choice at UK airports (% respondents), 2011

	Location and surface access	Routes and frequency	Cost	Third party decision	Other
London Heathrow	39	32	9	16	5
London Gatwick	35	21	17	22	4
London Stansted	40	19	33	6	2
London Luton	46	18	24	9	3
Manchester	66	17	4	8	5
Birmingham	64	10	7	9	11
East Midlands	64	15	8	6	7

Source: adapted from UK CAA (2012)

Table 3.4 Reasons for passenger airport choice at Washington Airports (% respondents), 2009

	Baltimore Washington International	Dulles International	Reagan National
Accessibility	60	57	79
Closest airport	56	53	72
Better public ground transportation	1	1	6
Better access roads and parking	3	3	1
Quality of air service	39	42	20
More convenient flight times	5	8	8
Only airport with direct/non-stop flight	4	11	2
Less expensive airfare	27	16	7
Frequent flyer with specific airline	1	4	2
Only airport serving market	1	3	1
Other	1	2	1

Source: adapted from Canan and Mohammed (2010)

cinema, an observation hill and terrace, an aviation shop, airport tours, old historic aircraft and an airport exhibition.

In terms of attracting other visitors to the airport, this will very much be influenced by the nature of the product provided, be it a medical centre such as at Frankfurt Airport, wedding facilities such as at Stockholm Arlanda Airport, or a more fully developed airport city or aerotropolis that may include sport, cultural, entertainment and conference amenities, business parks and shopping centres. Local customers for these facilities will tend not to make choices between different airports but will compare the product at the airport with other similar ones nearby (e.g. out-of-town shopping malls) and make their decision based on general factors such as price, quality and accessibility.

'Other organisation' customers will take into account different factors. For instance, retailers will only want to operate at an airport if they have proof that the passenger, non-travelling visitor and employee profile is attractive enough for their product, and that the airport has sufficient traffic throughput. The average dwell time and the penetration rate – namely the proportion of passengers that use facilities – will also be considered. For instance, facilities such as duty free or F&B tend to have a wide appeal and high penetration rate, but more specialist shops may only interest a smaller share of passengers. For this reason, smaller airports often find it hard to attract the specialist retailers. For some organisations, such as those providing F&B, car hire and other surface access services, their product will be closely linked to travelling and flying to and from the airport, and will be in limited competition with other such organisations. However, retailers may have to take into account the volume and quality of retail space in nearby city centres and shopping malls.

3.2 Airport market segmentation

Once customers are identified and an understanding of their behaviour has been gained, it is appropriate to consider market segmentation, which is crucial for the development of a successful marketing strategy. In general, there are three key stages to market segmentation: the segmentation process itself, targeting and positioning.

3.2.1 The segmentation process

The process of market segmentation consists of dividing total markets, of either individuals or organisations, into submarkets or segments of potential customers with characteristics in common that can lead to similar demand for a product. There are many variables that can be used to segment markets, all of which should relate in some way to the customers' needs for, or uses of, the product. Pride and Ferrell (2008) identify a number of these variables, dividing them between consumer and business markets. For consumer markets they have four categories: demographics (e.g. age, gender, income, ethnicity, family life cycle), geographic (e.g. population, market density, climate), psychographic (e.g. personality traits, motives, lifestyles) and behaviouristic (e.g. volume usage, end-use, expected benefits, brand loyalty, price sensitivity). For the business market they have other variables such as geographic location, type of organisation, customer size and product use.

In selecting the most appropriate variables for market segmentation certain conditions must exist in order for the process to be effective. Dibb *et al.* (2006) identify six such conditions. First, the needs for the product should be heterogeneous or there will be no value in trying to divide up the market. Second, the segments must be easy to identify and measure. Third, each segment must be substantial enough to justify developing and maintaining its own specific marketing mix. Fourth, the segment must be easily accessible with the marketing mix. Fifth, the segments must be reasonably stable over time so that they can be used as a basis for future marketing plans. Finally, they must be useful to managers to help them better satisfy the needs of their customers. Similarly, Kotler *et al.* (2008) argue that the effectiveness of the process of segmentation depends on finding segments that are measureable, accessible, substantial and actionable.

Table 3.5 Segmentation variables for key airport customers

Customer	Variable	Example
Airlines	Type	Passenger, cargo, general aviation
	Nature of route	Domestic, international
	Passenger business model	Network, charter, LCC, regional
	Cargo business model	Combination, freight-only, integrators
	Alliance membership	Star, oneworld, SkyTeam
Passengers	Trip characteristics	Purpose, transfer or terminal, group size, length of stay, seasonality, surface access mode
	Passenger characteristics	Nationality, income, age, gender, life stage, education and occupation
	Travel behaviour and attitudes	Loyalty to airport, product preferences and requirements, frequency of travel
	Shopping behaviour	Price sensitivity, product and quality preferences, propensity to spend, shopping motivations and average dwell time
Commercial service providers	Product type	Duty free, specialist retail, F&B, car park
	Location	Airside, landside
	Size	Outlets, square metres
	Customer type	Arriving, departing, transferring
	Product purpose	Essential, souvenir, impulse buy

Source: compiled by the authors

As a first step for successful airport market segmentation, variables for key airport markets need to be identified. This will vary for consumers (e.g. passengers and other individuals) and business markets (e.g. trade and other organisations). Table 3.5 provides a summary of common variables for key airport markets: airlines, passengers and commercial service providers.

The most common segmentation for airlines is to distinguish between types of airline or business models. Many major airports still rely on the traditional market of network carriers (also known as flag carriers, full-service airlines, national airlines, mainline airlines or legacy carriers) which used to be, or in some cases still are, government-owned flag carriers. Such carriers tend to have some competitive advantages in terms of grandfather slot rights at many of the world's large airports and bilateral air service protection in some areas. Many of the world's network carriers also belong to one of the three global alliances (Star, SkyTeam and oneworld). If an airline joins a global alliance, its network scope may be increased and it may gain access to wider markets, but the number of direct flights from a certain airport may reduce. Alliance members will expect shared facilities, such as check-in and airline lounges, and efficient transfer facilities. A number of network carriers have also merged, such as Air France and KLM or British Airways and Iberia, which again has important implications for airports served by these airlines.

Another segment is airlines that offer all-business class services and hence demand premium services at airports. This is a relatively new model. Originally, in 2002, Lufthansa contracted the

Swiss-based airline Privatair to provide premium services on its Dusseldorf–Newark service. It subsequently expanded services on the Munich–Newark and Dusseldorf–Chicago routes, but has now shifted services to a few Middle Eastern and Indian destinations. Swiss and KLM have also used Privatair for some transatlantic services, and in 2004 Air France launched its Dedicate service on routes to oil industry destinations in the Gulf, Central Asia and Africa. Meanwhile, British Airways launched the Paris-based all-business transatlantic operator OpenSkies in 2008, and in 2009 added an all-business service out of London City Airport. Singapore Airlines also has such services to the US, and in 2012 Hong Kong Airlines launched business-only flights to London. There have also been examples of independent business airlines – notably EOS, Maxjet and Silverjet – which all operated business class services between London and the US for a couple of years but all ceased operations by 2008 when general economic conditions became more challenging.

As discussed in Chapter 2, there has been a considerable growth in the LCC sector (also known as no frills, budget or low fares airlines) over the last 15 years or so, which has stimulated new and existing markets and placed different demands on airports. While the term LCC is often used to refer to a homogenous product, in reality there are many variations of the model. Francis *et al.* (2006) divide them into five groups: Southwest copy-cats, subsidiaries, cost cutters, diversified charter carriers, and state subsidised competing on price. Each type will have slightly different airport requirements, but common needs tend to be efficient, simple and low cost services for fast turnarounds (e.g. no airbridges, no buses, no transfer facilities), which have encouraged some airports to introduce specialist LCC areas or even terminals (see Chapter 6). Table 3.6 shows the results of a survey of LCCs, which were asked to rank the most important factors that influenced their choice of airport.

Table 3.6 Factors influencing LCCs' choice of airport

Factor	Ranking (1 being most important)
High demand for LCC services	1
Quick and efficient turnaround facilities	2
Convenient slot times	3
Good aeronautical discounts	4
Positive forecasts for business and tourism	5
Cost conscious airport management	6
High airport competition	7
Good surface access	8
Spare airport capacity	9
Good environmental policy	10
Ambitious expansion plans	11
Privatised, deregulated airport	12
Good non-aeronautical revenues	13
Good experience of LCCs	14
High level of airline competition	15

Source: adapted from Warnock-Smith and Potter (2005)

Regional airlines tend to provide hub-feeder traffic (e.g. regional feeders) or point-to-point services for regions or local communities (e.g. independent regionals). Many of the routes will be low density, focused on business travel and will typically be served by regional jets or turbo-prop aircraft. Ownership can vary from independent companies (e.g. Skywest Airlines or Bangkok Airways) to wholly owned subsidiaries of network carriers (e.g. American Eagle and Lufthansa CityLine). In addition, some of the independent carriers will operate as franchises for the larger carriers, such as Air Nostrum for Iberia in Spain or Comair for British Airways in South Africa.

Charter or leisure airlines are mainly a European phenomenon, having developed during the 1950s and 1960s package holiday boom. They traditionally served short- and medium-haul seasonal routes but have diversified over the years to serve long-haul destinations, as well as having year-round operations. They tend to serve dense routes with relatively large aircraft out of regional and secondary airports, rather than those serving capital cities. Increasingly, this market is dominated by large pan-European travel companies such as TUI and Thomas Cook. However, in recent years such carriers have lost considerable market share to LCCs and have adopted a number of response strategies, such as developing a LCC product themselves or focusing on more specialist holiday products like those associated with adventure travel or new faraway destinations.

For cargo traffic there are three types of business model, which again have different needs at the airport. There are combination carriers, which may carry cargo in the cargo holds or in combi-aircraft with passenger flights, or alternatively may operate a network of scheduled, all-cargo flights. Some airlines such as Lufthansa and Singapore Airlines have hived off their cargo operations into a separate subsidiary company. Then there are a few all-cargo carriers, the most notable being Cargolux and Atlas Air. The third type of operator is the express carrier or integrator, such as Federal Express and UPS, which integrate the full logistics chain within one company. Unlike the two other types, which tend to operate an airport-to-airport service, the integrators offer a multi-modal door-to-door service (usually road and air) to their final customer, with features such as guaranteed delivery times. This puts different demands on the airport operator. The other two types of operator often rely on intermediaries, such as freight forwarders or global logistics suppliers, to provide the interface between the freight shipper and airline.

One of the problems with segmenting airlines by their business model, especially for the passenger market, is that the models are becoming increasingly blurred and hybrids are emerging. For instance, network carriers are adopting pricing structures introduced by LCCs, while LCCs are adding on frills such as assigned seats, fast-track boarding, frequent flyer points or even joining global alliances (e.g. Air Berlin and oneworld). Some airlines that traditionally served regional services have transformed themselves into LCCs, such as Flybe in the UK. Many charter carriers are now selling seat-only flights or have changed to LCCs, while some LCCs now sell accommodation through their website and may have gone one stage further by setting up a tour operator (e.g. easyJet). Shaw (2011) argues that this blurring of models has produced a number of different airline businesses based loosely around Porter's sources of competitive strategy related to differentiation, cost leadership and focus. Porter's model is considered within an airport context in Chapter 5.

Another popular way of segmenting airlines is according to the routes they operate, such as whether they have domestic or international services, or short-haul versus long-haul routes. This may have an impact on their airport operational requirements, especially in the terminal. For example, in the UK Virgin Atlantic has specialised until very recently in long-haul services, while Flybe only operates domestic and short-haul flights. Globally, domestic RPKs accounted for 37 per cent of total traffic in 2011, of which the largest markets were in North America, Latin America (due to Brazil) and Asia-Pacific (due to India, China and Japan) (IATA, 2012). A further distinction can be made regionally, as at European airports, where EU and non-EU airline segments may be covered by different aviation rules and regulations in certain areas of operation. Airlines can also be segmented by nationality, although as regards marketing activities it needs to be acknowledged that international aviation regulation prohibits discrimination on the basis of nationality.

There are many ways that passengers can be segmented at airports. The easiest and most basic way is to use the airline models. Then, further segmentation can take place within each of these groupings. For example, Martinez-Garcia and Royo-Vela (2010) found four segments for LCCs in Spain: price-sensitive travellers, destination and flight-conscious travellers, non-sensitive and business travellers, and educational and second residence travellers. Passengers can also be segmented according to the type of airline service. For instance, domestic and international passengers have needs for different facilities (such as customs and immigration) and may have access to additional commercial facilities (such as duty free and tax free retailing). Passengers can also be segmented according to whether they are terminal or transfer passengers. For example, in 2007 at London Heathrow Airport, connecting traffic accounted for 35 per cent of all passengers. Of these, 24 per cent were domestic–international transfers and 76 per cent were international–international; 66 per cent of connections were with British Airways and oneworld, 19 per cent with the other alliances and 15 per cent with non-aligned airlines (UK CAA, 2008).

Other variables related to travel characteristics can be used, such as group size, length of stay and seasonality. One of the most popular variables is trip purpose. At the most basic level, passengers can be grouped by business and leisure, and then each of these categories can be further subdivided. Business passengers can be grouped according to whether they are travelling for internal business, meetings with external customers, conferences, trade fairs or exhibitions. Leisure passengers may be going on short breaks, long holidays or package tours, or may be VFR or travelling to study. Linked to this, there can be segmentation by travel class (such as premium or economy). Typically, business passengers are thought to be more time-conscious and demanding, travelling for short periods of time and requiring easy parking, executive lounges, higher-end branded commercial products and speedy processes. In contrast, leisure passengers often travel in groups, are more price sensitive but less demanding, have more dwell time and require a wider range of retail, F&B and entertainment facilities. Each segment can still be broken down much further, as at Amsterdam Schiphol Airport where leisure passengers are divided into three groups: price seekers (42 per cent), comfort seekers (35 per cent) and short distance seekers (23 per cent) (Martens, 2012). Table 3.7 shows the segmentation variables related to travel characteristics used at Frankfurt Airport. It is important to note that the same person may belong to different passenger segments depending on the nature of their trip. For instance, an individual may travel alone on business and be a demanding and time-poor passenger, whereas they may then travel for leisure with their family and have totally different priorities for their ideal passenger experience.

Other models use passenger characteristics to segment demand. This can include general demographic and geographic variables such as nationality, income, age, gender, life stage, education and occupation variables. Table 3.8 presents the passenger characteristic variables used at Athens International Airport. Airports also use psychographic and behaviouristic market segmentation. For example, Graham (2008) describes a segmentation process that grouped passengers according to whether they are agoraphobics, euphorics, confident indulgers, airport controllers and self-controllers. With regard to loyalty, Freathy and O'Connell (2000) discuss a classification devised by Ballini that identifies passengers as loyalists, defectors, mercenaries and hostages. Amsterdam Schiphol Airport defines passenger segments according to their likely propensity to switch between Amsterdam Schiphol and other airports (Martens, 2012). It divides the market between users and non-users. Within the user groups there are committed customers (entrenched or average) and uncommitted customers (shallow or convertible). Among non-users there are

Table 3.7 Passenger segmentation variables related to trip characteristics at Frankfurt Airport, 2011

Variable	Category	Share of passengers (out of 100%)
Flight distance	Short-haul	61%
	Medium-haul	10%
	Long-haul	29%
Alliance use	Star	77%
	oneworld	4%
	SkyTeam	3%
	Other	16%
Type	Terminal	46%
	Transfer	54%
Destination	International	88%
	Domestic	12%
Seasonality	1st quarter	21%
	2nd quarter	26%
	3rd quarter	28%
	4th quarter	24%
Purpose	Business	40%
	Other	60%

Source: adapted from Fraport (2012)

open non-customers (available or ambivalent) and unavailable non-customers (weakly unavailable or strongly unavailable).

Some of these segmentation models for passengers will also be useful for consideration of commercial facilities. Charter passengers have traditionally been favourites for impulse buys, while LCC passengers tend to be heavy users of F&B facilities because of the limited offer on board aircraft. International passengers or long-haul passengers tend to have more time to shop than domestic and short-haul ones. Transfer passengers will not need access to car hire or car parking facilities but may want to make some retail purchases if there is sufficient time between flights. Some airports, such as Dubai International and Singapore Changi, place much emphasis on providing and marketing their retail offer to transfer passengers to encourage them to choose the airport.

Business travellers tend to make purchases relatively infrequently, although their average spend is usually quite high. Inbound and arriving passengers are likely to spend on car hire and currency conversion, whereas outbound and departing passengers are likely to use car parks and make retail purchases. Nationalities and culture will also influence spending and shopping behavioural patterns. For example, Scandinavians – who are used to relatively high duties and taxes in their home countries – are regular spenders on duty and tax free shops, while Americans tend not to be, especially because of the many downtown shopping malls selling discounted products in the US.

As with the aeronautical areas it is useful to segment passengers using psychographic and behaviouristic variables. This can include factors such as price preferences, product and quality preferences, propensity to spend, shopping motivations and average dwell time. Echevarne (2008)

Table 3.8 Passenger segmentation variables related to trip characteristics at Athens International Airport, 2010

Variable	Category	Share of passengers (out of 100%)
Gender	Male	53%
	Female	47%
Age	18–24	14%
	25–34	30%
	35–44	23%
	45–54	17%
	55+	16%
Education	None/Elementary	2%
	High School	23%
	College/University	75%
Nationality	Greece	53%
	Other EU	25%
	Other Europe	6%
	USA/Canada	9%
	Middle East	1%
	Asia-Pacific	4%
	Africa	1%
	South America	1%
Frequency of travel to/from	Up to 2 times	55%
Athens per year	3–9 times	29%
	10+ times	16%

Source: adapted from Athens International Airport (2011)

describes a classification devised by Pragma Consulting/ARC Retail Consultants based on motivation. There is travel necessity (e.g. books, toys, music, confectionery), souvenirs (e.g. local produce, t-shirts, ornaments), gifts for those at home or in the destination, personal self-treats (e.g. designer label clothing, watches, jewellery and accessories), convenience (e.g. ties for executives), exclusive opportunities to buy (e.g. reduced prices or unique merchandise in duty free shops), and trip enhancement (e.g. sunglasses for holidays). Tables 3.9 and 3.10 present examples of segmentation models that have been devised at both US and European airports to assist in the marketing of commercial facilities.

Finally, there are a number of ways to segment the commercial service providers at airports. The simplest way is related to the product they sell, such as duty free goods, specialist merchandise, F&B, car parking, conference facilities and hotel beds. Another method, especially in the terminal, is to divide the facilities by location. This has become particularly important in recent years as security restrictions on LAGs in hand luggage have pushed more emphasis onto airside shopping. Other segmentation models may differentiate by size (e.g. number of outlets, square metres), customer type (e.g. arriving, departing, transfer) or product purpose (e.g. necessity, souvenir, impulse buy).

Table 3.9 Passenger lifestyle segmentation based on demographic variables at Dallas/Fort Worth International Airport, 2009

	% terminal passengers	% connecting passengers
Dream weavers	21	9
New suburbs families	17	8
Young cosmopolitans	10	5
Small town success	7	6
Urban commuter families	5	7
America's wealthiest	5	3
Prime middle America	4	7
Second generation success	3	0
Steadfast conservative	0	7
Stable careers	0	6
Minority metro communities	0	3
Status conscious consumers	0	2
Professional urbanites	0	2
Latino Nuevo	0	2
Affluent urban professionals	0	2
Other segments	28	31
Total	100	100

Source: adapted from LeighFischer (2012)

Table 3.10 Passenger segmentation related to shopping behaviour at selected European airports

Amsterdam Schiphol	Lisbon	Brussels	Manchester
Satisfied atmosphere tasters	Shopaholics	Mood shoppers	Shopaholics
Certainty seekers	Supporters	Apathetic shoppers	Agitated passengers
Active pleasure seekers	Pure convenience	Shopping lovers	Unfulfilled shoppers
Trendy shoppers	Minimalists		Value seekers
Exclusivity claimers	Controlled		Unlikely shoppers
Well to do functional	Value seekers		Measured shoppers
	Unlikely shoppers		

Sources: adapted from Martens (2012), Madeira (2011), Geuens *et al.* (2004) and Agbebi (2005)

3.2.2 Strategies for airport market targeting and positioning

After the market has been segmented, the next stage is to decide on the targeting strategy. This involves deciding which and how many segments to target, and how they should be prioritised. This decision process is likely to be quite complex. Dibb *et al.* (2006) describe how such targeting judgements will be based on a number of factors such as needs and wants of end-users, product market size and structure, company and brand market share, resources and capabilities of the company, intensity of competition, and production and marketing scale economies. The choice will basically be to go for no segmentation, target a number of different segments or focus on just one or a few. Kotler *et al.* (2008) define these alternatives as undifferentiated marketing, differentiated marketing and concentrated marketing respectively. Once target markets have been selected, positioning can take place; this involves creating product benefits, features, prices and promotional messages that appeal to the needs of the preferred segments. This process can lead to a formalised marketing strategy that establishes the importance of the different target markets and the marketing activities related to them.

Jarach (2005) identifies five key market positioning strategies related to primary hubs, secondary hubs, regional airports, low cost airports and cargo airports. However, he then argues

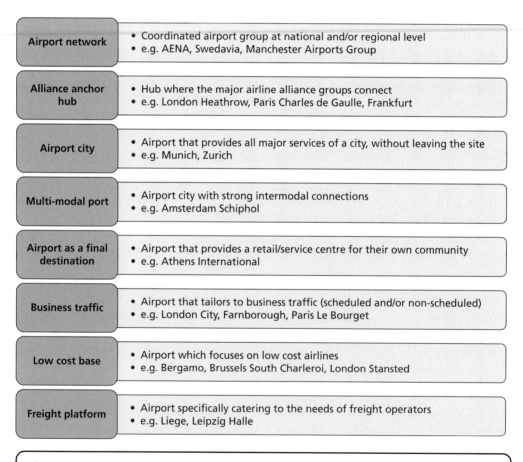

Airport network	• Coordinated airport group at national and/or regional level • e.g. AENA, Swedavia, Manchester Airports Group
Alliance anchor hub	• Hub where the major airline alliance groups connect • e.g. London Heathrow, Paris Charles de Gaulle, Frankfurt
Airport city	• Airport that provides all major services of a city, without leaving the site • e.g. Munich, Zurich
Multi-modal port	• Airport city with strong intermodal connections • e.g. Amsterdam Schiphol
Airport as a final destination	• Airport that provides a retail/service centre for their own community • e.g. Athens International
Business traffic	• Airport that tailors to business traffic (scheduled and/or non-scheduled) • e.g. London City, Farnborough, Paris Le Bourget
Low cost base	• Airport which focuses on low cost airlines • e.g. Bergamo, Brussels South Charleroi, London Stansted
Freight platform	• Airport specifically catering to the needs of freight operators • e.g. Liege, Leipzig Halle

Figure 3.2 Key positioning strategies for airports in Europe
Source: adapted from ACI Europe (2010)

that this is a simplification of the actual situation in the airport industry and explains that there is much higher variance between market positions. He lists 19 different types, including airports acting as a county's sole gateway, airports attracting overflow traffic, greenfield airports, airports integrated within a system and airports operating within the same catchment area. Similarly, ACI Europe (2010) identifies eight key positioning strategies of airports. These are airport network, alliance anchor hub, airport city, multi-modal port, airport as a final destination, business traffic, low cost base, and freight platform (see Figure 3.2).

In positioning themselves, airports need to consider a full range of questions, such as whether they have enough spare capacity and slots for a hub or whether positioning themselves as a feeder airport would be better. They also need to consider whether targeting LCCs or charter traffic might have a negative impact on existing business traffic. Different target segments will have different risk factors. Charter airlines have always been subject to considerable competition and can be very vulnerable to external factors, while a number of LCCs have proven to be very footloose customers.

Numerous examples of different positioning strategies exist. For example, at Salzburg Airport, LCCs have been vital to the tourism industry in making Salzburg a year-round destination. However, the airport has also wanted to maintain incoming and outgoing traffic connectivity via the major hubs, and so in the mid-2000s targeted 'quality' rather than 'quantity' markets, particularly in an attempt to re-establish the Amsterdam and Paris flights it used to have (Schano, 2008). Elsewhere, London City Airport has positioned itself as 'the airport for discerning travellers'. Business travel is its key focus and it aims to provide services that reduce both time and stress. Around two-thirds of the passengers are male with a higher than average income. They take an average of around eight business trips a year, nearly half of these being for just one or two days (Gooding, 2006; London City Airport, 2011). Chapter 5 provides further examples of positioning strategies within the broader context of marketing planning.

References

Accent (2011) *2131 Consumer Research*, London: Accent.
ACI Europe (2010) *An Outlook for Europe's Airports*, Brussels: ACI Europe.
Agbebi, Y. (2005) 'How do traffic structure and leisure preferences drive airport retail and investment strategies?', presented at *Hamburg Aviation Conference*, Hamburg, February 2005.
AMPG (2007) *2006 Air Passenger Survey Final Report: Los Angeles International Airport*, Los Angeles: AMPG.
Athens International Airport (2011) *Aerostat Handbook 2010*, Athens: Athens International Airport.
Canan, T. and Mohammed, A. (2010) *2009 Washington-Baltimore Regional Air Passenger Survey*, Washington, DC: Metropolitan Washington Council of Governments Online.
Dibb, S., Simkin, L., Pride, W. and Ferrell, O. (2006) *Marketing: Concepts and Strategies*, 5th European edn, Boston: Houghton Mifflin.
Echevarne, R. (2008) 'Impact of attracting low cost carriers' in A. Graham, A. Papatheodorou and P. Forsyth (eds) *Aviation and Tourism: Implications for Leisure Travel*, Aldershot: Ashgate.
Francis, G., Humphreys, I., Ison, S. and Aicken, M. (2006) 'Where next for low cost airlines? A spatial and comparative study', *Journal of Transport Geography*, 14(2); 83–94.
Fraport (2012) *Frankfurt Airport: Air Traffic Statistics 2011*, Frankfurt am Main: Fraport.
Freathy, P. and O'Connell, F. (2000) 'Market segmentation in the European airport sector', *Marketing Intelligence and Planning*, 18(3); 102–111.

Gardiner, J., Humphreys, I. and Ison, S. (2005a) 'Freighter operators' choice of airport: a three-stage process', *Transport Reviews*, 25(1); 85–101.

Gardiner, J., Ison, S. and Humphreys, I. (2005b) 'Factors influencing cargo airlines' choice of airport: an international survey', *Journal of Air Transport Management*, 11(6); 393–399.

Geuens, M., Vantomme, D. and Brengman, M. (2004) 'Developing a typology of airport shoppers', *Tourism Management*, 25(5); 615–622.

Gooding, R. (2006) 'Surviving the low cost carrier challenge: London City Airport's business model', *Journal of Airport Management*, 1(1); 6–8.

Graham, A. (2008) *Managing Airports: An International Perspective*, 3rd edn, Oxford: Butterworth-Heinemann.

Hermann, N. and Hazel, B. (2012) *The Future of Airports: Part 1 – Five Trends That Should Be on Every Airport's Radars*, New York: Oliver Wyman.

IATA (2012) *2011 ends on a positive note – capacity, economy loom as issues in 2012*, Montreal: IATA. Online. Available at: http://www.iata.org/pressroom/facts_figures/traffic_results/Pages/2012-02-01-01.aspx (accessed 1 March 2012).

Jarach, D. (2005) *Airport Marketing: Strategies to Cope with the New Millennium Environment*, Farnham: Ashgate.

Kotler, P., Armstrong, G., Wong, V. and Saunders, J. (2008) *Principles of Marketing*, 5th European edn, Harlow: Prentice Hall-Pearson Education.

LeighFisher (2011) *ACRP Report 54: Resource Manual for Airport In-Terminal Concessions*, Washington, DC: Transportation Research Board.

London City Airport (2011) *The Airport for Discerning Passengers*, London: London City Airport.

Madeira, C. (2011) 'Building retail practices for the new Lisbon airport', *Journal of Airport Management*, 6(1); 40–50.

Martens, H. (2012) 'How to win back markets', presented at *ACI Economics and Finance Conference*, London, March 2012.

Martinez-Garcia, E. and Royo-Vela, M. (2010) 'Segmentation of low-cost flights users at secondary airports', *Journal of Air Transport Management*, 16(4); 234–237.

Pride, W. and Ferrell, O. (2008) *Marketing*, 14th edn, Boston: Houghton Mifflin.

Schano, R. (2008) 'A "balanced approach" to airport marketing: the impact of low cost airlines on tourism in Salzburg', *Journal of Airport Management*, 3(1); 54–61.

Shaw, S. (2011) *Airline Marketing and Management*, 7th edn, Farnham: Ashgate.

Sykes, W. and Desai, P. (2009) *Understanding Airport Passenger Experience*, Independent Social Research.

UK CAA (2008) *Connecting Passengers at UK Airports*, London: UK CAA.

UK CAA (2012) *Heathrow: Market Power Assessment: Non-Confidential Version*, London: UK CAA.

Warnock-Smith, D. and Potter, A. (2005) 'An exploratory study into airport choice factors for European low cost airlines', *Journal of Air Transport Management*, 11(6); 388–392.

Chapter 4

Airport marketing research

This chapter investigates how airports can use marketing research as a function for linking customers to the marketer: the information obtained helps airports to address marketing issues such as the identification of marketing opportunities, solving of marketing problems, refinement of marketing actions and monitoring of marketing performance. The chapter begins by examining the role of marketing research in general. This leads on to exploring the specific nature of airport marketing research, giving special attention to the ASD process. The rest of the chapter considers the different research methodologies and the sources of information available to the airport marketer both from secondary and primary research.

4.1 Definition and the role of marketing research

Marketing research is 'the systematic design, collection, interpretation and reporting of information to help marketers solve specific marketing problems or take advantage of marketing opportunities' (Pride and Ferrell, 2008: 240). This means that for successful marketing, organisations need to have practical and unbiased information to enable them to make appropriate and effective marketing decisions. Any information an organisation uses in assisting their marketing decision-making process, collected through marketing research or gathered more informally (e.g. by developing ideas within the organisation), is usually defined as marketing intelligence (Dibb *et al.*, 2006).

A distinction needs to be made between market research and marketing research. The former has a specific focus on the characteristics, attitudes and behaviour of customers. Marketing research includes a much wider spectrum of research that covers not only market research but also types of research such as an assessment of the product and price on offer, or an analysis of the competitive situation or the effectiveness of a promotional or distribution strategy. While a considerable amount of marketing research effort tends to be concentrated on researching products and services, it is still likely to cover the whole marketing process from initial data collection and identifying marketing opportunities to monitoring marketing strategies and the marketing mix that has been used. Thus, marketing research is designed to help marketers reach decisions and monitor the results of those decisions.

Many different marketing research activities can be undertaken but all have a common process that consists of four stages: defining the problem and the research objectives, developing the research plan, implementing the research plan, and interpreting and reporting the findings (Kotler *et al.*, 2008). The first stage involves focusing on a problem or issue that needs exploring and defining specific research objectives or questions related to this. These objectives or questions tend to be linked to explanatory research for gathering information to define the problem, descriptive research (that investigates characteristics or attitudes of certain customer groups), or causal/experimental research to test a cause-and-effect relationship (e.g. between price and sales). Examples of general research questions could be: why are there so many complaints or why have sales decreased?

Having established the objectives or questions, the research plan is developed. Decisions need to be made regarding the information required and how it will be collected. The latter will be through quantitative or qualitative research, or a combination of the two. Quantitative research can be described as relatively objective, producing numerical data or information that is often factual in nature. Qualitative research is a more subjective research discipline that goes beyond the figures and probes areas where deeper insight is needed, exploring attitudes, preferences and feelings.

Such information can be gathered from secondary sources (sometimes referred to as desk research), primary sources (sometimes referred to as field research), or both. Secondary sources include internal data (e.g. sales figures and customer databases) or external sources such as the general and trade press (e.g. newspapers and trade journals), government agencies (e.g. official economic statistics), international organisations (e.g. the World Trade Organization (WTO)), and specialist market research companies (e.g. Mintel). Secondary sources offer instantly available and accessible information, but it may not be entirely up-to-date, reliable or free from bias, especially from sources available on the internet. In addition, information from secondary sources will have been collected for another purpose. This means that it may not be focused enough on the specific research objectives of the marketer, even though it may be possible to reanalyse the information.

Information from secondary sources provides a useful starting point for marketing research but when the data is inadequate, unreliable or even non-existent, it is necessary to gather information from primary sources. This means that information will be collected in connection with specific research objectives. It is a more up-to-date, but usually more expensive, means of gathering information compared to using secondary sources. In addition, there can still be the problem of biased or unreliable data if the research is not undertaken correctly. Information can be gathered in a number of ways such as from surveys (telephone, e-mail/internet, postal, face-to-face), personal diaries, focus groups or panel discussions. Observational research can also be undertaken; this involves observing relevant people, actions or situations, such as recording the time it takes a customer to make a purchase or how they interact with a product in a real-world environment. Additionally, experimental research can analyse the results of adjusting how a product is sold. This is carried out by certain retail outlets under controlled conditions (keeping everything else the same) to try to establish a link between product position and sales.

In designing the research plan the most appropriate research methods have to be selected, not only to ensure that the information collected will allow the research questions to be answered but also so that practical considerations such as costs, availability of resources, and planning time deadlines are taken into consideration. Once methods have been selected, research details need to be agreed. With surveys, for instance, decisions need to be made concerning the selection of the population, sample size, sampling technique, questionnaire design, and how to pretest and pilot the survey. Similarly, for observations, decisions need to be made concerning who or what is going to be observed, where and when the research will take place, and what method is going to be used to record information (e.g. manual, computer, video, audio). This may require using 'mystery shoppers'.

The third stage of the research process involves implementing the plan by collecting, processing and analysing the data. If quantitative research methods have been used, it should be possible to conduct statistical analysis of the data. This may be descriptive analysis such as calculating averages (e.g. means) and the dispersal of data (e.g. standard deviation), but may also include measures of association (e.g. correlation and regression) and inferential statistics (e.g. analysis of variance (ANOVA), t-tests or chi-square). If qualitative research has been undertaken, the analysis will usually involve identifying categories, patterns, themes and relationships in the data; techniques such as content and semiological analysis can also be used. The final stage of the research process consists of interpreting and reporting the findings, and it may be appropriate to use the findings to make relevant and informed estimates (e.g. for current and potential demand).

4.2 The nature of airport marketing research

For airports, just as any other organisation, marketing research is essential for effective marketing planning. As airport operators have become more engaged in marketing their services in recent years, the quality of their marketing research has also improved, with a vast array of different research now being undertaken. In some respects marketing research for airports may be considered easier than for other industries because airport marketers have access to a considerable amount of data regarding passenger numbers, airline services and air transport trends that is generally available as a by-product of the information that has to be collected for operational requirements. This means that providers of commercial facilities also have access to details about their customers, which is something that high street retailers struggle to obtain. It could also be argued that undertaking primary research at airports, especially among passengers, is easy, given that they all go through common processes at airports and in many cases have time to spare that can be occupied by participating in surveys.

However, there are many factors that make airport marketing research quite challenging. The wide range of different airport customers (e.g. passengers, visitors, airlines) means that it is a complicated task to fully research the needs and trends of all customers. In addition, as airline deregulation sweeps through more world regions, a consequence is that the airline industry has become progressively more competitive, so it has become much more difficult for airport marketers to access airline-specific data. Furthermore, the continual tightening of security regimes at airports has also made survey work in the airside area more problematic.

Clearly the amount of marketing research an airport operator can undertake will depend largely on the size of airport and resources available. For example, the large airport company the Schiphol Group has a department called Schiphol Marketing Research, which employs seven people and is dedicated to marketing research connected not only to Amsterdam Schiphol Airport but also to other airports such as John F. Kennedy International Airport (IAT Terminal 4), Brisbane Airport, Lelystad Airport, Rotterdam The Hague Airport and Eindhoven Airport. At smaller airports, marketing research may be just one of the functions that marketing staff undertake. At some airports marketing research is carried out by one department, whereas at other airports aeronautical and commercial research may be the responsibility of different departments. Many small airports will not have the resources to undertake much marketing research themselves and may therefore need to focus on developing partnerships (e.g. with tourism organisations, regional development agencies and other stakeholders at the airport) to pool resources and information. Partnerships such as these will be discussed in Chapters 7 and 8.

While there are airport-specific factors that need to be taken into account when conducting marketing research, airport marketers still need to go through the general four-stage process already discussed. The question or problem that needs to be addressed by airports could relate to a wide range of issues including exploring unserved or underserved routes, assessing the price sensitivity of customers to inform pricing decisions, identifying features of airport product and service quality that need improving, and monitoring the effectiveness of promotional campaigns. The research requirements vary for each of these areas, but in practice a large part of airport marketing research can be divided into three different categories covering customer characteristics, product and service quality issues, and the use and performance of commercial facilities. While separate marketing research may be undertaken for each of the three areas, there is likely to be a considerable amount of overlap. For instance, information about passengers' characteristics that may be gathered for market assessment purposes can be used to determine the best commercial offer mix. Similarly, customer satisfaction scores may offer insight into attitudes towards commercial facilities. In addition, external economic information such as income and GDP will be useful for predicting the potential for new routes and also for assessing trends in commercial revenues.

There is a considerable amount of information that can be gathered concerning market characteristics for airlines, passengers and other customers. Some of this has already been discussed in Chapter 3 in relation to market segmentation choices. For example, airline data can be collected by type of airline, nature of route, passenger business model, cargo business model and alliance membership. Similarly, passenger data can be collected by trip and passenger characteristics. This data and the associated market segments can be used to identify strategies for airport market targeting and positioning, and to plan the marketing mix in terms of product design and delivery, pricing strategies, promotional activities and distribution channels. The data also plays a key role in the ASD process, which is discussed later in this chapter.

Research concerning service quality and customer satisfaction can broadly be undertaken in two ways. First, an objective approach can be adopted by measuring the services delivered; this can cover areas such as flight delays, availability of lifts, escalators and trolleys, and other factors such as queue length, space provision, waiting time, and baggage reclaim time. To be accurate and reliable, these measures need to be collected regularly and at varying time periods when different volumes and types of passengers are being processed through the airport. The advantages of these measures are that they are precise and easy to understand. However, this approach to researching service quality can only cover a limited range of issues and service dimensions. For instance, while they can evaluate the reliability of equipment, they cannot tell whether consumers feel safe, assured and satisfied with their use of the equipment. Similarly, a passenger's perception of the time they have spent waiting in a queue may be very different from the actual waiting time. Therefore, more subjective research looking at passenger satisfaction ratings is also needed, to enable the quality of service to be assessed through the eyes of users rather than airport marketers.

Any information an airport has gathered on market characteristics may be useful for research related to commercial facilities, as passenger profile information can be important in explaining price sensitivity, product and quality preferences, and propensity to spend with commercial facilities (LeighFisher, 2011). More specific information on customers of commercial facilities (e.g. passengers, employees and visitors) in terms of their characteristics, dwell times and attitudes and behaviour towards commercial facilities can also provide insight, as can sales and performance data.

4.3 The ASD process

An important area of airport marketing research is associated with the marketing of new services (STRAIR, 2005; Martin, 2008). For this, the airport marketer will typically go through an ASD (sometimes referred to as route development) process, which will have different data and research requirements at each stage. The overall task is to identify potentially viable routes that are not currently being served, and ultimately to produce route by route forecasts and a feasibility

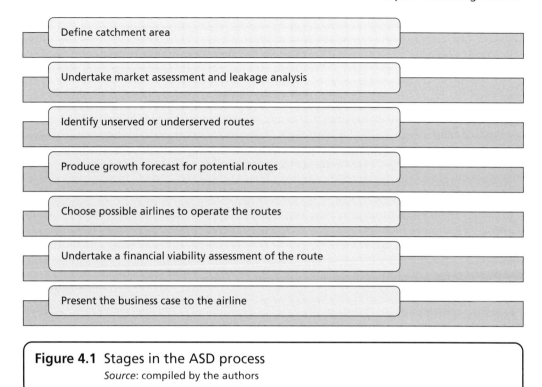

Figure 4.1 Stages in the ASD process
Source: compiled by the authors

assessment. Marketing research is an essential component that provides the foundations for this. The typical stages of the ASD process are outlined in Figure 4.1.

The first stage involves determining the catchment area of the airport: this refers to the geographic reach of the airport services on the surrounding population and economy they serve. Hence, it is the area where most of the outbound passengers originate from, or where most of the inbound passengers are travelling to, so airport marketers will tend to concentrate their marketing effort on this area.

Catchment areas can be formally defined using isochrones that identify an area within which it is possible to reach the airport within a certain time. These can be identified with different time periods (e.g. 1-hour isochrones, 2-hour isochrones) and can be more complicated if different forms of ground transport modes are taken into account (e.g. 2-hour drive time, 2-hour public transport time). The appropriate drive time is dependent on the passengers' willingness to travel to the airport, which needs to be assessed by considering the true origins and destinations of passengers. Various types of passenger will have different preferences and willingness to accept certain travel times. For instance, more time-sensitive business passengers will tend to demand shorter travel times than leisure passengers; long-haul (or perhaps international) travellers are likely to be less concerned with this element of travel time than short-haul (or perhaps domestic) travellers, since it accounts for a smaller share of their overall journey time. Hence, the airport marketer needs to take into account the nature and purpose of journey when defining its catchment areas. The distinction between the primary catchment area – where most travellers (both residents and visitors) are likely to consider the airport as their first choice based on proximity – and weaker or secondary catchment areas – where the airport will not necessarily be the first choice – can also be made based on isochrones of longer times.

Airport marketing research

The catchment area information on The Route Shop website (see Chapter 8 for a discussion about this website) provides examples of how different airports define their catchment area. Drive time isochrones are the most popular. For example, Brussels Airport identifies almost 20 million people living within one and a half hour's drive, while a number of other airports (such as Toronto Pearson International, Copenhagen, Prague and Cancun International) provide population information for 30-minute, 60-minute and 120-minute drive times. Haikou Meilan International Airport provides details of major cities that can be reached within these time limits, while others use distance criteria such as 100 kilometres for Dubrovnik Airport or 250 kilometres for Rome Fiumicino Airport. Dublin Airport provides population data for a 10-mile radius of the airport (nearly one million), 40 miles (1.7 million) and 50 miles (1.9 million).

Once the airport operator has established its catchment area boundaries, it must quantify the level of air travel demand generated in the area, which is the second stage of the ASD process. The number of potential passengers travelling to or from a catchment area will depend on many variables. This is especially the case for outbound traffic factors such as population size and propensity to travel, demographic characteristics of the residents and past immigration patterns. Influencing factors for inbound travel will include the business and tourist activities in the area. If the airport has a central location, it can potentially draw traffic from all areas around the airport, which would not be the case if it was located near a coast. In addition, catchment area size will be dependent on the quality of the road network or public transport services (depending on how the isochrone has been defined), with better quality increasing the catchment size. If subsequent improvements are made to transport links, the catchment area will increase.

It is important to note that any estimate of the level of demand in the catchment area is only a hypothetical maximum measure of the traffic-generating power of the area, as it will fail to take account of nearby competitor airports and the impact such airports will have on potential traffic volumes. In reality many airports have overlapping catchment areas, so potential passengers within these areas will make their choice of airport dependent on a number of factors such as fares levels, services levels (frequency or whether the service is non-stop or connecting), preferred airlines, parking and so on. For short-haul travel to popular destinations there may be significant competition from other airports, and so catchment areas will probably overlap considerably, whereas this may not be the case for less popular or longer-distance destinations. Overlap typically occurs with regional airports or when there is more than one airport serving a major city. The larger the overlap of the two catchment areas, the higher the likelihood that the two airports will compete directly for the same passengers. However, the relative attractiveness of overlapping airports will vary constantly as improvements are made to the road infrastructure or public transport, new or additional air services are offered, or there is some other change such as a reduction in car parking prices.

A good example of overlapping catchment areas occurs in the UK. The UK CAA (2011) found that the catchment area of London Stansted Airport overlaps with that of London Luton Airport, Bristol Airport, Birmingham Airport and East Midlands Airport, but has very little direct overlap with Manchester Airport. However, this concept of overlap is only relevant if the airports are providing substitutable air services or products. For instance, within the London area there are the two business and general aviation airports London Biggin Hill Airport and Northolt Airport, whose catchment areas overlap considerably with London Heathrow Airport and London Gatwick Airport, but who offer distinctly different aviation products and are therefore not really in direct competition.

If past data exists that shows passengers' use of a number of airports categorised by small residential regions (e.g. planning or postal districts), it may be possible to determine whether each region is within each airport's catchment area, and therefore whether any of the catchment areas overlap. For example, an assumption could be made, as in the UK CAA study, that an airport is considered to be serving a region if it captured a quarter of its originating passengers. Therefore, such past usage data can provide some insight into the market share each airport is likely to achieve but, as conditions are constantly changing, this cannot necessarily be a realistic guide for future marketing planning.

In reality, the competitive strength of an airport and the success of its marketing effort can be assessed by determining its effectiveness in capturing all the potential passengers in its catchment area. When traffic is lost or diverted away from its 'natural' catchment area to another airport as a result of factors such as insufficient airline capacity or frequencies, higher air fares, or a lack of non-stop services at the airport in question, this is defined as traffic leakage. Reverse leakage is the opposite situation, when passengers will use a given airport even though they have not been directly associated with its catchment area. In recent years, LCCs have been particularly successful in attracting passengers from outside catchment areas and causing leakages because of the lower prices they offer. This has been especially the case with leisure passengers because of the lower value of their own time. An example is BSCA in Belgium, which is situated in a region that has traditionally attracted very little air travel, although it is located near other more populous and affluent areas. A survey of Ryanair passengers showed that only 18 per cent came from southern Belgium, which is the natural catchment area of BSCA. The Brussels area accounted for a further 25 per cent of passengers, with the rest coming from northern Belgium, the Netherlands, Luxembourg, France and Germany (Dennis, 2007).

The airport operator can use this assessment of the market within its catchment area and the associated leakage analysis to determine the adequacy of air services at the airport, and to identify routes not served satisfactorily, or at all, by considering the schedules of current air services. This is the third step of the ASD process. By weighing up the factors that passengers take into account when considering different flight and airport options such as air fares, frequencies and schedules, and accessibility of the airport (in terms of cost and time), the airport operator can then estimate the likely market share of new services to and from the airport.

The next stage of the process will involve estimating the potential future demand for the route, which will usually require the input of other marketing research data related to key drivers of demand such as income, population, propensity to travel and journey purpose. Forecasting methods may vary from simple time series projections of past traffic performance into the future to more complicated procedures such as regression analysis. Reference to aviation industry forecasts may also be useful here. One of the most challenging situations will be when there is no relevant historical data to use as a basis for the forecasts. There also needs to be consideration of the amount of stimulation or generation of new demand, which may be caused, for example, by a significant reduction in air fares, reduced ground time, the introduction of a non-stop route or a route which has reduced connection points or time. It is generally assumed that LCC services stimulate a certain amount of new demand because of the low fares offered. Indeed, a survey by NFO Infratest found that 'new' demand amounted to 59 per cent of the total demand (ELFAA, 2004). However, this is probably a considerable overestimate of LCCs' demand-generating abilities, given the more mature nature of this airline sector in many countries now.

Once future demand has been forecast, the airport marketer will need to research which airline would be the most suitable to operate the route, in terms of having the most appropriate network, flying aircraft that can reach the destination, and having the capacity to carry the projected traffic. In addition, the general strategy (e.g. expansion plans, hub development, alliance membership) and business model (e.g. network versus LCC) of the airline, as well as its attitude towards the airport in question and market characteristics of the new route, need to be considered to ensure a good match with the new route requirements.

As a final stage, the airport operator may undertake a feasibility assessment of the route by bringing together the forecast traffic, yield and load factor data and estimating the airline's operating costs. This will require additional research to ensure that the estimates are realistic and credible when they are presented to the airline, even though the airline will undoubtedly undertake its own assessment if it is interested.

Initially, some of the research concerning the market assessment and potential for new routes may be presented on websites such as The Route Shop to encourage dialogue with airlines, or discussed during informal meetings at conferences such as Routes (see Chapter 8). If an airline is interested in the airport proposal, the airport will normally make a formal business presentation to the airline. Table 4.1 summarises the typical information presented during one of these meetings. To present a convincing and compelling business case, in addition to the traffic and financial assessment, other information relating to the attractiveness of the catchment area such as demographic and economic data needs to be provided (as well, of course, as details about price incentives, marketing support and airport facilities). While this information will primarily be used by airport marketers to make a business case to the airlines, it can also be used to encourage other organisations such as tourist boards or development agencies to cooperate by financially supporting price incentives and marketing assistance to encourage the airlines.

A statistical tool called the quality service index (QSI) estimates passenger behaviour by quantifying the relative attractiveness of different flight options. It is used by airlines when assessing their networks, but can also be used by airport marketers during the ASD process to evaluate route opportunities and perhaps to add credibility to the business case proposal to airlines. The inputs to the model are the factors that passengers consider when choosing different flight options such as air fare, flight frequency, travel time, aircraft time and number of stops. A coefficient is then applied to each of these factors, which can have a relative value (e.g. non-stop flight = 1, single connection = 0.25) or an absolute value (e.g. number of frequencies). By imputing data related to the city pair market size, airline schedules, air fares, stimulation factors and so on, the model can calculate market share and other variables such as load factor and airline revenues (Weatherill, 2008). Some airports have chosen to develop their own QSI models, even some small ones such as Grenoble Airport and Chambéry Airport, while others have bought software packages offered by, for example, IATA, the Official Airline Guide (OAG) and Sabre. These models can be useful but require a considerable amount of data,

---

Table 4.1 Typical information provided by airport marketers for airlines at ASD meetings

Information	Examples
Route forecasts	Nature of traffic, traffic forecasts, stimulated traffic, schedule, load factor
Financial evaluation	Operating costs per block hour, yields, forecast revenues, costs and profits
Catchment area characteristics	Population, travel propensity, demographics, business/tourist activity, surface transport links
Marketing support	Fee deductions or incentives, joint advertising campaigns, sharing of market research data
Airport facilities and profile	Infrastructure, services, other airlines at the airport

Source: compiled by the authors

as well as realistic assumptions related to the coefficients, to ensure that credible estimates are produced.

4.4 Secondary research

One of the key decisions to be made in developing any research plan once the problem or issue to be considered has been identified is the choice of the most appropriate research method, and whether secondary, primary or both information sources are going to be used. For the airport industry a range of sources are in many cases available, but all have their benefits and limitations. Therefore, cross-checks should be made whenever possible, using all available sources. In making choices, consideration has to be given to the accuracy, reliability, relevance and timeliness of the data, as well as to practical considerations related to the cost, resources and time involved. The rest of this chapter will discuss the types of research that can be undertaken, starting with secondary research and concluding with primary research.

4.4.1 Air transport statistics

Internally, particularly for operational reasons, a considerable amount of traffic data is available to airport marketers. This includes volume figures such as the number of movements, passengers and cargo tonnes. Each of these can be broken down into further detail, for instance, by flight destination or airline and by daily, weekly and monthly patterns. ACI undertook a survey among its member airports of the internal sources used to produce these air transport statistics. In many cases, a mixture of sources were used, the most popular being directly from airlines (72 per cent), followed by air traffic control and civil aviation departments (62 per cent), internal airport company records (57 per cent) and airlines via handling agents (49 per cent) (ACI, 2011).

In addition to internal traffic statistics that are directly available to the airport operator, there are a number of global publications of data that can prove useful to the airport marketer. ACI's traffic reports provide passenger, cargo and movement data, such as its annual world airport traffic report, which covers over 1,400 airports in more than 150 countries, and the corresponding monthly report. Since these reports include a considerable number of airports they cannot be published until several months after the data has been collected, so there are also monthly summary reports called PaxFlash and FreightFlash; these cover a smaller size (60 per cent of total passenger traffic and 70 per cent of total freight traffic worldwide) but provide a snapshot of up-to-date traffic trends. Some of ACI's regional offices such as ACI Europe and ACI North America also produce reports of airport traffic in their regions.

ICAO reports monthly and annual traffic data at major international airports, but again there is some lag before this data becomes available. National government departments or agencies often publish airport traffic data, sometimes on their websites. Other relevant sources of air transport data include OAG, which publishes airline schedules from all over the world and sells a number of software packages that enable further analysis of the schedule data. IATA produces a considerable amount of airline data that, although not directly related to airport operators, can be particularly useful in the later stages of the ASD process when the airline evaluation is being undertaken. ICAO airline data may also be useful here.

While airport traffic volumes can be helpful for assessing the comparative performance of competing airports, for ASD planning purposes more detailed passenger traffic between city pairs is needed. ICAO has two publications related to this. The first is the on-flight origin and destination report, which shows, on an aggregate basis, the number of passengers, freight and mail tonnes carried between all international city pairs on scheduled services. This is based on ticket sales but does not take into account additional flight segments bought at the same time (e.g. if the passenger has connecting flights). The second is the traffic by flight stage report, which contains annual traffic on board aircraft on individual flight stages of international scheduled services. This gives each airline and aircraft type used, the number of flights operated, the aircraft capacity offered and the traffic (passengers, freight and mail) carried. There are also other sources for certain markets, such as Eurostat in Europe and the Bureau of Transportation Statistics (BTS) in the US. A number of government bodies in other individual countries report such data, although the coverage, reliability and timeliness of statistics vary considerably.

The major problem with all these sources is that they do not normally show the true origin and/or destination (O–D) of a passenger. For each route, all will include passengers who are connecting at both ends, but will not count passengers who have flown indirectly between the two points. In addition, they do not take into account leakage when passengers have travelled out of their way to another airport to reach the same destination. For some airports the difference between route data and O–D data may not be very large, but for others it may be very significant.

This problem is usually overcome by using passenger surveys or airline booking data. There are two major sources of booking data: market information data tapes (MIDT), which come from the global distribution systems such as Sabre and Amadeus used by high street and online travel agents, and billing and settlement plan (BSP) data from IATA and its accredited travel agents. The typical information gathered is passenger volume by origin or destination, travel routing, operating and ticketed airline and ticket class, and average airfare. A specific example of how airport operators use the BSP data can be seen in Nice Côte d'Azur Airport's opportunities survey, which can be found on The Route Shop website (The Route Shop, 2012a) (Tables 4.2 and 4.3).

There are a number of shortcomings with the MIDT and BSP datasets. First, in terms of measuring travel to, from or via an airport, they do not include tickets sold through direct distribution channels such as airline call centres and airline internet sites, and so do not provide complete coverage, especially with the trend towards more direct selling (e.g. with the LCCs). In addition, they do not cover charter activity. Therefore, the total market size may have to be estimated by airport marketers (e.g. by assessing total schedules with OAG data), although some data sources such as IATA's AirportIS and Sabre's Airport Data Intelligence already come with such estimates. In terms of traffic leakage, there are other limitations. The data sold by travel

---

Table 4.2 Examples of types of data obtained from BSP sources used by Nice Côte d'Azur Airport to support its ASD activities in 2012

Characteristic	Details
Region	Total direct and indirect traffic between Nice and the region
Country	Ranking of traffic and growth patterns
Selected routes	Indirect and direct traffic 2008–2011
	Market share of hubs used by indirect traffic
	Origin/destination split of traffic 2008–2011
	Low and high fare split of traffic 2008–2011
	Seasonality of route (average 2010–2011) – separate indirect and direct traffic

Source: The Route Shop (2012a)

Table 4.3 Examples of traffic data used by Nice Côte d'Azur Airport to support its ASD activities in 2012

Region	Nice Airport share of direct traffic in 2011	Routes from Nice identified with potential
France	97%	Brest, Rennes, Biarritz, Lorient
Other Europe	84%	Stockholm, Moscow, Prague, Gothenburg, Warsaw, Hamburg, Budapest, Kiev, Porto, St Petersburg, Malaga, Sofia, Stuttgart, Tallinn, Vilnius
North America	27%	Montreal, Toronto, John F. Kennedy International Airport, Miami, San Francisco, Los Angeles, Vancouver
South/Central America	0%	Sao Paulo, Rio de Janeiro, Mexico City, Buenos Aires, Fort de France, Pointe à Pitre
Middle East	34%	Beirut, Riyadh
Africa	27%	Johannesburg, Cairo, Dakar, Cape Town, Mauritius, St Denis de la Réunion, Marrakech
Asia/Oceania	0%	Tokyo Narita, Bangkok, Seoul, Hong Kong, Beijing, Shanghai, Osaka, Sydney, Singapore, Delhi, Mumbai

Source: The Route Shop (2012a)

agents in the catchment area may be used to estimate leakage by assuming that the place of ticket issuance represents the passenger's residency, but in many cases travel agencies now process bookings through a centralised office, which invalidates this assumption. Also, while such data may pick up some of the outbound leakage, it will not identify the inbound leakage, although this is usually a smaller amount.

MIDT and BSP data sources tend to be rather expensive and may be beyond the reach of many small airports, particularly as there may be a minimum cost that will not be suited to small requests. O–D and traffic leakage data may be purchased separately (e.g. AirportIS has a leakage report that gives information solely about the passengers and revenues lost to competing airports and trends through time, which is separate from the O–D airport database).

4.4.2 Survey and performance data

In addition to air transport statistics, there are some secondary sources of survey data that airports may use for marketing research. While many airport marketers design and undertake airport surveys themselves, there are also organisations that carry out such research. For example, the UK CAA undertakes passenger surveys at airports annually, with interview numbers ranging from 3,000 to 70,000 depending on the size of the airport. The face-to-face interviews usually take place in the gate rooms, using a stratified sample (by carrier, route and quarter), which is then

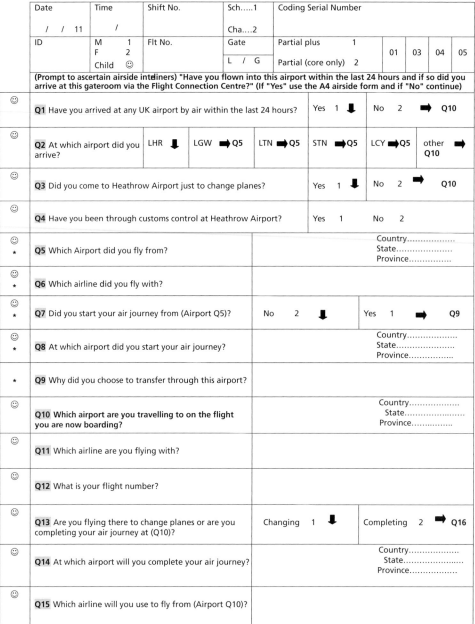

Figure 4.2 UK CAA passenger survey for London Heathrow Airport
Source: courtesy of the UK CAA
(http://www.caa.co.uk/default.aspx?catid=81&pagetype=90)

☺	Q16 What nationality passport do you hold?	Passport 1	Passport 2
☺	Q17 In which country have you been living for most of the last 12 months?		Non UK/IE ➡ Q20 Non UK/IE Int/Lin ➡ Q26 except from LGW/LTN/STN/LCY ➡ Q20

☺ M	Q18 Where is your home in the UK/Ireland?	Town
		District Council or London Borough
		County

☺	Q19 What is your postcode?	1st part	2nd part
		Int/Lin ➡ Q26 except from LGW/LTN/STN/LCY ⬇	

☺ M	Q20 Where, in the UK, did you start your journey to catch this flight?	Home ➡ Q22	
		Town	
		District Council or London Borough	
		County	
	What is the postcode?	1st part	2nd part

☺	Q21 Was this a transit stop or did you have a reason for being in (place in Q20). If transit re-ask Q20. **If not transit through LGW/LTN/STN/LCY go back and ask Q20 again, deleting Q's 5* to 9***	Home (partial only) 1	Business 2	Leisure 3	72 hours √	Other 4

☺	Q22 Could you tell me in detail how you travelled from (place in Q20) to Heathrow Airport today?

Private Car		Bus/Coach		
1	driven away	30	hotel bus	1st Mode
2	short term car park	31	charter coach	
3	short term car park – meet/greet	32	London bus companies	
4	business car park	33	local bus companies	
5	mid stay car park bus	34	Terravision	
6	airport long term car park bus	35	National Express coaches	
7	private long term car park bus	36	other national/regional coach services	
8	hotel car park bus	37	Rail Air bus (Reading/Woking/Feltham)	
9	valet service – off airport	38	courtesy bus	
10	valet service – on airport	39	airport to airport coach service	2nd Mode
11	staff car park bus	40	Luton airport parkway shuttle bus	
12	type of car park unknown	41	Luton airport parkway not via shuttle bus	
Rental Car		42	Luton station not via shuttle bus	
20	short term car park	43	bus/coach company not known	
21	rental car courtesy bus	45	LHR-LTN coach service	
22	airline car	**Rail**		
Taxi/Minicab		50	tube	
23	taxi	51	tram	3rd Mode
24	minicab	52	Docklands Light Railway	
Other		53	Heathrow Connect	
70	ship/boat	54	Heathrow Express	
71	Walk (where only mode)	55	Gatwick Express	
72	cycle	56	Stansted Express	
73	motor cycle	57	National railways	
74	chauffeur	58	National railways (MAN only) – changed trains	
99	Other (write in mode box)	59	National railways (MAN only) – not changed trains	

Figure 4.2 continued

☺	**Q23** How long did your journey take from (place in Q20)?	Hours		Minutes	
☺	**Q24** How many people came into the Terminal to see you off today?				
☺	**Q25** Including yourself, how many people are travelling in your immediate group?				

☺ □1	**Q26 What is the chief purpose of your present trip?**	Single Code		B	L
		Accompany on Business (comp tkt) AC		1 with	
		Accompany on Business (own tkt)		15 with	

☺ □2	**Q27** Which of these age groups do you come into?	Int/Lin ➡ Q30			
		except from LGW/LTN/STN/LCY ⬇			

☺ AC	**Q28** Is this your outward, return or a single journey?	Outward mirror image 1	Return mirror image 2	Single 3 ➡ Q30
☺ AC	**Q29** How long will you/have you been away?	Weeks	Days	Hours

□3 AC	**Q30** What type of ticket do you have?	Number	Letter	IT passengers ➡ Q32
				Multiple sector ➡ Q32
	Q31 How much was paid for your flight, including ticket, tax and other charges excluding insurance?	Cost	Currency	Single 1	Return 2

☺ □M	**Q32** On arrival at (airport in Q10 or Q14) where is your main destination?	**Europe** – Including Malta, Cyprus, Greece, Turkey & Ireland country prefix and number, country code or county
		North America - Town/State **Canada** - Town/Province
		Domestic routes -Town/City/County/District Council
		UK Business ➡ **Q34**
		Non UK passengers ➡ **Q35**

	Q33 Do you own a property (at place in Q32)?	Yes 1		No 2	
	Q34 When was this trip booked?	< 1 mth 1<2 mths 2-<3 mths 3-6 mths >6 mths 1 2 3 4 5			

☺	**Q35** How many times have you flown in the last 12 months:- on this route? (excluding current trip)	Total		Leisure	
☺	**Q36** How many times have you flown in the last 12 months:- on any route? (excluding current trip)	Total		Leisure	
	Q37 What single improvement would you like to see at Heathrow Airport?				

Figure 4.2 continued

4	**Q38** Why did you choose to fly from Heathrow Airport today?				
☺	**Q39** Do you have a disability or impairment that makes accessing and/or using this airport difficult?	Yes	1	No 2 ➡	**Q42**
☺	**Q40** Did you ask for assistance?	Yes	1	No 2 ➡	**Q42**
☺	**Q41** Were you satisfied with the assistance provided by the airport?	Yes	1	No	2
☺ 5 AC	**Q42** Looking at this card, to which of these ethnic groups do you consider you belong?	Number Specify	Letter	Business ➡ **Q47**	
	Q43 How many people live in your household including yourself?				
	Q44 How many are children under 16?			Non UK ➡ **Q46**	

	Q45 What is the occupation of the chief income earner in your household?	Job Title	SP	S/E
		Qualifications		
		Location size	Dept. size	Responsible for
		Nature of Business		

6	**Q46** Can you indicate from this card the total ANNUAL income of ALL people living in your household BEFORE tax and other deductions?		**End Interview**	

AC	**Q47** What is the main business of your firm or organisation?	Manufacture		Materials
		Sales	Retail	Whole
		Other		
			Non UK ➡	Q49

AC UK	**Q48** What is your occupation and job title?	Job Title	S/E
		Qualifications	
		Location size	Dept. size Responsible for

6 AC	**Q49** Can you indicate from this card, which ANNUAL income group applies to you BEFORE tax and other deductions?		**End Interview**	

Figure 4.2 continued

weighted to actual traffic levels. The major London airports of Heathrow, Gatwick, Stansted and Luton, as well as Manchester Airport, are surveyed every year; other airports are surveyed every three to five years. Around 30 questions are asked, covering passenger characteristics (e.g. trip length and purpose, group size, income levels, socio-economic grouping and family make-up) (see Figure 4.2). There are also questions that relate to the origin and destination of passengers and modes of surface transport used, which are particularly useful for ASD purposes. For example, Birmingham Airport identified over ten routes with potential on The Route Shop using the UK CAA data and a 1-hour catchment area, ranging from Madrid with an estimated market of 184,000 passengers to Athens with 89,000 passengers (The Route Shop, 2012b). It is possible for airport operators or other organisations to request additional questions to be asked. For example, in 2009 the UK Department for Transport asked for questions about the passenger experience to be added. The advantage of surveying groups of airports (unlike the surveys carried out by airport operators themselves, which will usually only cover the one specific airport unless there is multiple airport ownership) is that leakage to, and reverse leakage from, different airports can be considered.

Service quality is another area where secondary survey data is available. Although a number of airports survey this area themselves, the advantage of secondary information is that it allows for cross-airport comparisons and benchmarking. The major source of data is ACI's airport service quality (ASQ), data which is obtained from a quarterly survey undertaken at more than 190 airports in more than 50 countries (ranging from 0.5 million to 85 million passengers). Over 250,000 passengers are interviewed per year, with a requirement for each airport to have a minimum of 350 responses per quarter to ensure a representative sample, although in practice most airports survey considerably more passengers. This is a self-completion survey: questionnaires are distributed to passengers at the departure gate. It includes 34 service quality areas, including check-in, passport/personal ID control, security, airport facilities, the airport environment and overall satisfaction.

There is also the newer and more specialist ACI ASQ retail measures passenger satisfaction survey, which focuses on three key areas: F&B, duty and tax free, and general retail. Its 30 measures cover performance aspects (e.g. the number of passengers spending at outlets and the amount spent) and passenger characteristics and behaviour (e.g. who are the typical shoppers, how many shops did they visit, how much time did they spend there, whether purchases were planned or on impulse). Again, the survey is undertaken at the gate but this time for two quarters of the year, with a minimum sample size of 1,000 per survey period. In the retail area another publication called the Airport Commercial Revenues Study, published by the Moodie Report, provides useful performance data (such as sales figures and passenger penetration rates) from a number of airports. This can be used, perhaps together with customer surveys, to assess the commercial aspects of the airport product.

In addition, the Skytrax airport customer satisfaction survey, which is based on 12 million passengers and 388 airports, covers 39 different airport service and product areas from check-in, arrivals, transfers, shopping, security and immigration through to departure at the gate. While precise details about the methodology are not available, the website states that the research includes passenger-completed questionnaires (online and via e-mail), telephone interviews, business research groups/travel panel interviews, and corporate travel questionnaires and interviews.

As well as all this survey information, there is other secondary data that provides details about service delivery. The ACI ASQ performance measures assess the service performance actually delivered, focusing on 16 key measures such as waiting time at check-in, security and immigration, and the number of available trolleys. The data is obtained through a series of observations during peak hours. Flight delay statistics are also available from central sources such as Eurocontrol, the Association of European Airlines (AEA) and the BTS, as well as being accessible from a number of national sources. Another area of performance airport marketers may be interested in when devising their pricing policies is the comparative level of airport charges at different airports. This information is usually available on individual airport websites, or from IATA or ICAO sources, and there are specialist publications by organisations such as Leighfisher and Airportcharges.com that undertake benchmarking analysis in this area. However, the drawback with all these sources is that they primarily consider published fees and will not take account of any incentive arrangements agreed between airport marketers and airlines.

4.4.3 Other secondary information

Internally, airport operators can access other types of information that may prove useful for marketing research. For instance, there will be records of customer complaints such as letters, e-mails, comment and complaints cards, and on social networks such as Twitter and Facebook. This can provide extra insight into the level of customer satisfaction and key issues that need to be addressed. Databases set up for CRM purposes such as loyalty schemes (see Chapter 9 for details) may also provide useful information. For the commercial aspects of the business, airports may also have access to the point of sale data, which contains flight information about passengers obtained from boarding passes shown when purchases are made in the airside area.

Externally, in addition to specific air transport data, airport marketers need to collect and analyse other information that will help them understand the trends and characteristics of passengers and cargo flows, especially for market assessment purposes. Tourism data from national statistics or global organisations such as the World Tourism Organization (UNWTO) can give an indication of the volume of tourists and current trends, and will be relevant if most tourists arrive by air. A limitation with such sources is that they often do not differentiate by mode of transport. They also tend to focus on inbound tourism, so it may not be possible to evaluate outbound flows. The UNWTO, as with air transport organisations such as IATA, ICAO, ACI, Boeing and Airbus, produces demand forecasts that may be useful during the ASD process when future traffic patterns are being predicted. Airport marketers may need to access general economic, social and demographic data to assess the key drivers of demand. Various organisations such as the Organisation for Economic Co-operation and Development (OECD), IMF, Eurostat and the US Census Bureau produce datasets that may be relevant.

4.5 Primary research

The previous section has discussed the range of secondary information available to airport marketers as they undertake their marketing research. As explained, a considerable amount of data is routinely collected at the airport or is available from other organisations. However, in some cases, this information will not be sufficient to address the specific research issue or problem that has been identified. In such a situation, the airport operator will need to carry out primary research, for which the most popular method is surveys.

4.5.1 Surveys

Surveys can be undertaken among various airport stakeholders including passengers, employees, airlines, tenants, local residents, local businesses and travel companies, and air cargo businesses (Biggs *et al.*, 2010). The overall purpose is usually to gather more information about the stakeholder under consideration (on both aeronautical and commercial sides of the airport business) and to assess the levels of satisfaction with the airport product. Less commonly, airport surveys cover other marketing areas such as the effectiveness of an airport promotional campaign or the perceived strength of brand used at the airport. Clearly, one of the key advantages of an airport undertaking its own survey in any area is that it can be focused on issues that are specific to the airport in question.

Many aspects of planning these surveys are common across the different types. For instance, once the purpose of the survey has been established, the method of either interviewer-completed questionnaires (face to face or telephone) or self-completed questionnaires (paper or e-mail/internet) has to be selected. Choices have to be made regarding the survey population and sample, the sampling strategy and plan, and the detailed design and wording of the questionnaire. Decisions have to be taken concerning where and when the survey will take place and for how long, as well as how to pretest and pilot the chosen method.

In undertaking survey work, especially with passengers, choices have to be made as to whether the surveys are performed in-house or with an external agency. There are a number of factors that make surveying passengers in the terminal challenging, such as their international nature, the time constraints they face, the 24-hour day of the airport, and the security clearances all interviewers need to obtain if they are working airside. These specific factors mean that some airports choose to have their own team of interviewers. For example, London Heathrow Airport chooses to have its own staff that carry out passenger and employee surveys and can also be used to perform research for other organisations. By contrast, Manchester Airport – also in the UK – has a specialist agency that undertakes the surveys.

4.5.1.1 Passenger and visitor surveys

Passenger surveys are by far the most popular type of survey. A study undertaken in the US relating to airport surveys found that over half of all respondents had carried out air passenger surveys in the last five years, compared to less than a third with all other types of airport surveys (see Figure 4.3). Even some of the small US airports have undertaken passenger surveys (Kramer *et al.*, 2010). Passenger surveys may often be the only way that airports can gain detailed information about passenger characteristics and their attitudes towards the airport overall, as well as detailed views about the commercial offer (LeighFisher, 2011). Vital information about passengers' true origins and destinations can be obtained for ASD reasons, although such surveys tend not to cover passengers who have leaked or diverted to other airports.

As regards the choice between interview-completed or self-completed questionnaires, the airport marketer is faced with balancing cost and accuracy requirements and taking into account a number of other practical considerations. Personal interaction may increase response rates, particularly as further explanations to questions can be given, but will tend to increase costs. Face-to-face surveys can also be subject to interviewer bias and provide no anonymity to the respondent. By contrast, self-completion methods usually produce more responses for a given budget (as they can use a larger sample), but the questions will have to be simple, with no probing possible, and there will be no control over questionnaire completion. The international nature of airports also means that consideration needs to be given to whether the questionnaire should be translated into other languages or whether interviewees need to speak other languages.

Increasingly, electronic data collection devices such as personal digital assistants (PDAs) or laptops and tablets, as well as commercial software packages, are being used for passenger surveys. These have the advantage of eliminating the need to enter data manually and being more user-friendly for more complex questionnaires. However, they may increase the cost, and their standard features might not be easily adapted to meet the specific needs of airports.

The survey location is very important. A popular area is the gate room, where passengers are more relaxed, having passed through all the essential processes and made all their retail purchases,

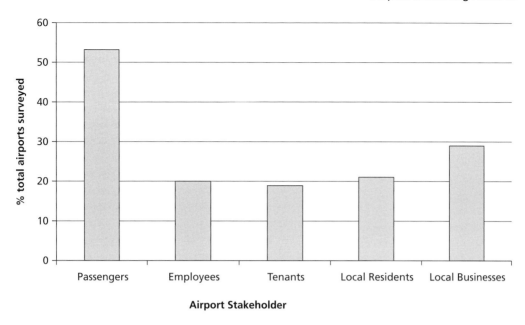

Figure 4.3 Types of survey performed in the last five years at US airports
Data source: Biggs at al. (2010)

and so in most cases have nothing else to do but to wait for their flight. However, this may introduce bias into the results as the responses will be limited to passengers travelling on certain flights. An alternative approach is to intercept passengers just after they pass through security and enter the airside area, but at this stage passengers may be too anxious to get to their gates or too keen to visit the shops. This location may also fail to pick up transfer passengers. In some cases it may be useful to obtain the views of arriving passengers, but this is more difficult since most are reluctant at this time to participate in a survey as they will be keen to return home or get to their final destination. A possible interview point is in the baggage reclaim area, if they have to wait for their luggage.

If any interviewing is done in the secure airside part of the terminal, thorough security checks will clearly need to be undertaken for all interviewers, which will complicate the process and may lengthen the time period needed for the research. If surveys are undertaken in the landside area, they can provide information not only on passengers but also on visitors and meeters and greeters. This can be particularly useful when surface access aspects of the airport product are being considered, or when information regarding non-passenger usage of commercial facilities is needed. Sometimes a special survey of just these non-passenger groups may be undertaken.

The timing of the survey needs to be carefully chosen as the volume of passengers and their characteristics will vary by time of day, day of week and month of year. Therefore, depending on the purpose of the survey, it may need to be undertaken at a number of different times or designed as a continuous survey to be undertaken on an ongoing basis throughout the year. The survey may be undertaken on an ad hoc basis or may become a regular activity undertaken every year, as is the situation at many large airports. The experience within Europe shows considerable variation in the sample sizes used for passenger surveys. For example, in 2010 at Dublin Airport over 17,500 departing passengers were surveyed regarding their characteristics, while similar

Budapest Questionnaire

1) Do you currently travel between London and Budapest?

○ Yes   ○ No

2) Do you travel for business or leisure reasons?

○ Business ○ Leisure

3) From which airport do you currently fly?

○ Heathrow   ○ Gatwick   ○ Luton

4) How many times do you fly between Budapest and London each month?

○ 1 - 4   ○ 5 - 10   ○ 11 - 14   ○ 15 +

5) How many people within your organisation do you think fly to/from Budapest?

○ Up to 5   ○ 6 - 10   ○ 11 - 15   ○ 16 - 20   ○ 21 +

6) Does your company have a travel policy?

○ Yes   ○ No

7) Does your company's travel policy dictate which airline you have to travel with?

○ Yes   ○ No

8) What's most important to you?

○ Frequency   ○ Convenient Schedule   ○ Price
○ Punctuality   ○ Value for money   ○ Time saving/Ease of airport

9) Does the cost of ground transport to/from the airport (i.e. the cost of a train or a taxi to/from the airport) influence your airport choice in any way?

○ Yes   ○ No

10) What would be your ideal number of flights per from LCY to Budapest or Budapest to LCY?

○ 2   ○ 3   ○ 4   ○ 5   ○ 6   ○ 7   ○ 8   ○ 9   ○ 10

11) What time would you like to leave London?

○ 0700 - 0800   ○ 0800 - 0900   ○ 0900 - 1000   ○ 1000 - 1100
○ 1100 - 1200   ○ 1200 - 1300   ○ 1300 - 1400   ○ 1400 - 1500
○ 1500 - 1600   ○ 1600 - 1700   ○ 1700 - 1800   ○ 1800 - 1900
○ 1900 - 2000   ○ 2000 - 2100

Figure 4.4 London City Airport Budapest questionnaire
Source: © Copyright London City Airport 2012

12) What time would you like to arrive in Budapest?

○ 1000 - 1100   ○ 1100 - 1200   ○ 1200 - 1300   ○ 1300 - 1400

○ 1400 - 1500   ○ 1500 - 1600   ○ 1600 - 1700   ○ 1700 - 1800

○ 1800 - 1900   ○ 1900 - 2000   ○ 2000 - 2100   ○ 2100 - 2200

○ 2200 - 2300   ○ 2300 - 0000   ○ 0000 - 0100

13) What time would you like to leave Budapest?

○ 0700 - 0800   ○ 0800 - 0900   ○ 0900 - 1000   ○ 1000 - 1100

○ 1100 - 1200   ○ 1200 - 1300   ○ 1300 - 1400   ○ 1400 - 1500

○ 1500 - 1600   ○ 1600 - 1700   ○ 1700 - 1800   ○ 1800 - 1900

○ 1900 - 2000

14) What time would you like to arrive in London?

○ 0800 - 0900   ○ 0900 - 1000   ○ 1000 - 1100   ○ 1100 - 1200

○ 1200 - 1300   ○ 1300 - 1400   ○ 1400 - 1500   ○ 1500 - 1600

○ 1600 - 1700   ○ 1700 - 1800   ○ 1800 - 1900   ○ 1900 - 2000

○ 2000 - 2100   ○ 2100 - 2200

Please add in any comments you would regarding your request for a new service

First name

Surname

Company Address

Email

Add into newsletter: ○ Yes ○ No

Submit answers

Figure 4.4 continued

information was obtained at Copenhagen Airport using a sample of 130,000 passengers. Sample sizes for passenger satisfaction surveys also range from 2,000 a year at Geneva Airport, 24,000 at Frankfurt Airport, 34,000 at London Heathrow Airport, and 40,000 at Athens International Airport.

Some airports have used passenger surveys in more unusual ways to research passenger characteristics and opinions. For example, in 2012 visitors to the London City Airport website had an opportunity to provide opinions about a number of destinations that were then not served by the airport, such as Budapest, Dusseldorf and Hamburg. Respondents were asked which airport they currently used to fly to the destination and their travel preferences (e.g. frequencies and schedules) if a service were to operate from London City Airport (see Figure 4.4).

Many airports now conduct destination surveys online via their website, or even via social media sites such as Facebook or online survey tools such as QuestBack. Mineta San José International Airport used the strapline 'Airlines need to hear from YOU!' for its 2012 destination survey, which could be completed online via a computer or mobile device. The survey asked respondents for basic personal information (name, e-mail address, city of residence and company they work for), and then offered them the opportunity to select any destinations from a list of 19 domestic and 33 international destinations. Respondents were also asked to e-mail the airport if a desired destination was not listed. During 2012, Southampton Airport and London Stansted Airport used an online destination survey that asked respondents for their name and e-mail address, offered an open box for respondents to list as many destinations as they wanted, and asked respondents to select whether the destinations would be mainly for business or leisure purposes, or both. Cambridge Airport used a fairly detailed online destination survey during 2012 that asked respondents for their name and e-mail address, place of residence (according to travel time from the airport), current travel behaviour by air, and UK and European destinations desired from Cambridge Airport, with separate lists of major cities and holiday destinations that respondents could select from.

Another more unusual example of airport surveys is the use of a 'zip code kiosk' at Daytona Beach International Airport. This was placed on the landside before security and passengers were asked to enter their zip code into the kiosk. The airport estimated that it captured about a quarter of its passengers with this, and by combining this data with mapping software was able to gain a greater understanding of both where its local passengers lived and the residency details of its visitors (Biggs *et al.*, 2010).

4.5.1.2 *Employee surveys*

A number of airports undertake surveys of employees working at the airport. While the purpose for such surveys is sometimes beyond the scope of direct marketing activities (e.g. to measure employment to assess the airport's economic impact), employees nevertheless also need to be considered for marketing research, primarily for two reasons. First, employees contribute to the airport product and so knowledge about their characteristics and attitudes to the workplace is important for ensuring that an attractive product is offered to airport customers. Second, employees act as customers themselves for certain commercial facilities, such as F&B and car parking, so an understanding of their behaviour and preferences related to these can be important.

As with passengers, airport operators may undertake continuous or ad hoc surveys of employees, although the continuous surveys tend to be less regular, partly because of resources and cost implications, and partly since the findings are likely to change less rapidly over time. Unlike with passengers, because the identity of employees is known, common survey methods are e-mail/internet surveys, telephone surveys or even just handing out questionnaires at the workplace. Internet surveys are low cost and allow a large sample to be reached but tend to have a low response rate. They have the advantage of automatically processing the data but can only be relatively simple as no probing can be undertaken. By contrast, telephone surveys are more expensive and have a smaller number of respondents, but do have instant responses and may enable more detailed or more complicated questions to be asked. Issues covered with all types of employee surveys can range from assessing their general understanding of and satisfaction with their specific role and relationship with management, to evaluating their use of and needs for commercial facilities and ground transport modes. Employee job satisfaction surveys (although arguably perhaps falling outside the usual boundaries of marketing research information) are particularly popular at many airports such as Amsterdam Schiphol, Lisbon, Frankfurt and with airport operators in Spain and Sweden.

4.5.1.3 Airline, concessionaire and tenant surveys

Airline, concessionaire and tenant surveys will usually be undertaken to identify the needs of the respective customer groups and to gauge their satisfaction with the airport operator. They may also be undertaken to provide insight into the economic impacts of the airport. However, at most airports there is usually a regular dialogue between airlines, concessionaires, tenants and other service providers, and so additional information through more formal surveys may not be necessary. In addition, the smaller number of organisations involved with all but the largest airports, compared to passenger or employee groups, means that airports may be able to survey all or most of the target population rather than having to select a representative sample. Airports that formally survey these groups of stakeholders include the large airports of Frankfurt, Paris and Amsterdam in Europe. Elsewhere, at the major airports in Australia there are both airline and border agency surveys.

4.5.1.4 Local resident surveys

While passenger surveys can provide invaluable information about those who are already flying from an airport, particularly for ASD reasons, airport marketers frequently want to obtain information about local residents who are either using other nearby airports or not flying at all. The target population here would be the airport's catchment area and a possible sample could be chosen using postal or telephone codes. Postal, telephone or door-to-door surveys might be possible. Issues covered would be the factors influencing choice of airport and reasons that would make them use the specific airport.

4.5.1.5 Local business and travel company surveys

As with local residents, surveys of local businesses can provide valuable information for airport marketers, about both the potential market for air services and customer needs in terms of the airport product. The advantage of this group, compared with local residents, is that contact details (e.g. e-mail addresses) are much more readily available. Such views are important to research, since one organisation may represent many individuals who may have the potential to become passengers if the air services and other features of the airport product meet their needs. Travel agents and corporate travel businesses are also useful groups to contact and survey on customers' travel needs, preferences and views of the airport. Suppliers of tourist products and information (e.g. hotels, attractions, tourist boards) may also be able to provide some useful research material.

4.5.1.6 Cargo businesses surveys

Finally there are cargo surveys. A different approach to passengers has to be adopted here as cargo itself cannot be surveyed and so the focus has to be entirely on the organisations involved with handling the cargo such as the airlines, integrators and freight forwarders. In some cases, if relevant, airline surveys can cover both passenger and cargo markets. However, in general the amount of data related to cargo operations is much more limited and less available to airport operators. In some countries such as Australia, data (e.g. on total cargo throughput) is not available at all to airport operators. Information in this area tends to be more commercially sensitive

Table 4.4 Most popular airport survey methods

Stakeholder	Most popular survey method
Passenger	Self-completion paper questionnaire
Employee	Hand-out/hand-back questionnaire
Tenant	Mailed questionnaire
Local resident	Mailed/internet questionnaire
Local business	Mailed questionnaire

Source: Biggs *et al.* (2010)

and more complicated because of the unidirectional nature of much of the traffic and because cargo capacity is often provided as a secondary by-product of passenger capacity.

In summary, there are a number of different stakeholder surveys that airport marketers may make use of with their marketing research. These may differ quite considerably in the specific methodology used, the survey frequency and the pressures exerted on the marketing research budget and resources. As an illustration of this, Table 4.4 presents the results of a US study that shows the most popular survey method for each target group.

4.5.2 Other primary research methods

With many of the stakeholders mentioned above it may be useful to undertake in-depth interviews, focus groups or panel discussions, which will give the airport marketer a chance to discuss certain issues in more depth than could be achieved with a survey. In this case more qualitative information will be gathered, which will typically investigate opinions and attitudes rather than gathering data about stakeholder characteristics. With group discussions the selection of the members will be very important, and ideally a trained facilitator should lead the discussion to maximise the effectiveness of this approach. However, this research method tends to be rather time-consuming and expensive, and because only small groups will be used the findings cannot be generalised and applied to a broader population.

Observation methods can also be used. Most large airports regularly observe service delivery performance (e.g. waiting time and queue length for essential processes). However, if there is a certain issue related to one aspect of the airport product or one part of the airport terminal, they may want to undertake additional ad hoc research. Mystery shoppers can be used for assessing the passenger experience in the terminal overall or the quality of the commercial facilities. Other methods can include tracking, when passengers are monitored throughout their journey in the terminal to see where they spend their time and where they are held up with bottlenecks in the processes. This may help shed some light on how available time influences retail spend, and any other issues related to passenger flows that have not been identified through other research methods. Technology, for instance, which enables the identification of mobile phone signals, has made passenger tracking much easier in recent years. Observation methods can even take place outside the terminal, such as recording vehicle registration licence plates which may, in some countries such as the US, give an indication of the residences of the passengers who have parked the cars.

References

ACI (2011) *ACI Statistics Manual: A Practical Guide to Addressing Best Practices*, Montreal: ACI.

Biggs, D.C., Bol, M.A., Baker, J., Gosling, G.D., Franz, J.D. and Cripwell, J.P. (2010) *ACRP Report 26: Guidebook for Conducting Airport User Surveys*, Washington, DC: Transportation Research Board.

Dennis, N. (2007) 'Stimulation or saturation? Perspectives on the European low cost airline market and prospects for growth', *Transportation Research Record: Journal of the Transportation Research Board*, 2007; 52–9.

Dibb, S., Simkin, L., Pride, W. and Ferrell, O. (2006) *Marketing: Concepts and Strategies*, 5th European edn, Boston: Houghton Mifflin.

ELFAA (2004) *Liberalisation of European Air Transport: The Benefits of Low Fares Airlines to Consumers, Airports, Regions and the Environment*, Brussels: ELFAA.

Kotler, P., Armstrong, G., Wong, V. and Saunders, J. (2008) *Principles of Marketing*, 5th European edn, Harlow: Prentice Hall-Pearson Education.

Kramer, L., Fowler, P., Hazel, R., Ureksoy, M. and Harig, G. (2010) *ACRP Report 28: Marketing Guidebook for Small Airports*, Washington, DC: Transportation Research Board.

LeighFisher (2011) *ACRP Report 54: Resource Manual for Airport In-Terminal Concessions*, Washington, DC: Transportation Research Board.

Martin, S.C. (2008) *ACRP Report 18: Passenger Air Service Development Techniques*, Washington, DC: Transportation Research Board.

Pride, W. and Ferrell, O. (2008) *Marketing*, 14th edn, Boston: Houghton Mifflin.

STRAIR (2005) *Air Service Development for Regional Agencies: Strategy, Best Practice and Results*, STRAIR.

The Route Shop (2012a) *Nice Côte d'Azur Airport*. Online. Available at: http://www.therouteshop.com/nice-airport (accessed 20 September 2012).

The Route Shop (2012b) *Birmingham Airport*. Online. Available at: http://www.therouteshop.com/birmingham-airport (accessed 20 September 2012).

UK CAA (2011) *Empirical Methods for Assessing Geographic Markets, in Particular Competitive Constraints between Neighbouring Airports*, London: UK CAA.

Weatherill, J. (2008) 'Quality of service index review', presented at *ACI North America Air Service Data and Planning Seminar*, New Orleans, January 2008.

Chapter 5

Airport marketing planning

This chapter considers airport marketing planning: a systematic process that can be used by airports to anticipate the best ways in which to exploit their future business environment. It introduces the marketing planning process, including its role and importance for airports. The chapter also examines individual elements of the marketing planning process, such as corporate intentions, situation analysis, marketing decisions and implementation.

5.1 Introduction to the marketing planning process

Marketing planning is 'the logical sequence and a series of activities leading to the setting of marketing objectives and the formulation of plans for achieving them' (McDonald and Wilson, 2011: 24). The marketing planning process is illustrated in Figure 5.1. It typically involves a description of corporate intentions that are represented by the vision, values, mission and objectives of the airport. Corporate intentions are not a specific marketing function but it is important to include them in the marketing planning process because they help to guide marketing decisions. A situation analysis investigates internal strengths and weaknesses of the airport and any external

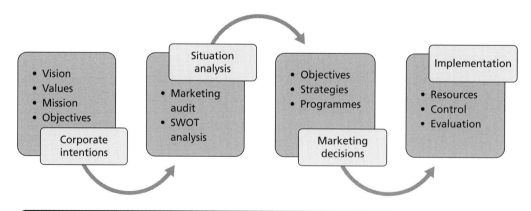

Figure 5.1 Main stages in the marketing planning process
Source: compiled by the authors

opportunities and threats. This also guides marketing decisions because it encourages the airport to assess both the environment in which it operates and how it should position itself in that environment for the future. Marketing decisions are a key part in the process. They determine the marketing objectives for the airport and the strategy and specific programmes to be used to achieve the objectives. The final part of the process involves the implementation of any marketing programmes including the allocation of resources, and any mechanisms for control and evaluation. The findings of any control and evaluation should then feed into future cycles of the process.

Figure 5.1 gives the impression that marketing planning is a simple process, and, conceptually, that might be the case. In practice, it is difficult to implement because it seeks to combine different and often complex elements of marketing into a single plan. In addition, the process is dependent on being incorporated into an institutionalised management system (McDonald and Wilson, 2011). Airports may therefore find that the process is affected by their style of corporate governance, the culture and organisational structure of the airport, and the size and nature of the airport's activities.

Marketing planning is also likely to be one of a number of planning functions at an airport. In addition to a marketing plan, airports produce plans for business, operations, and planning and development. These are all linked in one way or another and may come under the umbrella of an overall airport strategic plan that has subsequent implications for resource allocation including finance and staff training and development (Ashford et al., 2011).

Marketing planning is important for all airports, regardless of their role or individual objectives and resources for marketing. It is particularly important given the challenging business environment in which airports find themselves (see Chapter 2). This chapter provides a general description of the individual elements of the marketing planning process in Figure 5.1. However, it is important to note that plans themselves must be unique to each airport, and the extent to which plans vary will depend largely on the marketing objectives of each airport.

At larger airports, marketing objectives are likely to target many different market segments and affect a range of strategic business units. It is therefore important to develop a plan that reduces the complexities that come with being a large organisation, exploit the strengths of the airport, and produce marketing decisions that are relevant to any opportunities that exist. At smaller airports, marketing objectives are likely to target more narrowly defined market segments and affect fewer strategic business units. In this instance, developing a marketing plan can help smaller airports to find a niche and deliver key messages to the community and customers (Thompson, 2009). For many airports, the marketing plan will form the basis for securing funding for marketing and will need to be approved by a board of directors or a relevant authority.

5.2 The airport marketing planning process

5.2.1 Airport corporate intentions

Corporate intentions underpin the marketing planning process because they describe the desired priorities and purpose of the airport, and how the airport is positioned in its main markets. They are typically presented as vision, value or mission statements that say something about what the airport hopes to achieve.

A vision statement says something about the future scenario the airport wants to achieve for its stakeholders, while a value statement represents what the airport wants its stakeholders to say about the way it conducts itself. A mission statement puts the vision into practice and says something about the purpose of the airport and what it ultimately wants to achieve. Corporate objectives can then be used to show how the airport intends to achieve its mission. Objectives

---

Table 5.1 Sydney Airport's corporate intentions

Intention	Description
Vision	To deliver a world-class airport experience and foster the growth of Sydney Airport for the benefit of Sydney, New South Wales and Australia.
Values	Integrity and openness: acting honestly and openly to achieve corporate and social objectives. Safety and security: delivering the highest levels of safety and security. Excellence: striving to deliver an outstanding airport experience through operational efficiency, superior customer service and innovation. Teamwork: fostering a collaborative and supportive work environment that values diversity. Creativity and flexibility: working with our partners to achieve superior business outcomes. Sustainability: responsible growth through balancing community and environmental needs with corporate objectives.
Mission	Sydney Airport is committed to meeting the responsibilities of a leading airport owner, operator and partner to create long-term value by working with stakeholders to meet objectives.
Objectives	Ensure that Sydney Airport is managed responsibly and delivers the requirements of airlines, passengers and airport businesses. Deliver market leading performance for our investors through sustainable long-term growth at Sydney Airport. Ensure the highest standards of safety and security. Provide a rewarding and safe workplace for Sydney Airport employees by recognising good performance, valuing teamwork and fostering equality of opportunity. Promote proactive and transparent engagement with all levels of government, stakeholders and the communities in which Sydney Airport operates. Operate in a socially and environmentally responsible manner.

Source: adapted from Sydney Airport (2012)

may focus on different aspects of performance such as finance, market share, service levels or safety. They should be listed in order of priority because this will subsequently help to guide the focus of the airport, including any marketing objectives. The corporate intentions of Sydney Airport are provided as an example (see Table 5.1).

Although not directly relevant to the marketing planning process, corporate intentions are important because marketing strategy needs to be compatible with the overall intentions of the airport and to support the strategies of other departments at the airport. According to Brassington and Pettitt (2007), corporate strategy guides, directs, controls and coordinates marketing strategy, while marketing strategy informs, achieves and operationalises corporate strategy. This means that there should be a fair amount of overlap between the two, and emphasises the need for some degree of consistency between them.

5.2.2 Situation analysis

The next stage in the marketing planning process is to conduct a situation analysis for the airport, which provides a systematic way of organising information for planning. It is typically based on the findings of a marketing audit, which is:

> A systematic, critical and unbiased review and appraisal of all the external and internal factors that have affected an organisation's commercial performance over a defined period. It answers the question: 'Where is the organisation now?' The marketing audit is essentially a database of all market-related issues for the company, which forms part of the company-wide management audit. By providing an understanding of how the organisation relates to the environment in which it operates, the marketing audit enables management to select a position within that environment based on known factors.
>
> (McDonald, 2008: 39)

The marketing audit requires airports to conduct an internal audit of their own strengths and weaknesses and an external audit of their business environment, which provides a means for reflecting on the airport's business environment and its actual or planned ability to respond to that environment. As shown in Chapter 2, airport capabilities – as well as the environment in which they operate – are constantly changing, often with dramatic consequences. As a result, the marketing audit should be continuous, and based on current market research.

5.2.2.1 Internal marketing audit

An internal audit will typically assess the marketing effectiveness of the airport according to absolute market position, but also its market position relative to competitors. The assessment is typically carried out in the form of a portfolio analysis that focuses on individual strategic business units (e.g. aviation, retail, advertising, property or consultancy) or sets of products within a strategic business unit (e.g. for aviation this could be domestic, intra-regional and intercontinental routes). It is therefore important to define what units or products the airport has or would like to develop. Brassington and Pettitt (2007) suggest that a number of key questions should then be addressed by the internal audit. Are there enough strong units or products to support the weak ones? Do any of the weak units or products have development potential? Are there new units or products that should be developed to take over declining ones?

Figure 5.2 provides adaptations of two well-known models that may be used in support of portfolio analysis: the Boston Consulting Group (BCG) matrix and the McKinsey/General Electric (GE) matrix. Airports can plot individual units or products in the matrix cells, using different circle sizes to represent the contribution of each unit or set of products to total volume (e.g. turnover or the movement of passengers, cargo or aircraft). An arrow can be included to indicate the expected direction of movement in the matrix for the unit or set of products in the future. Each cell in each matrix represents a different competitive position, along with opportunities and threats to the airport, and the main strategic choices have been added to the respective matrices in Figure 5.2. A third model, called the Shell directional policy matrix, is sometimes used. It has two dimensions: competitive capabilities (weak, average, strong) and prospects for sector profitability (unattractive, average, attractive). As with the GE matrix, units or products can be plotted in one of the nine cells that represent different strategic choices.

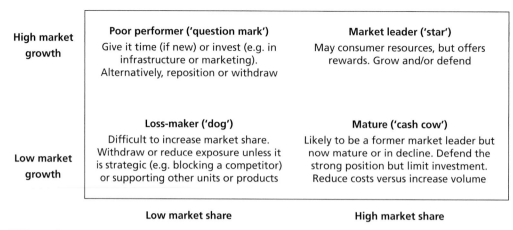

BCG matrix

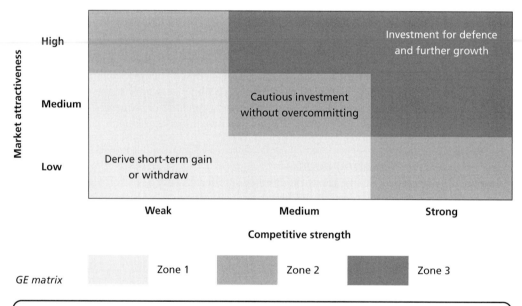

GE matrix

Figure 5.2 Portfolio analysis models
Source: adapted by the authors from the original models

Brassington and Pettit (2007) recommend that companies should try to develop a balanced portfolio with units and products that generate resources which can then be invested in those that should be defended or offer opportunities for growth. Portfolios that are unbalanced will result in either too few resources for investment or too few opportunities for future growth.

Criticisms of each model are well documented in marketing literature (e.g. see Brassington and Pettitt, 2007), and those criticisms are relevant to the airport context. For instance, owing to the presence of multiple competitors, airports may find it difficult to decide who their market share should be relative to in the BCG matrix. Alternatively, some airports have a monopoly or quasi-monopoly situation or are exposed to structural or regulatory constraints that affect their ability to compete. Quantifying values for the different dimensions should be possible for aviation-related products such as air services, but may be difficult for products in non-aviation areas such as retail, advertising, property or consultancy. In addition, the models become less appropriate for smaller airports with few units or products to assess, and for airports with limited opportunities for growth. A further criticism of the BCG matrix relates to the use of market growth and share because it does not take account of possible return on investment, which is sometimes more important to an airport than market share. Finally, some airports are more focused on being better at what they do than pursuing increased market share in growth markets, and this strategy is not really represented by any of the portfolio analysis models.

Despite the criticisms, portfolio analysis models are a useful part of the internal audit. Airports can develop their own model with dimensions that meet their needs, which can then be used to plot elements of the airport portfolio conceptually, visualise the marketing effectiveness of the airport, and subsequently assess the opportunities and problems associated with different elements of their portfolio. This knowledge and understanding can then be used to make marketing decisions later in the marketing planning process.

In addition to portfolio analysis, airports can use the dimensions of the GE matrix to conduct a more general and descriptive audit of their key attributes. For market attractiveness, this may include the size and growth or diversity and profitability of markets served, the level of competitive intensity experienced by the airport, and any market trends and behaviour that have an impact on it. For competitive strength, this may include location (e.g. proximity to a central business district or holiday destinations), accessibility (e.g. surface access), operational capabilities (e.g. handling, runway dimensions, capacity, navigational aids and designations such as for customs, immigration or foreign trade), management capabilities (e.g. experience and qualifications), company assets and financial resources (e.g. to support future investment needs), how the airport is perceived (e.g. image and brand recognition, community support, service levels, customer satisfaction and loyalty) and economic or operational performance (e.g. pricing and economic or operational efficiency).

A more general and descriptive audit of this nature can be used by airports to indicate how they should position and promote themselves in order to gain a competitive advantage. It can also be used to assess how any planned or recently completed improvements (e.g. in infrastructure or services) will have an impact on the airport's market attractiveness and competitive strength.

5.2.2.2 External marketing audit

An external audit should cover aspects already discussed in this book, such as the influence of macro- and microenvironmental factors (Chapter 2), and market forecasting and potential (Chapter 4).

Macroenvironmental factors provide a range of opportunities and threats for airport marketing. For instance, policy decisions influence the planning and development of airport infrastructure and services, while regulatory forces such as price regulation affect the extent to which airports are free to make decisions (e.g. about pricing). Airports may need to focus on cost control and reduction during times of economic hardship, which may subsequently have an effect on which markets they position themselves for. Socio-cultural trends such as changes in population or travel trends and behaviour may influence which markets airports should target, while public attitudes (e.g. towards the airport and their level of corporate responsibility) may influence the extent to which an airport concentrates its efforts on public relations. Technological change may influence marketing decisions by offering new ways of conducting business that can help the airport to be more cost-efficient and productive, or by offering different products and services. It is important that the external audit identifies key factors and the way they influence airport marketing decisions.

Another important part of the external audit is to identify microenvironmental factors, especially competition, because this can influence airport marketing decisions and determine the success or failure of an airport in its chosen markets. It is therefore important for airports to identify their competitors and the unique advantages they have over them that can then be exploited through marketing. Competition has already been discussed in Chapter 2 but is covered again here within the context of Porter's five forces: a model developed by Michael E. Porter in 1979 (see Porter, 1979). The model identifies five competitive forces that are experienced in an industry and shape the characteristics of a market: threat of new entrants, threat of substitutes, bargaining power of suppliers, bargaining power of customers, and rivalry amongst existing companies. The model provides a wide definition of competitors that encourages airports to look beyond direct competition for end-users (e.g. for airlines, passengers and cargo) and to consider indirect and future competition for suppliers. Graham (2010) applies Porter's five forces to the airport industry and some of that discussion is repeated here.

The threat of new entrants is generally low in the airport industry because it is increasingly difficult to find suitable locations for new airports, the planning and regulatory processes involved tend to be long and complicated, and high levels of investment are needed. The threat of substitutes provides a few potential sources of competition, such as the introduction of high speed rail as a threat to short-haul air services, although the growth of the LCC sector has meant that air travel may be a cheaper and more attractive option on routes where rail and air services compete. While it may have a negative impact on hub connections at airports, high speed rail may also provide opportunities; for instance, its connections may provide airports with rail-based feeder services, and it may also allow capacity-constrained airports to replace short-haul routes served by smaller aircraft with long-haul routes served by larger aircraft, resulting in fewer aircraft movements per passenger.

Airports that serve holiday destinations may experience a high threat of substitutes. Airlines that provide holiday traffic are less likely to serve an airport because of network or public service considerations and are less likely to be based at the destination airport; as a result, they are likely to have lots of alternative airports to choose from. Australia's Productivity Commission investigated substitution possibilities at a number of airports in Australia as part of a price monitoring process (see Productivity Commission, 2006). A summary of the findings is provided in Table 5.2, listing the airport, main market segments served and the extent to which the airport can be substituted by other airports, other modes of transport or other destinations. Possibilities for

Table 5.2 Substitution possibilities at a number of airports in Australia

		Substitution possibilities		
Airport	Main market segment	Other airports	Other modes of transport	Other destinations
Adelaide	Domestic: business 49%, VFR 29%; International: holiday 41%, VFR 34%	Low with no nearby airports	Low for business travellers but some for VFR and holiday travel	Relatively low since mostly business and VFR traffic

Airport	Main market segment	Substitution possibilities		
		Other airports	Other modes of transport	Other destinations
Brisbane	Domestic: business 33%, VFR 27%; International: holiday 61%, VFR 21%	Low but increasing with airports in the Gold Coast and Maroochydore	Low for business travellers but some for VFR and holiday travel	Relatively low since mostly business and VFR traffic
Canberra	Domestic: business 64%, VFR 25%	Low with no nearby airports	High as 3 out of 4 visitors to Canberra arrive by car, go surface to Sydney and fly from there to a holiday destination	Relatively low since mostly business and VFR traffic
Darwin	Domestic: holiday 40%, business 37%; International: holiday 59%	Low for 'top end' visits but higher for visiting several areas within the territory	Low for business travellers but significant for holiday travel	High as mostly holiday traffic: can choose to go to other tourist destinations
Melbourne	Domestic: business 48%, VFR 27%; International: holiday 42%, VFR 26%	Generally low but Avalon Airport used by Jetstar for some of its flights	Low for business travellers but some for VFR and holiday travel	Relatively low since mostly business and VFR traffic
Perth	Domestic: business 42%, VFR 31%; International: holiday 51%, VFR 27%	Low with no nearby airports	Low since Perth is relatively isolated	Relatively low since mostly business and VFR traffic
Sydney	Domestic: business 52%, VFR 24%; International: holiday 51%, VFR 21%	Low with no nearby airports	Low for business travellers but some for VFR and holiday travel	Relatively low since mostly business and VFR traffic

Source: Graham (2008) using information from Productivity Commission (2006)

substitution are generally low with the exception of Darwin Airport, which competes with other airports for holiday traffic, and Canberra Airport, which competes with other modes of transport.

Airports may also experience a threat of substitutes for commercial activities, especially retail. For instance, hub airports with a high proportion of transfer traffic such as Dubai International Airport, Singapore Changi Airport and Amsterdam Schiphol Airport compete in retail with other airports and with downtown or internet shopping. They also compete as stop-over destinations.

Airports offer a composite product that consists of many different services provided by the airport, airlines operating at the airport or a third party provider. The way services are provided will affect the extent to which airports face competition in terms of the bargaining power of suppliers. For some operational services, such as air traffic control and security, the airport may have no choice over suppliers as this will be determined by government policy. However, the airport may not have to pay for all these, especially if they are provided by a state agency. For ground handling services, there may be regulations such as the EC's directive on access to the ground handling market at community airports, which stipulates the number and nature of suppliers that must be used. The situation is complicated further because suppliers of some services, such as air traffic control or ground handling, charge airlines directly for use of their services. For commercial activities such as retail, airports are likely to be less restricted and may have a greater choice of suppliers. In extreme cases, entire terminals may be managed by different suppliers.

The bargaining power of customers – especially airlines – can vary significantly, and is likely to be influenced by the extent to which airlines serving the airport are able to switch to an alternative airport. It is likely to be higher for more footloose airlines such as charter and LCCs than for airlines serving the airport as part of their wider network or for public service considerations. In developed areas, a national carrier can often have strong political power due to its role in encouraging trade or tourism. The degree of power may also be influenced by other factors such as the amount of spare capacity at the airport, the extent to which an airport needs or wants to attract new business, the degree to which an airport is dependent on just one or a few airline customers, and whether an airport's airline customers belong to an airline alliance. Such considerations will determine the balance of power between airports and their airline customers. The degree of power wielded by an airport is likely to influence its approach to pricing although, as will be discussed in Chapter 7, airport aeronautical charges may be controlled directly by governments or indirectly through some type of economic regulation in order to limit an airport's ability to abuse its strong bargaining power.

The scope for competitive rivalry between existing airports varies considerably. Rivalry is likely to be low at airports located in remote regions with limited touristic appeal because such airports are most likely to appeal to traditional scheduled carriers who serve the airport for network or public service considerations, and may not necessarily have alternative airports to choose from. The greatest scope for rivalry will be at airports that are physically close, have overlapping catchment areas, and have a high concentration of point-to-point services, especially inbound services provided by charter or LCCs. Rivalry will be particularly high in major cities such as London that are served by a number of different airports, or in regions where catchment areas can be continually expanded or contracted, depending on the nature of air services and surface links on offer at neighbouring airports (e.g. see Lian and Rønnevik, 2011). It may also be high at airports competing for the role of hub by aiming to provide good flight connectivity and efficient passenger transfers.

Porter's model is fairly broad and focused largely on macro-level forces. Airports also need to consider micro-level forces, identifying current and potential competitors, their characteristics such as infrastructure and markets served, their relative strengths and weaknesses (including the extent to which market needs are currently being met and are likely to be met in the future), and their current and potential reaction to changes in the business environment. Micro-level competitive forces were discussed in Chapter 3.

Airports need to be careful about selecting relevant competitors for comparison. For instance, comparing a large international airport with a small local airport may not be worthwhile, even though each may have certain unique advantages over the other. In addition, many airports have identified weaknesses such as capacity constraints at competing airports that allow them to carve out a niche for themselves in a different market by focusing, for example, on leisure, low cost or business-related markets. In this instance, airports are competing, although not necessarily for the same markets.

Airports need to be specific about identifying companies that realistically compete or have the potential to compete. For airports serving large and diverse markets, it may be useful to group competitors into clusters depending on their focus and strategy. As mentioned in the internal audit section of this chapter, the identification of strengths and weaknesses could cover a broad range of areas including infrastructure or services available, organisational and managerial capabilities, spatial factors such as airport location and environmental restrictions, financial strength and success, customers and market segments served, operational performance and position in the market. Consideration of market position should include areas where competing airports are strong, areas where they are weak and vulnerable, and the direction they seem to be moving in. Competitive reaction is also worth considering, such as the speed and decisiveness with which competing airports tend to react to the actions of others or to changes in the business environment. The competitor analysis will need to be continuous, not just for marketing planning, and be based on sound and current research.

The external audit should also consider market potential and forecast the size of future markets the airport wants to compete in and the proportion of the market they want to capture. This relies on airports being able to make a precise definition and quantification of market size, which is difficult given that they operate in an uncertain environment affected by many factors: not just the behaviour of competitors but wider macroenvironmental factors too. The dynamic nature of the airport industry also makes it difficult to estimate the proportion of the market the airport wants to capture and results will always need to be considered relative to how the market changes over time. Despite the challenges, it is important to base marketing decisions on forecasts of market size and potential; it is therefore worth investing in accurate and effective means of forecasting. Estimating market potential is important for marketing planning as it helps set marketing objectives, guides marketing strategy, and determines any marketing programmes to be used. It also provides a measurable indicator for success or failure that can guide future planning.

Dallas Airport System (2010) provides an example of how competition and market potential guides marketing decisions at Dallas Executive Airport. The airport is located 10 kilometres southwest of the city of Dallas in Texas, US. The airport serves the general aviation market and acts as a reliever for Dallas Love Field Airport. The Dallas Executive Airport marketing plan of 2010 identifies opportunities for growth in terms of aircraft operations (take-offs and landings) and based aircraft. An airport market area analysis based on a 30-minute drive time radius for each airport identifies seven airports located close enough to Dallas Executive Airport to be considered competitors, especially for based aircraft. Market growth for based aircraft has stagnated in recent years and market share analysis suggests that the airport is underperforming its rivals. There were 1,782 based aircraft at Dallas Executive Airport and its seven competing airports in 2009. Dallas Executive Airport found that it had 10 per cent market share (179 aircraft) compared to 12.5 per cent (223 aircraft) if each airport had equal market shares. This is a shortfall of 2.5 per cent (44 aircraft), which represents a market share deficiency but also an opportunity for growth. A number of airport characteristics are compared in the competitor analysis, including those related to airport rates and charges and airport infrastructure and services, in order to identify the position of Dallas Executive Airport relative to its competitors. The airport has also implemented a number of enhancements to infrastructure and services in recent years that improve its competitive position. Marketing objectives and the marketing programme of activities subsequently focus on ways to enhance the airport's image, increase airport visibility and exposure, inform local aircraft owners about the enhanced infrastructure and services, and promote the benefits of using the airport.

5.2.2.3 SWOT analysis

A large amount of information may be generated by the marketing audit and the diverse nature of that information can be difficult to make sense of. A SWOT analysis is commonly used as a method for structuring audit information and for providing a critical analysis that helps drive the marketing plan forward (Brassington and Pettitt, 2007).

SWOT is an acronym for strengths, weaknesses, opportunities and threats. Strengths and weaknesses focus on internal factors that can, to some extent, be controlled by an airport. They

---

Table 5.3 SWOT analysis for Muskoka Airport

Strengths	Weaknesses
Community transportation link	Lack of apron space in the summer
Aviation business community	Un-serviced land
Access to vacant land for development	Seasonal traffic activity
Community support	Competition from road travel
6,000 foot runway	Unknown commodity
Existing tenant base	Transportation service to and from site
Reputation as a tourist destination	(e.g. car rental and taxi)
Close proximity to highway	No scheduled service
Central location in district of Muskoka	Ageing and small terminal facility
Visible from the highway	Signage
Enhances the economy (tourism, industry)	Maintenance costs
	Lack of temporary hangar space in winter

Opportunities	Threats
Potential market for serviced lots	Lack of government support
Partnerships with community groups	Over-regulation in the aviation industry
Muskoka is presently promoted by other organisations (Muskoka Tourism)	Security in the aviation industry
Off-season development	Economic issues
Possible closing of airports to the south	9/11-like situation
Lack of development space at airports to the south	Rising fuel prices
Cooperative marketing	Security issues
Community hangar space for rent	Increasing costs of operation

Source: adapted from Muskoka Airport (2006)

are inward-facing factors that affect an airport's past or present situation and typically include individual elements of the marketing mix as well as corporate strengths and weaknesses. Less controllable factors such as characteristics of main markets served may also be included. Opportunities and threats focus on outward-facing external factors that cannot be controlled by an airport but are likely to affect an airport's current or future situation. They tend to have a more strategic orientation.

Strengths and opportunities tend to help airports achieve their marketing objectives while weaknesses and threats tend to hinder airports. There may be some degree of overlap. For instance, a small airport may view its size both as a strength (allowing it to be dynamic and able to react quickly to change) and as a weakness (restricting the ability of the airport to invest and diversify its business). Similarly, an opportunity may also pose a threat. This is typical where the emergence of a new market may provide an opportunity for an airport but may also pose a threat to existing markets. This is sometimes the case for airports in holiday destinations that are served by charter carriers and view the possibility of attracting scheduled LCCs as an opportunity for growth and diversification of their business but also as a threat to services provided by existing charter carriers. A similar situation is experienced at airports seeking to replace public air services with commercial ones. Commercial air services may be more competitive (e.g. offering lower fares, larger aircraft and a higher frequency) but are more likely to base their decisions on commercial versus public service considerations and may therefore reduce or withdraw services at short notice.

Table 5.3 provides a SWOT analysis produced by Muskoka Airport, while Table 5.4 provides a SWOT analysis for Cardiff International Airport produced by a team of academics based on interviews with airport management. Similarly, Rankin (2011) produced a SWOT analysis for King County International Airport, based on a review of airport corporate publications.

Some airports employ external experts or survey stakeholder opinions to help develop their SWOT analysis. For example, in 2011 the Greater Orlando Aviation Authority offered

---

Table 5.4 SWOT analysis for Cardiff International Airport

Strengths	Weaknesses
Support through national identity, position and customer demand	Future of the market provision
Capacity, infrastructure and hinterland, which allow for growth	Demand as a destination market
Strong charter market and expanding LCC/ business routes	Surface leakage and poor access infrastructure

Opportunities	Threats
Route provision to meet local demand	The gravity effect of other airports
Congestion and growth limits at competing airports	Market dominance of airlines operating from competing airports
Regeneration of hinterland driving demand and improving access	

Source: adapted from Davison *et al.* (2010)

Table 5.5 Most common SWOT factors cited by British Columbia's northern airports

---

Item	% airports	Item	% airports
Strengths		*Weaknesses*	
Geographical location	15.4	Deteriorating infrastructure	13.8
Infrastructure condition	15.4	Maintenance costs/revenue shortfalls	12.8
Infrastructure size	14.3	Lack of capital funding	9.6
Land for development and expansion	8.8	Runway length	8.5
Opportunities		*Threats*	
Growth of regional industries	12.0	Lack of capital/operations funding	20.0
Tourism flights	12.0	Maintenance costs	12.9
Land development (airside/commercial)	12.0	Competition/airport leakage	7.1
Aircraft maintenance and engineering/manufacturing facilities/flight training	8.0	Federal regulations	7.1
		Financial viability	7.1

Source: adapted from Sypher (2006)

community leaders and business partners the opportunity to submit suggestions online for a SWOT analysis to be considered in developing the strategic plan for Orlando International Airport. In 2006, Northern British Columbia and Alberta Aviation Communities commissioned consultants to conduct a review of airport strategies in relation to the airport strategy of the federal government. As part of that review, the consultants produced individual SWOT analyses for 36 of British Columbia's northern airports based on the findings of airport questionnaires and workshop sessions. Table 5.5 provides a summary of the most common SWOT factors cited by British Columbia's northern airports.

It is not always easy for airports to decide what factors to include in their SWOT analysis and in which cell of the matrix to place them because of overlap between some factors. The most important task is to list the main factors somewhere in the matrix where it makes sense to the airport and helps to identify key issues and their impact. Creative analysis may be required to make sense of the information and it helps to think of strengths and weaknesses as representing where the company is now and opportunities and threats as representing where the company could be or wants to be in the future. Marketing decisions can then represent what the company needs to do in order to close the gap (Brassington and Pettitt, 2007).

5.2.3 Marketing decisions

5.2.3.1 Marketing objectives

Marketing objectives must be based on the findings of the situation analysis. They should also be linked to the corporate intentions of the airport, especially corporate objectives that describe what the airport is trying to achieve as an organisation. Compared to corporate objectives that have a more visionary and strategic orientation, marketing objectives are specific and functional and describe what the airport is trying to achieve through its marketing activities. Some airports use the terms marketing goal and marketing objective interchangeably, so it is important to emphasise that a goal is a general statement about what an airport wants to achieve through marketing while an objective is a specific and measurable target. For instance, an airport may have a goal to increase air service provision at the airport. Marketing objectives may thus include targeting a new market segment or growth in an existing market segment (e.g. by attracting new air services or increasing frequency or capacity on existing air services). Tasks will be set; these are the specific activities that support the achievement of this objective (e.g. deliver a proposal for a new air service to an airline or offer a growth incentive to an airline to encourage added frequency or capacity to an existing air service). Objectives should be achievable within the timeframe of the marketing plan and therefore tend to have a short- to medium-term focus of between one and five years. A range of example marketing objectives for different areas of the airport business is provided in Table 5.6.

Marketing objectives are a vital part of the planning process. They guide decisions relating to marketing strategies and underpin any marketing programmes. They also provide purpose and direction, with ultimate goals for attainment that form the basis for controlling and evaluating marketing performance. Objectives will benefit from being SMART. SMART is a mnemonic used to set objectives. The first known use of the term was by Doran (1981), and while there are different adaptations and interpretations of the mnemonic, it typically refers to the need for objectives to be specific (state exactly what is to be achieved), measurable (in quantitative terms such as number of movements, market share or turnover), achievable (realistic given the circumstance within which they are set and the resources available), relevant (to the airport and to those responsible for achieving them) and time-orientated (framed within a specific and realistic time period).

5.2.3.2 Marketing strategies

Marketing strategies 'allow an organisation to concentrate its limited resources on the greatest opportunities to increase sales and achieve a sustainable competitive advantage' (Baker, 2008: 3). Strategies underpin the marketing plan and should be designed to meet market needs and achieve the marketing objectives. Plans and objectives tend to provide time-related milestones that can be measured and assessed. Marketing strategies tend to be more long-term visions for the marketing activities of the airport and tend to be dynamic and interactive, changing as changes take place in the business environment or in response to competitor behaviour.

5.2.3.2.1 ANSOFF'S GROWTH MATRIX

Some airports may be pursuing survival or the status quo. The latter may involve a focus on being better at what they do without seeking growth, which is sometimes referred to as 'harvesting'. The growth matrix developed by Igor Ansoff (see Ansoff, 1957) provides a useful framework for airports that do seek growth. It helps identify strategic options in terms of product and market growth and offers four main strategies (market penetration, market development, product development and diversification), depending on whether an airport decides to market new or existing

Table 5.6 Example airport marketing objectives

Business area	Example marketing objectives
Aviation	Increase total passenger movements at our airport by 10% within 3 years.
	Increase market share of passenger movements vis-a-vis our main competitor by 5% within 3 years.
	Reduce airport leakage (of passengers to neighbouring airports) by 5% within 5 years.
	Attract at least 2 scheduled, year-round passenger services to an international destination not currently served from our airport within 2 years.
Property	Achieve 75% hangar utilisation within 3 years.
	Achieve 60% occupation of airport commercial rental property within 3 years.
	Increase income from property leases by 15% within 4 years.
Consultancy	Increase turnover from business consultancy projects by 5% within 2 years.
	Secure a minimum of 3 new process optimisation projects each year for the next 3 years.
	Increase the number of consultancy projects that our airport does through joint venture by 5% within 3 years.
Retail	Contract a master concession to assume overall responsibility for retail management at the airport within 1 year.
	Increase income from airport retail activities by 5% within 4 years.
	Attract 3 new concessions within 1 year.
Other areas	Achieve 75% brand awareness in each of the airport's main target markets within 3 years.
	Create and launch a new airport logo within 1 year.
	Reach 10,000 followers on Facebook within 3 years.
	Offer free wi-fi in the airport terminal within 1 year.

Source: compiled by the authors

products to new or existing markets. As with the BCG matrix discussed earlier in this chapter, it is useful for airports to have a balanced mix of growth strategies in order to avoid an overreliance on one type.

Market penetration is where the airport focuses on existing products in existing markets. This is a safe option for airports because it involves focusing on known markets and products and is not likely to require much investment. The strategy can be achieved through increasing use of the airport by existing customers such as passengers and airlines (e.g. with loyalty schemes, growth incentives or promotions), maintaining or increasing market share of existing products (e.g. by using more competitive pricing or promotions), or dominating growth markets. Many airports have introduced loyalty schemes for passengers in recent years that offer free or exclusive offers on retail, catering, car hire and parking, fast track services, lounge access and exclusive competitions (see Chapter 9). Similarly, airport price incentives are widely used to stimulate market growth in air services (see Chapter 7). Another strategy for achieving market penetration would be to restructure a mature market by driving out competitors and securing market dominance, although this is less common in the airport industry.

Market development is where airports focus on existing products in new markets: for instance, by entering new geographical areas with existing products. Some airport operators such as Changi Airports International have pursued growth in new markets through overseas airport investment, consultancy and management projects. However, these types of global expansion rarely seek to offer the same product. One exception is where common approaches to retail are used.

Airport mergers, or the formation of airport alliances and franchises, may also be seen as a way of entering new markets with existing products. For instance, Amsterdam Schiphol Airport and Frankfurt Airport established the Pantares agreement in December 1999 that aimed to offer a common range of services to, and subsequently gain market share in, the global airport market, as well as to achieve cost synergies from optimising hub operations at the respective airports. Six key areas for cooperation were targeted: passengers and retail; aviation, ground handling and cargo; real estate development; facility management; information and communications technology; and international activities. However, the agreement achieved very little and was eventually phased out. In December 2008, the Schiphol Group and AdP acquired 8 per cent of each other's share capital and signed an agreement for industrial cooperation for an initial period of 12 years. As with Pantares, this aims to achieve cost synergies but also sets up synergies in management structure that place the chief executive officer of each group on the board of directors of the other group. It also aims to enhance operational performance of the Air France–KLM route network.

The trend for cooperation between airports has been slow to develop since Pantares in 1999; however, it has sped up rapidly in recent years (e.g. see Stone, 2011). Table 5.7 provides examples of airport agreements, often referred to as 'sister agreements', signed during 2012. Many of these include a memorandum of understanding (MoU) concerning working jointly on developing and supporting new routes between the airports, while others involve sharing information and best practice or the provision of consultancy services. In addition, many of the agreements involve airports in the Asia-Pacific region, which is not surprising given the growth in those economies. Many airports have multiple agreements. For example, Airports of Thailand signed sister agreements with airports in four different countries: Munich International Airport in Germany in 2010, Incheon International Airport in South Korea in 2010, Narita International Airport in Japan in 2010, and Beijing International Airport in China in 2011. The agreements are for cooperation in the areas of information exchange, airport operations, marketing, staff training and technological and business innovations. They also include opportunities for staff exchange, meetings, seminars and workshops (Suvarnabhumi Airport, 2012).

Product development is where airports focus on new products in existing markets. Although the markets will be familiar to the airport, the product may not, unless it is simply a modification of an existing one. The strategy may require development of new competencies to ensure that new or modified products appeal to existing markets. Product development might be considered a form of differentiation, which will be discussed later in this chapter.

Diversification is where airports focus on new products in new markets. This is generally considered a high risk strategy because it involves moving into markets in which the airport has little or no experience, and with products of which the airport again has little or no experience. Airports pursuing diversification should therefore conduct a thorough and honest appraisal of the risks and be clear about what they expect to achieve. A common approach is when airports diversify their revenue sources in order to exploit opportunities for non-aeronautical revenue and reduce their dependency on aeronautical revenue. Athens International Airport provides a good example of this with the development of their Airport Retail Park, which is located two kilometres

> **Table 5.7** Selection of agreements made between airports during 2012

Airports	Agreement
Christchurch, New Zealand Adelaide, Australia	MoU to secure direct air services between the two cities with a NZD 7.5 million support package to the first airline to operate a daily service
Dallas/Fort Worth International, US Seoul Incheon International, S.Korea	Partnership agreement for joint promotion of existing non-stop services between the two cities; share information and best practice (e.g. in sustainability, customer service, engineering, airport amenities and airfield operations)
Birmingham, UK Chicago O'Hare International, US	MoU/sister agreement to formalise a working relationship and commit to the development of new opportunities, especially reinstating direct flights between the two cities
Delhi Indira Gandhi International, India Sydney, Australia	Partnership with the aim of introducing direct flights between the two cities
Melbourne, Australia Chengdu Shuangliu International, China	Sister airports to attract direct services and boost travel between the two cities; share knowledge and best practice (e.g. in route development, operations, planning and retail); staff liaison and exchange
Seoul Incheon International, S.Korea Kuala Namu International, Indonesia	Sister agreement for Seoul Incheon to assist Kuala Namu with its management and development
Singapore Changi, Singapore Narita International, Japan	MoU to intensify their partnership; undertake joint projects to improve the network between them; exchange information to improve management and operations; staff liaison, exchange and study trips
Hamburg, Germany Lübeck, Germany	The two airports are just 50 kilometres from each other and will continue to compete for air services but signed a cooperation agreement for partnership in technical support, staff training and procurement
Seoul Incheon International, S.Korea Bangladesh Airports	Agreement to provide consultancy services for a new airport in Bangabandhu, Bangladesh and on upgrading Dhaka International Airport; sharing Incheon's business expertise with Bangladesh

Source: compiled by the authors from various sources

south of the main terminal building and offers megastore shopping opportunities with companies such as IKEA (home furnishing), Kotsovolos (electrical appliances), Factory Outlet (a 'shop in shop' concept with more than 400 well-known brands of apparel, footwear, sportswear and accessories), and the Olympus Plaza Food Park.

Diversification is also important for the aeronautical side of the airport business because an overreliance on one airline customer can leave an airport exposed to risk from airline failure or a reduction or withdrawal of air services. This was the case at Brussels Airport, which lost most of its air services when its main airline customer Sabena went bankrupt in 2001. The airport still serves Brussels Airlines (formed after taking over part of Sabena's assets) but has diversified its customer base to include a wider range of traditional scheduled and LCCs, along with a number of airlines offering charter and cargo services.

5.2.3.2.2 GROWTH STRATEGIES BASED ON MARKET DOMINANCE

An alternative to market growth strategies are those based on market dominance. Within this category, four main types of competitive position have an impact on airport marketing strategy: market leader, challenger, follower and nicher.

Market leaders occupy a dominant position in their main markets. For example, Dallas/Fort Worth International Airport is the busiest airport in Texas and serves the Dallas/Fort Worth area with a range of regional, national and international services. Strategies for market leaders may involve expanding the market or their share of the market, defending their position or maintaining the status quo.

Challengers pursue aggressive strategies to gain market share: for instance, by attacking the market leader or other competitors. Dallas Love Field may be considered a challenger to Dallas/Fort Worth. The airport is about 10 kilometres northwest of the central business district of Dallas. Love Field was the primary airport for scheduled air services in Dallas and one of the 10 busiest airports in the US until 1974 when Dallas/Fort Worth opened and immediately assumed its dominant position as market leader. Love Field lost most of its passenger services after Dallas/Fort Worth opened but the airport has worked hard to regain market share since the 1970s, especially in recent years following the completion of a number of modifications to airport infrastructure and services that coincide with an end to restrictions in the Wright Amendment. (This is a federal law governing traffic at Dallas Love Field that limited most non-stop flights to destinations within Texas and neighbouring states from 1979. Limits were phased out in 1997 and 2005 but some restrictions remained and are due to be lifted in 2014.)

Followers are not in a dominant position. Instead of pursuing aggressive strategies to gain market share from a market leader, followers are more likely to play it safe and take any overflow from the market leader (Huff, 2011). This is common in situations where competing airports are owned and operated by the same company: if one of those airports is a market leader, others may become followers. Los Angeles International Airport is a market leader, operated by Los Angeles World Airports, which also operates Van Nuys Airport, Palmdale Airport and Ontario Airport. Ontario Airport has served the overflow from Los Angeles International Airport for years but a recent severe drop in passenger numbers has prompted Ontario city officials to question the way the airport is operated, claiming that there is a conflict of interest because Los Angeles World Airports is largely concerned with bolstering traffic at Los Angeles International (see Pierceall, 2011).

Nichers specialise in serving one or a few specific markets, focusing on developing expertise and a marketing mix that meets the needs of those markets (e.g. Frankfurt Hahn as a low cost airport, London City Airport for business travellers, and Liege Airport for cargo). The niche strategy is discussed again later in this chapter.

Strategies may also be based on innovation, where airports pursue cutting edge technology and business innovation as pioneers (risk-takers that like to be first to try new technologies or approaches to business), followers (who are more risk averse but recognise the value of investing in new technologies and business innovations) or late followers (who like to adopt new technologies and business innovations, but after others have done so) (Huff, 2011). Exambela Consulting (2009) conducted a survey of leaders at 22 European airports to identify which other European airports (or airport operators) they thought were 'best in class' in terms of innovation. Airports or airport operators that received between one and four mentions were Vienna, Aeroporti di Roma, Fraport, Dublin, Manchester, AENA (Spanish Airports and Air Navigation), AdP, BAA and TAV (Tepe and Akfen Airports Group). Athens, Brussels, Zurich and Copenhagen received between five and ten mentions, while Munich and Amsterdam Schiphol received ten or more mentions . Munich Airport provides a good example of an airport that is committed to innovation (Feldman, 2009), as it has both a team and a budget dedicated to innovation. The team has implemented various innovation-based products such as the MUC card (a payment and loyalty scheme card for staff and other airport users), the winter market (a themed market held in winter, offering opportunities for Christmas shopping and ice skating), ramp process improvements and the use of biofuels for ground service equipment.

5.2.3.2.3 PORTER'S GENERIC STRATEGY FRAMEWORK

Michael E. Porter, who developed the five forces model introduced earlier, also described a framework consisting of three general types of strategy used by businesses to achieve and maintain competitive advantage (see Porter, 1980). Porter's generic strategy framework provides a useful model within which airports can frame their strategic decisions. It uses dimensions of strategic scope (market penetration) and strength (competitive advantage). The framework comprises three main strategies: cost leadership, differentiation and focus or niche. Graham (2010) applies Porter's generic strategy framework to the airport industry and some of that discussion is repeated here.

Companies pursuing a strategy based on cost leadership aim to compete by offering lower prices. In order to achieve this, companies may need to focus on achieving reduced costs, offering a standardised product, achieving high sales volume, or taking advantage of economies of scale. Some airports are committed to a cost leadership strategy. For example, Saskatoon Airport Authority has a publicly stated objective for Saskatoon Airport to be a low cost airport for both passengers and airlines, and has pursued this strategy since taking over the management and operation of the airport in 1999. The Authority immediately reduced the aviation fees published by Transport Canada by 11 per cent and has endeavoured to maintain the lowest possible aviation rates and charges ever since, despite the challenges of increased security, regulatory compliance and administrative costs. Saskatoon Airport Authority (2005) describes how it views price as a determining factor in generating traffic throughput at the airport and how cost leadership provides a strategic advantage for future growth and development. The Authority feels that a prudent approach to financial management demonstrates to the public, passengers and airline customers that Saskatoon Airport offers an efficient and economical base from which to travel by air.

Cost leadership is not an easy strategy for airports to pursue, partly because of their high operating costs and investment needs, but also because their fixed location and apparent lack of economies of scale beyond a certain size mean that it is difficult for them to achieve cost savings. In addition, the relationship between costs and prices is weak at some airports, especially those where public sector owners subsidise airport operations to achieve a broader objective such as to stimulate regional economic development, or those operated as part of a group where uniform prices across the group do not reflect the costs of individual airports. It could also be argued that cost leadership is not necessary for many airports on the basis that their main markets may be fairly price insensitive.

Companies pursuing a strategy based on differentiation aim to develop products or services perceived as being different from those of their competitors or indeed unique. Differences may be real (e.g. through differences in design) or perceived (e.g. through the use of advertising). There is scope for airports to pursue differentiation strategies. For instance, an airport may differentiate itself from its competitors through its being in closer proximity to a particular area, or by offering enhanced service features, having a superior brand image, being more innovative, using more advanced technology, or offering more advanced operational capabilities.

Airports may develop differentiated products or services for different target markets. For instance, airports with multiple terminals often have separate terminals for different types of passenger or airline (e.g. short-haul versus long-haul, domestic versus international, or by airline alliance). Some airports even have competing terminals such as at John F. Kennedy International Airport, where the terminals are operated by different airlines or consortiums of airlines that use them, with the exception of Terminal 4, which is operated by the Schiphol Group. Airports may offer dedicated products and services for different types of passenger (e.g. fast track for first and business class passengers) or airline (e.g. dedicated low cost terminals for LCCs such as Terminal billi at Bordeaux Airport, mp^2 at Marseille Provence Airport, Piers H and M at Amsterdam Schiphol Airport, Low Cost Carrier Terminal (LCCT) at KLIA, and Budget Terminal at Singapore Changi Airport).

KLIA's LCCT was designed and built with only basic terminal amenities so that construction and operating costs could be minimised and savings passed onto LCCs by way of lower landing fees, handling fees and airport taxes. The 35,290 square metre terminal commenced operations in December 2008. It did not offer airbridges, rail connectivity, elaborate physical structures or decorations in the passenger terminal building. In addition, there was no transfer facility to the main terminal, meaning that transfer passengers needed to clear immigration, collect their luggage, clear customs and make their way to the main terminal in order to check in with the respective airline. LCCT was just a temporary solution until the new budget terminal, KLIA 2, opened in 2012. Similarly, Changi's Budget Terminal was built in response to the growth of LCCs in Asia. The 28,200 square metre terminal commenced operations in March 2006. In order to meet the demands of the LCC business model, the operating costs of Budget Terminal are kept low. It is a single-storey terminal without airbridges, moving walkways or lifts. However, Budget Terminal will be replaced by a hybrid terminal that can accommodate widebody aircraft used by low cost long-haul carriers such as Singapore Airlines' Scoot. It is not only LCCs that have had separate terminals developed for them: Dubai International Airport has Al Majalis VIP Pavilion, Dubai Executive Flight Terminal and Cargo Mega Terminal for VIP, executive and cargo operations respectively.

Focus or niche strategy is sometimes used by airports that are not large enough to target the whole market. Instead, the airport will specialise in serving one or a few specific markets such as a particular type of airline (e.g. charter, LCC or cargo) or services to a particular geographic area. Focus or niche strategies can be focused either on cost (e.g. airports that offer price incentives to LCCs) or on differentiation (e.g. airports that provide specialist facilities, such as for cargo at Liege Airport or for short-haul business at London City Airport).

In reality, many airports fit into what Porter's framework would define as being 'lost-in-the-middle'. This includes airports whose costs are too high to lead on cost, whose product is too standardised to differentiate, and whose appeal is too broad to be a focus or niche airport. There are also many airports that have multiple strategies. For instance, Christchurch International Airport is pursuing strategies that focus on diversification of revenue through expanded commercial activities and new revenue opportunities, operating cost focus and improvements in business efficiency, and being better at what it does to improve overall performance and engagement of their people (Christchurch International Airport, 2012).

5.2.3.3 Marketing programmes

Marketing programmes provide a detailed implementation of the marketing objectives and strategies: a written account of the actual tasks that need to be carried out. This typically includes an assessment of how each element of the marketing mix should be used to meet each marketing objective. Programmes should provide a written account of the person responsible for each task, allocated resources and any timescales involved. The dynamic nature of the industry means that they need to be reviewed continually. They need to be affordable, realistic and relevant. They also need to be budgeted, controlled and evaluated, which will be considered later in this chapter.

5.2.4 Implementation

The final element of the marketing planning process is to implement any marketing programmes. This may be straightforward at larger commercial airports with dedicated marketing staff working in a marketing or similar department. The head of that department may occupy a senior position within the airport hierarchy, meaning that marketing is considered a core business function of the airport with its own resources and responsibility for decision-making.

Smaller commercial or general aviation airports may not have personnel dedicated to marketing; in many cases it will be the airport manager or their assistant who assumes responsibility for marketing. This will be in addition to other operational and managerial functions, meaning that marketing may not be given a top priority even though the corporate objectives of the airport may be heavily dependent on marketing, such as the desire to develop air services, increase passenger throughput, improve public relations or enhance the image of the airport.

If the airport is operated as part of an airport group, responsibility for marketing may be complicated further since it may be assumed by someone at the corporate head office as opposed to someone at each individual airport. In this situation, there is always a risk that marketing decisions made by head office may be in conflict with what individual airports and their local stakeholders want to achieve. Similarly, airports may be owned by a government department, agency or regional or local authority. The owner is likely to have an interest in airport marketing but may not necessarily be forthcoming in funding any marketing activities. As with airports operated as part of an airport group, there is always a risk that the owner's opinions about marketing the airport may be in conflict with what the airport and their local stakeholders want to achieve.

Regardless of how the airport is owned or operated, it is important that overall responsibility for the implementation of any marketing programmes is assumed by one person, although individual tasks within each programme may be delegated to others. Responsibilities should be specified on any programmes in the marketing plan.

5.2.4.1 Resources

In addition to responsibilities, it is important for airports to specify the resources allocated to any marketing programmes. The amount of resources available is likely to depend on the source and allocation of funding for the airport. At larger commercial airports there may be a designated budget for airport marketing, while at smaller commercial or general aviation airports marketing may be funded from other budgets – such as for airport operations – so it may be difficult to determine what resources are specifically available. The situation may be complicated further if an airport is owned as part of an airport group or by a government department, agency or regional or local authority because the budget from which airport marketing activities are funded may not be owned by individual airports and may be used to fund a range of activities other than airport marketing.

Some airports seek support from stakeholders with an interest in supporting airport marketing such as a chamber of commerce and industry, regional or local government, a tourism or regional development agency, an employment agency, local businesses or individuals, interest groups or airlines. This may be in the form of an airport development group where resources are pooled and costs shared, and collaborations such as these will be discussed further in Chapter 9. For route development, individual airports can also pool resources with airports at the other end of the route.

Airports may hold fundraising events or try to access in-kind support (which is not financial but is free or provided in exchange for something from the airport) for marketing. For instance, airports may offer work experience opportunities for universities or colleges and their students in return for assistance with executing marketing activities. Airports may also seek opportunities for free advertising or publicity from local media or marketing and advertising agencies.

Grants are a common source of funding in the US. For instance, the states of Michigan, Minnesota and Wyoming provide grants for airport marketing. The US Department of Transport's Small Community Air Service Development pilot programme is also a source of funding for the marketing of small commercial airports (Kramer *et al.*, 2010).

The budget available for marketing will need to be specified in the marketing plan. Marketing literature often refers to four main methods for budget-setting (e.g. see Kotler *et al.*, 2008) that can be applied to airports. The affordable method involves setting a budget according to what management thinks the airport can afford or what the authority responsible for the airport can afford. The percentage of sales method involves setting a budget according to a set proportion of current or expected income. Some businesses will budget according to a set proportion of sales price but this is complicated for airports, given their range of customers and income sources. Instead, the budget may be calculated according to a set proportion of the overall budget for the airport. The competitive parity method involves setting a budget that is similar to competing airports. The objective and task method involves setting a budget according to specific marketing objectives and their desired outcomes. This involves defining specific objectives, determining tasks needed to achieve the objectives, and estimating the cost of performing each task and subsequently the overall cost for all tasks.

Affordable and percentage of sales methods are common at larger commercial airports because the diversity and complexity of their marketing programmes makes it difficult to use the competitive parity or objective and task method. However, they may use the objective and task method when budgeting for specific activities such as retail promotions or advertising campaigns. Smaller commercial and general aviation airports also tend to use a combination of methods. A budget may be set according to what management thinks the airport can afford or what the authority responsible for the airport can afford, but it may be negotiable if the objective and task method identifies a need to increase (or reduce) the overall budget.

As mentioned in Chapter 1, sales and marketing (including personnel costs) contributes 4.5 per cent of total airport operating costs (ACI, 2010). The figure will be much lower if personnel costs are excluded, and evidence from airports suggests that it is likely to be closer to 1 per cent. Many smaller commercial or general aviation airports will not have a budget for marketing, or will have a budget that represents a very small fraction of the total operating budget for the airport. In these circumstances, low cost or no cost opportunities for marketing will need to be sought to fund any marketing programmes. An element of prioritising may also be necessary: allocating a larger budget to the most important objectives and tasks. Airports then need to decide if the budget is sufficient to get the job done or whether certain objectives or tasks should be modified or withdrawn. Airports may also decide to seek additional funds, such as through collaboration with stakeholders or from in-kind support.

Table 5.8 Example marketing programme for an airport

Goal 2014–2016: Increase the provision of international passenger services
Total budget: $1mn for 3 years
Objective 1: 6 additional scheduled international passenger services within 3 years
Objective 2: 3 additional inbound international charter passenger services within 3 years

Tasks	Responsible	Timing	Budget	Operational control	Process evaluation
Deliver route proposals to operators at 2 route development forums p/year	Director	May, Sep	$100,000	Fortnightly meeting	Feedback from operators
Deliver route proposals to operators at their corporate offices	Director	When relevant	$40,000	Fortnightly meeting	Feedback from operators
Share a stand with our tourism partners at 2 travel trade exhibitions p/year	Director	Mar, Nov	$50,000	Fortnightly meeting	Feedback from trade
List unserved route opportunities for our airport on The Route Shop	Executive	Continuous	$20,000	Fortnightly meeting	Response to listed routes
Monitor airline requests for proposals on Route Exchange	Executive	Weekly	$0	Fortnightly meeting	Relevant opportunities
Guided tour of our airport and region for target operators	Director	When relevant	$35,000	Fortnightly meeting	Feedback from operators
Offer price incentives and marketing support for new routes	Executive	When relevant	$500,000	Fortnightly meeting	Feedback from operators
Advertise in *Airline Business* magazine (6 issues)	Executive	Feb–Jul	$75,000	Fortnightly meeting	Response to advert

Task	Responsibility	Timing	Budget	Review	Metric
Develop a market intelligence page on our website	Executive	Jan	$0	Fortnightly meeting	'Hits' on the page
Update tourism information page on our website	Executive	Jan	$0	Fortnightly meeting	'Hits' on the page
Generate interest and awareness for new routes on Twitter and Facebook	Executive	When relevant	$0	Fortnightly meeting	'Followers' and 'Fans'
Generate media coverage for route and tourism potential in our region	Director	When relevant	$0	Fortnightly meeting	Coverage
Launch events for new routes	Director	When relevant	$30,000	Fortnightly meeting	Feedback from attendees
Contingency budget for additional tasks	Director	When relevant	$150,000	Fortnightly meeting	Feedback from beneficiaries

Strategic control: review the marketing plan with the Board of Directors at annual Board meetings

Product evaluation: annual analysis of the number of international passenger air services (scheduled and charter) and the return on marketing investment

Source: compiled by the authors

Table 5.9 Example marketing programme for an airport

Goal 2014–2016: Raise community awareness and support for our airport
Total budget: $50,000 for 3 years
Objective 1: Increase community group visits to our airport by 15% within 3 years
Objective 2: Reduce the number of complaints to our airport by 10% within 3 years
Objective 3: Host 2 charity events at our airport within 3 years
Objective 4: Achieve 2 feature stories in the local media each year for 3 years
Objective 5: Increase hits on the community section of our website by 15% within 3 years

Tasks	Responsible	Timing	Budget	Operational control	Process evaluation
Host education and other community group visits to our airport	Assistant	When relevant	$10,000	Weekly meeting	Feedback form
Organise an annual open day at the airport	Manager	Jul	$10,000	Weekly meeting	Feedback form
Deliver at least 2 community outreach presentations p/year	Manager	Mar, Nov	$5,000	Weekly meeting	Feedback form
Generate feature articles and positive media coverage for our airport	Manager	When relevant	$0	Weekly meeting	Coverage
Organise an annual runway fun-run for charity	Manager	Sep	$10,000	Weekly meeting	Feedback form
Organise an annual community BBQ event for charity	Manager	Aug	$10,000	Weekly meeting	Feedback form
Improve the community section of our website	Assistant	Continuous	$0	Weekly meeting	'Hits' on the page

Use social media to generate awareness and support for our airport (e.g. airport presence on blog, Twitter, Facebook and Flickr)	Assistant	Continuous	$0	Weekly meeting	'Followers', 'Fans', 'Views' and social interaction
Produce and distribute a biannual newsletter (online and e-mail)	Manager	Jun, Dec	$0	Weekly meeting	Subscribers
Contingency budget for additional tasks	Manager	When relevant	$5,000	Weekly meeting	Feedback from beneficiaries

Strategic control: review the marketing plan with the Board of Directors at annual Board meetings

Product evaluation: annual number of community group visits, annual number of complaints to the airport, number of annual charity events and money raised, annual number of feature articles on the airport in the local media, 'hits' on the community section of our website, benchmark results from our annual community survey with the previous years

Source: compiled by the authors

Any budget an airport sets for marketing should be detailed enough to allow for the identification and allocation of necessary resources. It should also allow for any control and evaluation processes to be undertaken. However, there also needs to be a degree of flexibility built in, perhaps in terms of a contingency fund, which allows for amendments in response to any changes in the business environment.

During the implementation of any marketing programmes, it is important to have some form of budget control such as using a live budget to track any income and expenditure according to what was projected and the current status. Cash flow projections should be used to ensure that cash is available to pay any bills. Purchase orders and coded invoices should be used to record details of any payments. One designated budget holder should be responsible for managing the budget, including approving and recording all income and expenditure and any invoices.

5.2.4.2 Control and evaluation

Marketing control is used to monitor how the marketing plan is working in practice and to adjust it where necessary. Brassington and Pettitt (2007) distinguish between two main forms of control: strategic and operational. Strategic control is a long-term view of whether the overall marketing plan is driving the business in the desired direction, while operational control is a short-term view of whether any marketing programmes and their individual tasks are working in practice. Strategic control is typically conducted on an annual basis as part of the marketing planning cycle, while operational control will need to be frequent enough to assess progress, identify any issues or problems, and address them before they get worse. Operational control may be conducted during ad hoc or regular periodic meetings.

Evaluation assesses the effectiveness of any marketing programmes and their individual tasks. Evaluation can also be used as part of the control process to help identify issues or problems. The evaluation process should normally be designed at the same time as marketing decisions are made and should be documented in the marketing plan, as opposed to being designed or used as an afterthought. There are two main types of evaluation metric: product and process.

Product metrics help to decide whether to continue, modify or stop using a strategic business unit or set of products. For instance, they may measure elements of financial performance (e.g. return on investment or change in profit) or sales performance (e.g. increased sales or revenue). Metrics should assess whether enough new business has been generated as a result of marketing to justify the expense. Ideally, product metrics will allow airports to benchmark their performance with that of other airports or the airport industry in general.

Process metrics measure the response to, and effectiveness of, any marketing activities. For instance, they may measure advertising efficiency (e.g. enquiries generated as the result of an advertisement for the airport), promotions efficiency (e.g. the proportion of vouchers redeemed during a retail promotional campaign at the airport), networking effectiveness (e.g. business stimulated as a result of collaboration with airport stakeholders), sales conversion rate (e.g. success at securing a new concession rather than simply generating an interest), and the extent to which marketing activities have made it easier to sell the product or service (e.g. delivering an airline presentation for a new route opportunity that provides the information needed by an airline to make their decision).

Four main methods of evaluation can be used to investigate product or process metrics: top-down (e.g. by soliciting feedback from senior management), bottom-up (e.g. by soliciting feedback from customers), interactive (e.g. by soliciting feedback from a range of sources including potential, actual or lost customers, senior management, stakeholders, analysts and consultants) or objective (e.g. by using quantitative data). Evaluation metrics allow airports to measure the success or failure of marketing objectives. However, they will only measure what they have been designed to measure, so they need to be relevant and carefully designed. It is useful if the metrics are already widely used by other airports or by the airport industry in general so that benchmarking can be carried out. Metrics should be designed before any marketing programmes are implemented because it may be necessary to gather quantitative or qualitative information before, during or after implementation in order to measure any outcomes. It is also important not to change the metric to fit the situation because that will introduce bias, although there should be scope to consider using additional metrics where relevant, so that marketing opportunities or achievements that fall outside the scope of the metrics are not ignored.

5.3 Example airport marketing programmes

This chapter concludes by providing some example airport marketing programmes for goals to increase the provision of air services (see Table 5.8) and to raise community awareness and support (see Table 5.9). The examples are purely hypothetical: they illustrate how airport marketing programmes might be presented as opposed to providing recommendations for what airports should do to achieve the respective goals. Marketing objectives that may be used to reach the goals are shown along with tasks, responsibility, timing, budget, and mechanisms for control and evaluation. Objectives and tasks should be listed in order of importance and the programmes may be more or less detailed, depending on the specific needs of the airport. For instance, a detailed breakdown of the budget for each task can be provided (e.g. for staff travel and accommodation, registration fees for attending events, agency fees for the production of advertising materials and F&B costs for hosting any visitors to the airport), staff and non-monetary resource allocation can be specified, a more detailed breakdown of each task can be provided and a Gantt chart can be produced to provide a detailed schedule for the programme. Airports may also want to specify key messages and the target audience for each marketing programme.

References

ACI (2010) *Airport Economics Survey 2010*, Montreal: ACI.

Ansoff, I. (1957) 'Strategies for diversification', *Harvard Business Review*, 35(5); 113–24.

Ashford, N.J., Mumayiz, S. and Wright, P.H. (2011) *Airport Engineering: Planning, Design and Development of 21st Century Airports*, 4th edn, Hoboken: John Wiley & Sons.

Baker, M. (2008) *The Strategic Marketing Plan Audit*, Axminster: Cambridge Strategy Publications.

Brassington, F. and Pettitt, S. (2007) *Essentials of Marketing*, 2nd edn, Harlow: Pearson Education.

Christchurch International Airport (2012) *Statement of Intent for the Year Ending 30 June 2012*, Christchurch: Christchurch International Airport Limited.

Dallas Airport System (2010) *Dallas Executive Airport Marketing Plan, Briefing for the Transportation and Environment Committee*, Dallas: Dallas Airport System.

Davison, L., Ryley, T. and Snelgrove, M. (2010) 'Regional airports in a competitive market: a case study of Cardiff International Airport', *Journal of Airport Management*, 4(2); 178–94.

Doran, G.T. (1981) 'There's a S.M.A.R.T. way to write management's goals and objectives', *Management Review*, 70(11); 35–6.

Exambela Consulting (2009) *European Airport Leadership Peer Survey – 2009*, Geneva: Exambela Consulting.

Feldman, D. (2009) *Diversify, Differentiate, Innovate: Airport Strategies for Success in a New World*, Geneva: Exambela Consulting.

Graham, A. (2008) *Managing Airports: An International Perspective*, 3rd edn, Oxford: Butterworth-Heinemann.

Graham, A. (2010) 'Airport strategies to gain competitive advantage' in P. Forsyth, D. Gillen, J. Muller and H-M. Niemeier (eds) *Airport Competition: The European Experience*, Farnham: Ashgate.

Huff, A. (2011) *What's your airport's marketing strategy?* Fort Atkinson: AviationPros.com. Online. Available at: http://www.aviationpros.com/blog/10442121/whats-your-airports-marketing-strategy (accessed 10 October 2012).

Kotler, P., Wong, V., Saunders, J. and Armstrong, G. (2008) *Principles of Marketing*, 5th European edn, Harlow: Prentice Hall-Pearson Education.

Kramer, L., Fowler, P., Hazel, R., Ureksoy, M. and Harig, G. (2010) *ACRP Report 28: Marketing Guidebook for Small Airports*, Washington, DC: Transportation Research Board.

Lian, J.I. and Rønnevik, J. (2011) 'Airport competition – Regional airports losing ground to main airports', *Journal of Transport Geography*, 19(1); 85–92.

McDonald, M. (2008) *Malcolm McDonald on Marketing Planning: Understanding Marketing Plans and Strategy*, London: Kogan Page.

McDonald, M. and Wilson, H. (2011) *Marketing Plans: How to Prepare Them, How to Use Them*, 7th edn, Chichester: John Wiley & Sons.

Muskoka Airport (2006) *Strategic Business Plan for The Muskoka Airport – 2006*, Muskoka: The District Municipality of Muskoka.

Pierceall, K. (2011) 'Ontario Airport: city's bid to take reins short on rescue strategy', *The Press-Enterprise*, 5 April 2011.

Porter, M.E. (1979) 'How competitive forces shape strategy', *Harvard Business Review*, 57(2); 137–45.

Porter, M.E. (1980) *Competitive Strategy: Techniques for Analysing Industries and Competitors*, New York: Free Press.

Productivity Commission (2006) *Review of Price Regulation at Airport Services*, Melbourne: Productivity Commission.

Rankin, W. (2011) 'King County: a case study model for strategic marketing planning for airport managers', *Journal of Aviation Management and Education*, 1(March); 8–17.

Saskatoon Airport Authority (2005) *Saskatoon Airport Authority Business Plan 2005–2009*, Saskatoon: Saskatoon Airport Authority.

Stone, R. (2011) 'Sister act', *Airport World*, 14(4); 34–5.

Suvarnabhumi Airport (2012) *Sister airport agreement*, Bangkok: Airports of Thailand. Online. Available at: http://www.suvarnabhumiairport.com/about_sister_airport_en.php (accessed 15 October 2012).

Sydney Airport (2012) *What Sydney Airport Stands For*, Sydney: Sydney Airport.

Sypher (2006) *Alberta – British Columbia Northern Airports Strategy*, Ottawa: Sypher.

Thompson, J. (2009) 'Getting the word out about general aviation airports', *Advances*, Summer 2009.

Chapter 6

The airport product

This chapter examines the airport product. It begins by defining the product and goes on to discuss the main features of the airport product and the amount of control an airport operator has over these. The nature and use of branding by airports is also explored. The chapter concludes by assessing how the product can be evaluated and planned to meet the needs and expectations of the airport's customers.

6.1 Definition of the airport product

Chapter 1 discussed the differences between marketing goods and services and identified the problems in applying general marketing concepts, traditionally used with manufactured commodities, to airports. These difficulties become very apparent when the airport product is being considered. In its broadest sense, the product consists of the supply of facilities and services offered by the airport to meet the needs of different customers. It is extremely complex because of the wide range of features that are brought together by airport operators in order to fulfil their role within the air transport industry. These include air traffic control, security and police, fire and rescue in the airfield, and ground handling facilities so that passengers, their baggage and cargo can be successfully transferred between aircraft and terminals and processed within the terminals. Car parking infrastructure and approach roads need to be considered, as do immigration and customs services. Also included is the increasingly diverse offer of commercial or non-aeronautical facilities within and outside the terminal, ranging from shops, restaurants, banks and car hire to hotels, conference services, entertainment amenities and business parks. This airport product is composite, as many of these services – for example, in the ground handling or commercial areas – are often provided by other companies, or alternatively – for instance, in the case of security and immigration – by government agencies.

The product has tangible elements such as the physical infrastructure, and intangible elements such as the provision of services. Urfer and Weinert (2011) classify the tangible features as the airside infrastructure (e.g. runways, taxiways, navigational aids), landside infrastructure (e.g. terminals, parking facilities, ground transport interchanges), airport support infrastructure (e.g. aircraft maintenance, in-flight catering services, police and security facilities) and support areas such as industrial areas and duty free zones. The intangible components are defined as the organisational, structural and operational aspects such as state support, administration (e.g. airport planning and management), operations (e.g. air traffic control, airport safety and security), airport maintenance and external factors such as regulations and the environment.

The airport product

While dividing the product between tangible and intangible features goes some way to help understand its detailed nature, this definition gives little indication of how the product relates to customer needs and expectations, so a more demand-focused definition is needed. A popular approach adopted in marketing theory divides the product into the core, actual or physical, and augmented elements (Kotler *et al.*, 2008). The core product is the essential benefit the customer is seeking, while the actual product delivers the benefit. Product features, design and packaging all make up the physical product. The augmented product is then additional customer services and benefits that will be built around the core and actual products, and will distinguish the product from others. Much of the competition will typically take place at the augmented level.

It is common to differentiate between business-to-consumer (B2C) products purchased to satisfy personal and family needs, and industrial or business-to-business (B2B) products bought to use in a company's operations or to make other products (Dibb *et al.*, 2006). The airport industry has both types of product (Figures 6.1 and 6.2). For instance, it offers a B2B product to airlines and a consumer product to its passengers. For the airline, the core is the ability to land and take off an aircraft, while for the passenger it will be the ability to board or disembark an aircraft. For each customer there will be a core product: for instance, for freight forwarders it will be the ability to load and unload freight on the aircraft. In order to provide the core product for the airline, the actual product will need to consist of the runway, the terminal building, the equipment, and so on, as well as the expertise to provide all these facilities efficiently and safely. For passengers, the actual product will include check-in desks, baggage handling and other features such as immigration control that will enable passengers to fulfil their need of boarding or disembarking the aircraft. The actual product will also include adequate transport services to and from the airport and the provision of other facilities such as information desks and toilets.

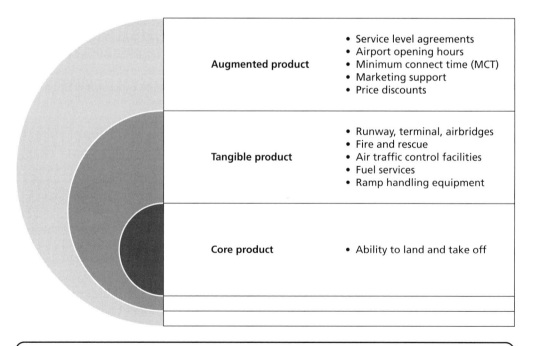

Augmented product
- Service level agreements
- Airport opening hours
- Minimum connect time (MCT)
- Marketing support
- Price discounts

Tangible product
- Runway, terminal, airbridges
- Fire and rescue
- Air traffic control facilities
- Fuel services
- Ramp handling equipment

Core product
- Ability to land and take off

Figure 6.1 The airport product for airlines
Source: compiled by the authors

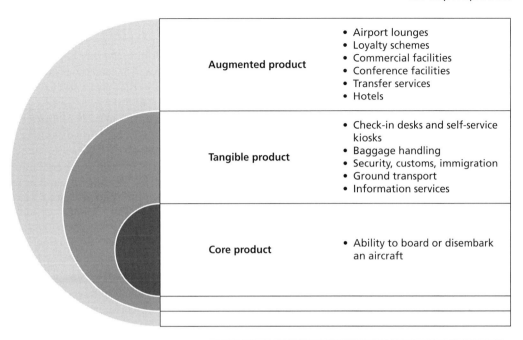

Figure 6.2 The airport product for passengers
Source: compiled by the authors

At the augmented level the airport may, for example, set service level agreements with its airlines to speed up processes or open for longer hours to improve accessibility. For the passenger, the range and diversity of shops, catering and other commercial facilities, as well as other features such as the ease of transfer between different aircraft, could all be considered part of the augmented product. Loyalty schemes that offer passengers additional benefits could also be included here, as could value and money-back guarantees associated with the commercial offer at the airport. A comparable product model can be applied to others in the airport's extended customer base such as meeters and greeters, visitors, employees and local residents.

Jarach (2005) adopts a similar approach to defining the product when he divides it into four levels of value proposition. He defines the core benefit (equivalent to the core product) as being to transfer passengers and goods between two points. His next two levels, the generic and expected product, are similar to the actual product. He gives examples of frequency of routes, service personalisation, cargo, comfort, baggage handling check-in, information, operational efficiency and ticketing for the generic product and multi-modal services for his expected product. His final level is the wide product (like the augmented product), which consists of logistic services, commercial services, congressional services, tourist services and consulting services.

Although such generic product definitions can be applied to the airport product, there remain some conceptual difficulties because of its composite nature. Indeed, from a passenger viewpoint the airport product includes the airline product, as well as the product of the concessionaire, handling agent, and so on. Hence, another way of looking at the airport product is by considering its 'raw' and 'refined' features. The raw product consists of both physical tangible elements (such as the runway, buildings, apron, lighting, navigation aids, fuel, fire and rescue) and intangible service elements provided by the airport operator's own staff and those of the customs, immigration and security agencies. In this case, the customer will be the trade markets such as airlines, concessionaires and tour operators. To produce the refined product involves adding the air travel elements, both tangible and intangible, provided by the airlines and the other services provided by concessionaires and other tenants. This product will appeal to general public markets.

A survey investigating the factors affecting passengers' choice of airport at the London airports of Heathrow, Gatwick and Stansted clearly showed the limited appeal of the raw airport product – other than its overall location ('easiest/nearest to get to'), which was identified by 49 per cent of Heathrow passengers, 39 per cent of Gatwick passengers and 46 per cent of Stansted passengers as being an influential factor. Next in importance were two airline factors: 'cheapest flight available', which was identified respectively by 10, 19 and 25 per cent of passengers and 'most convenient flight (time/day)', which was identified respectively by 24, 15 and 8 per cent of passengers. All raw airport product features had much lower percentages (UK CC, 2008).

6.2 Features of the airport product and its controllability

Irrespective of how the airport product is defined, its characteristics will have a major impact on the type and quantity of traffic that uses the airport. With product planning, it is the role of airport operators to design the features so that they are both appropriate to the target markets they are considering and attractive enough to give the airport a competitive edge over rival airports. With such a dynamic industry as aviation the needs and expectations of customers are continually changing, and the airport operator has to be responsive to the ever-evolving marketing environment (as discussed in Chapter 2). However, a major challenge is that, unlike many other industries, there are a number of parts of the product where the airport operator may have only limited control and influence. Most obvious is the actual location of the airport, which cannot be changed, and has already been shown to be one of the most important factors that influence choice.

Airports need to ensure that they meet all the physical airfield infrastructure requirements and associated technical capabilities of the airlines they are aiming to attract. This will include adequate runway length and capacity; appropriate air traffic control, instrument landing, lighting and weather monitoring systems; and sufficient ramp and apron space and gate capacity. These physical facilities will play a key role in determining what type of airline is able to use the airport, and by enhancing this part of the product – for example, by increasing the runway length – the airport might be able to accommodate new airlines with longer-range aircraft. Airports also need to react to new aircraft types, such as the Airbus A380, which requires a wider runway and specialised gates. Such infrastructure improvements in this area are invariably costly to implement, so the trade-off between increased costs that may in turn impact on the airport's price competitiveness has to be weighed up against the enhanced attractiveness of the airport product. At the same time, the airport must be careful not to be unduly influenced by other less relevant factors such as the prestige that such developments could bring. However, external factors here will also be important, and it may actually be the extent of environmental concern that determines whether such capacity enhancements can go ahead.

Governments may impose night curfews or quotas that will make airports unattractive to certain types of traffic, especially long-haul carriers, who may only have a certain limited time period when they can serve a country, or cargo operators and integrators. Cargo customers often require 24-hour operations in order to meet the demands of clients in different time zones and to achieve overnight delivery. If airports cannot operate around the clock, this may give them a competitive disadvantage in this area. While it may be difficult for the airport operator to have any effect on these environmental restrictions, or indeed on any planning decisions related to additional capacity, it is nevertheless always beneficial for the airport to try to develop good relations with the local community in the hope that some influence can be exerted. This can be undertaken primarily with public relations activities (as discussed in Chapter 8): for example, by emphasising the positive economic impacts of airport operations; by sponsoring or getting directly involved with local events; by arranging educational visits and open days; and by developing effective communications channels with the local and national press.

Another aspect of airfield operations where the airport operator may have limited control is slot allocation, particularly if the airport is congested and slots are allocated through the formal IATA scheduling committee processes, which favour incumbent airlines by giving them grandfather rights to slots (the right to use a particular slot time used in the previous equivalent season). However, if scarcity of runway capacity is not such an issue, it is the airport operator's role to ensure, by communicating with all its airline customers, that slots can be made available as much as possible, to suit all their needs.

Within the terminal, the product generally tends to be less influenced by external factors, so it is here that the airport operator can more readily have an impact on the product on offer. Good terminal design will be crucial, and at a general level decisions have to be made on the overall layout – such as making choices between linear or curvilinear terminals, or piers as opposed to remote satellites. Airport operators must ensure that they use planning standards related to space requirements, queuing and waiting that are appropriate to their target markets. Airports wanting to attract transfer traffic must possess the more sophisticated and costly passenger and handling systems needed for this type of traffic; likewise, if the airport wants to interest connecting cargo traffic, it must offer efficient transhipment facilities. If the airport wants to appeal to full-service airlines or global alliances it must be able to offer product enhancements such as dedicated VIP lounges and other dedicated facilities that their passengers desire, while if the airport wants to attract LCCs it must provide a product that fits in with the LCC business model, which requires simple, efficient and low cost facilities.

Many of the individual product features within the terminals are related to passenger, cargo and baggage processing. This includes areas such as security, customs and immigration. As discussed in Chapter 2, there have been considerable changes to such processes over the last few years and so there is a potential for airports to increase their use of biometrics and technology, in collaboration with the other service providers in this area, to enhance the passenger experience. At the actual product level, the airport clearly needs to ensure that it provides customs and immigration services if it is interested in attracting international passengers. Then, at the augmented product level, there may be the opportunity to provide pre-clearance services as offered, for example, with some flights to the US. In this case passengers go through US customs, immigration and agriculture inspections at their originating airport and as a result are treated as domestic passengers when they arrive; this allows a quicker process through the US airport. Such services are offered at Dublin and Shannon in Ireland, a number of Canadian airports and a few other locations such as Bermuda, the Bahamas and Aruba (Tretheway and Kincaid, 2010). However, a major complication for airport operators is that immigration and customs services will normally be provided by state agencies, as is often also the case with security, and in turn many practices will be determined by national and international regulation, which will consequently limit the airport operator's influence in this area.

Airport operators tend to have a greater control over the ground handling services provided, and again the major technological changes that are occurring may give an opportunity to the airport operator, with other service providers in this area, to gain a competitive edge here. The supply of ground handling services may be the responsibility of the airport operator, airlines or handling agents or a combination of these. At some airports there may be a monopoly provider (usually the airport operator or its main airline), which may not be popular with certain airline customers – although such practices are prohibited in some countries, most notably in Europe for all but the smallest airports, owing to the EC's directive on access to the ground handling market at community airports. Circumstances do vary but the ability of an airline to self-handle or to have a choice in handler may be significant in their choice of airport, so the airport operator needs to ensure that they take this into account.

In addition to these essential processes at the actual product level, there are also a diverse range of commercial or non-aeronautical facilities, many at the augmented level, which can be provided both within and maybe outside the terminal. These include not only traditional commercial outlets such as retail and catering but also entertainment, leisure, beauty and wellness facilities such as spas and salons. The airport operator will normally have considerable control over these, as even though they are typically provided by third party specialists or concessionaires, it is the operator who will choose the concessionaire and determine the conditions of the contract. While such product features will generally play an insignificant or only a small role in influencing a passenger's choice of airport, such facilities are nevertheless important in generating invaluable non-aeronautical revenues for the airport. For many passengers, particularly for those travelling for leisure purposes, they will also undoubtedly enhance the airport product and improve the overall passenger experience. With the specific case of transfer passengers, commercial facilities may have a greater impact on choice, if passengers cannot perceive other significant differences between the convenience and quality of the choice of connecting flights at different airports. With this in mind, airports such as Dubai International and Singapore Changi both offer a huge range of airside commercial facilities to their transfer passengers.

Within this list of commercial facilities can be included the provision of the internet, which can be offered through wi-fi for laptops or through internet kiosks or workstations. This is the norm now for airports. A recent study showed that 96 per cent of all airports provided wi-fi: three-quarters had it anywhere in the terminal and the remaining quarter within specific hotspots or within airline lounges or retail outlets. By contrast, 70 per cent of airports offered internet kiosks (ACI/DMKA, 2009). Other important features are charging stations for electronic devices, electrical plugs and working areas for laptop users. In a broader sense, many more airports are now also taking the opportunity to enhance the business features of their product by offering business, conferencing and/or event facilities. A survey in 2011 showed that just over two-thirds of airports provided such facilities (Halpern et al., 2011).

Another vital feature of the airport product relates to the airport's accessibility. This in turn will not only concern the various car parks (e.g. short term, long term, fast track) and product features of the car park (such as security and distance from the terminal) but also the availability of surface access links (e.g. direct rail, supply of taxis) and convenience of drop-off places. While the airport operator may have limited influence over surface transport issues, it may be able to support local road and rail improvements through the planning process or through public relations initiatives, or alternatively perhaps by providing financial support to such services. It may even decide that in order to meet the expectations of its customers it needs to operate some of the surface access links itself, as is the case with London Heathrow Airport and the Heathrow Express link in London.

Information provision and wayfinding is also an important part of the airport product. At the airport itself, information sources include both self-help tools (such as maps, leaflets and interactive kiosks) and staffed tools such as information counters and walking staff (e.g. the Changi Experience Agents at Singapore Changi Airport, each of whom speaks many languages and has the support of an iPad). There are some significant regional differences with the provision of such staff: a recent study found that in the regions of Africa, the Middle East and Asia-Pacific, 84 per cent of airports have walking staff compared with only 56 per cent in Europe (ACI/DMKA, 2011). Some airports – for example, London Luton Airport and Manchester Airport – have gone

one step further by introducing a new kind of airport helper in virtual assistants, which are actually life-size holograms.

Other rapidly changing parts of the airport product are its website and social media applications. These play an important and complex role not only in providing information but also in promoting the airport and acting as a distribution channel. Their function in these latter two areas is discussed in detail in Chapters 8 and 9. However, in terms of its role solely as a product feature, the airport website can enhance the product by providing useful information for passengers such as check-in periods, security arrangements, surface transport details and maps of the layout of the airport. Figures 6.3 and 6.4 provide examples of websites for Turin Airport and Gold Coast Airport, and show the use of common features on their homepages in terms of information provided (e.g. departures and arrival display, local time and weather, surface access details and links to commercial facilities and car parks). In a recent survey, 80 per cent of airports were found to provide a non-interactive map on their website, 29 per cent to have an interactive map and 9 per cent (mostly in North America) to have a movie that shows passengers the way around the airport (ACI/DMKA, 2011).

The growing use of mobile networks and specific smartphone applications allows passengers to use a mobile device as a virtual customer service desk. This can help passengers navigate the

Figure 6.3 Homepage of Turin Airport
Source: courtesy of SAGAT/Turin Airport

Figure 6.4 Homepage of Gold Coast Airport
Source: courtesy of Queensland Airports Limited

airport and give them details of where they are in the check-in process: for example, by providing gate numbers. It can also provide up-to-date information concerning the commercial services and facilities on offer. There is clearly an opportunity here for these two features to be linked so that, for example, when the passenger is informed of the boarding gate, they will be told which retail facilities they will be passing. As yet, however, this personalised approach has only been used by a relatively small number of airports such as Dallas/Fort Worth International Airport and McCarran International Airport. Chapters 8 and 9 will revisit this subject in more detail.

In providing the overall product, the airport operator must clearly take account of the changing needs and expectations of its customers, even though in some areas this will be particularly difficult because of limited actual control and the involvement of other bodies in providing the product. As with other industries, there may be dilemmas in trying to introduce changes in technology while still keeping a customer focus. There may also be challenges in producing the right balance between operational and commercial facilities to ensure that passengers can be moved efficiently from terminal to plane with a commercial offer that is attractive but not too much of a distraction, yet at the same time generates much needed non-aeronautical revenue for the airport.

6.3 The airport brand

The concept of an airport brand is related to the airport product. It is represented by tangible and intangible features such as a name, logo, design, signing, merchandising and advertising, which give the product an identity and differentiate it from rival airports. It can add more tangible cues to the intangible service that the airport offers, and can potentially promote preference and loyalty among target markets. Brand design and development is also an area where airport management can have very significant influence, unlike a number of other aspects of the airport product. If used successfully, Paternoster (2008) argues, branding can significantly improve customers' satisfaction with the airport experience.

The name of the airport is a key part of the brand and a number of different types of name exist (Halpern and Regmi, 2011) (see Table 6.1). The simplest option is to name the airport after the city that it serves, such as Auckland Airport or Brisbane Airport. Two names can also be included in the name, such as Leeds Bradford International Airport or Dallas/Fort Worth International Airport. An airport may decide to include the name of the nearest large city or town, even if it may not be particularly close. If it does this it may well make the airport easier to market and find in airline computer reservations systems and internet searches. This is typically the case with secondary airports that serve LCCs. Examples include Stockholm Skavsta Airport, which is 100 kilometres from Stockholm, Frankfurt Hahn Airport, which is 120 kilometres from Frankfurt, Chicago Rockford, which is 145 kilometres from Chicago, and BSCA, which is 46 kilometres from Brussels. This may result in many airports seemingly serving one city. A prime example is London, which appears to be served by eight airports: London Heathrow, London Gatwick, London Stansted, London City, London Luton, London Southend, London Biggin Hill and London Ashford.

Rather than including a city in the name of the airport, an airport may include the region it serves such as Gold Coast Airport in Australia or Girona Costa Brava Airport in Spain. Another example is Knock Airport in Ireland which was re-branded as Ireland West Airport Knock in 2005 to emphasise its importance as an access point to the west of Ireland. Basel-Mulhouse Airport was given the full name EuroAirport: Basel-Mulhouse-Freiberg in 1987 to reflect its central European location and bi-national (Swiss and French) ownership. East Midlands Airport in the UK is another example. In 2003 this airport decided to change its name to Nottingham East Midlands Airport to make its location seem more specific, but this was an unpopular move for the residents of the nearby towns of Leicester and Derby, which are nearer the airport. Hence, in 2006 the airport adopted a fuller title: East Midlands Airport: Nottingham-Leicester-Derby. The alternative is not to name the specific cities served, as with Tri-Cities Regional Airport in the US that serves a number of cities in Northeast Tennessee, Southwest Virginia and North Carolina. For small countries it might make more sense to name the airport after the country served, such as Malta International Airport.

Another option is to name the airport after nearby attractions. These may be natural (e.g. Lakselv Banak North Cape Airport and Annecy Haute-Savoie Airport Mont Blanc) or man-made (e.g. Bardufoss Snowman International Airport). Other airports use famous people associated with the location. These may be members of the royal family (King Abdulaziz International Airport and King Khaled International Airport), politicians (John F. Kennedy International Airport, Delhi Indira Gandhi International Airport, Paris Charles de Gaulle Airport), religious icons (John Paul II International Airport Krakow Balice), mythical gods (Quetzalcóatl International Airport), composers, entertainers and musicians (Warsaw Chopin Airport, Louis Armstrong New Orleans International Airport, Liverpool John Lennon Airport, Bob Hope Airport), artists (Pablo Ruiz Picasso Airport, Leonardo da Vinci-Fiumicino Airport), and others such as at Venice Marco Polo Airport and Skopje Alexander the Great Airport in Macedonia.

Table 6.1 Categories of brand names

Categories	Sub-categories	Examples
Place	Country, city-state, administrative region	Malta International Airport
	Region	Sunshine Coast Airport
	City, town, village	Melbourne Airport
	Multiple cities, towns, villages	Frankfurt Hahn Airport
Attraction	Natural attraction	Lakselv Banak North Cape Airport
	Man-made attraction	Bardufoss Snowman International Airport
Scope of services	International	Vienna International Airport
	National	Leros Island National Airport
	Regional	Asheville Regional Airport
	Domestic	Arar Domestic Airport
	Executive	Orlando Executive Airport
	Other	Page Field General Aviation Airport
Famous person	Royalty	King Abdulaziz International Airport
	Political leader/revolutionary	Delhi Indira Gandhi International Airport
	Other	Bob Hope Airport
Other	None	Linz Blue Danube Airport

Source: adapted from Halpern and Regmi (2011)

Serious consideration needs to be given to the appropriateness of the chosen name, to ensure that it has a positive impact on the airport image and operations. In Germany, Weeze Airport – which is 70 kilometres from Dusseldorf – wanted to include Dusseldorf in its name but this was blocked by a court ruling that considered this too misleading for passengers. Alternatively, the name may be too distinctive and attract too narrow a range of customers. Rovaniemi Airport in Finland is known as the official airport of Santa Claus in order to contribute to Santa-based tourism in Finnish Lapland. This type of traffic is very seasonal, however, and is dominated by charters; as a result, such naming may discourage other airlines that might provide a more regular service. In addition, when using famous names, airport operators need to ensure that the name they choose is closely associated with the airport and the surrounding area. In the UK there has been some debate as to whether the name 'Robin Hood' is appropriate for Doncaster Sheffield Airport, given that this legendary figure is more strongly linked with Nottingham (the logo for this airport is shown in Figure 6.5). Similarly, although the footballer George Best came from Northern Ireland and is therefore included in the name for Belfast City Airport, he is also closely associated with Manchester, where he played for many years for Manchester United Football Club.

The other key decision an airport has to make about its name is whether to give any indication of the size or scope of the services available. The most common situation is when an airport is called 'international', especially if it is quite small and wants to demonstrate that it serves international as well as domestic destinations. On the other hand, as airports become more developed and well known for their range of services, they might choose to drop the international part of their name, as Birmingham Airport did in 2010. Other names indicating the role of the airport include Leros Island National Airport in Greece, Asheville Regional Airport in the US, Afar Domestic Airport in Saudi Arabia, and Orlando Executive Airport, Homestead General Aviation Airport, Jean Sport Aviation Center and Mt Hawley Auxiliary Airport in the US.

In addition to this diverse range of names, airports throughout the world have also developed different slogans, taglines or straplines (Halpern and Regmi, 2011). Figure 6.5 provides some examples. In general, some slogans relate to the connectivity the airport provides, as in Dallas/Fort Worth International Airport 'The world connected', Munich Airport 'Service non-stop' or Barkley Regional Airport 'Your connection to the world'. Other airports have focused on location characteristics: for instance, Brussels Airport 'Welcome to Europe', Macau International Airport 'Gateway to China', Aéroports de Montréal 'Where Montreal meets the world', Halifax Stanfield International Airport 'You have landed at Nova Scotia', Cheddi Jagan International Airport 'The gateway to South America', Brisbane Airport 'Great for Queensland' and Christchurch International 'New Zealand's Tourism Gateway'. Stewart International Airport, which is owned by the Port Authority of New York and New Jersey, has an interesting slogan – 'Your neighborhood international airport' – aimed at branding it as an alternative gateway to the New York region.

The slogan may be less specific and relate to the travel and/or airport experience, such as Lyon Saint Exupéry Airport 'Going further to bring people together', Wichita Mid-Continent 'Convenient, friendly, affordable. It's a breeze!', Brisbane Airport 'Make the most of life', Moscow Domodedovo Airport 'Happy landings', Helsinki-Vantaa Airport 'For smooth travelling', Singapore Changi Airport 'The feeling is first class', London Heathrow Airport 'Making every journey better', ANA Portuguese airports 'Livening up airports' and Wellington International Airport 'Wild at Heart'. Others look at future opportunities, such as Malaysia Airports 'Creating the airport of the future', Vienna Airport 'Open for new horizons' and London Stansted Airport 'The opportunity to fly for'. In some cases, the slogan may be a play on words associated with famous people of the area. For example, Liverpool John Lennon Airport uses the slogan 'Above us only sky', quoting words from the Lennon song 'Imagine', and Glasgow Prestwick Airport adopted the popular Glaswegian colloquialism 'Pure dead brilliant' as its controversial slogan in 2005.

Re-branding can be particularly important when an airport has experienced a significant change that it wants to convey to its customers. For example, when London Gatwick Airport was sold by BAA in 2009 it launched a new brand with the slogan 'Your London Airport Gatwick' to differentiate itself from London Heathrow Airport and its previous owners BAA. Birmingham Airport also re-branded itself in 2010 with the new slogan 'Hello World' to reposition itself as a global airport when the original two terminals were merged into a single entity. Likewise, KLIA has developed a new brand with the slogan 'KLIA Next Gen Hub: The new way to the world' in preparation for the opening of the new LCC terminal, which is close to the main terminal rather than a considerable distance away as is the current situation.

A comprehensive study of 1,562 world airports gives some insight into the typical uses of names and slogans (Halpern and Regmi, 2011) (see Table 6.2). Over three-quarters of the airports were named after a single place, with almost half of these including a reference to the scope of services available. Regional differences existed with other names. For instance, calling an airport after natural or man-made attractions was most common in Europe, while

Figure 6.5 Airport logos
Source: courtesy of the individual airports

names associated with political leaders and/or revolutionaries were most popular in Latin America and the Caribbean. Royalty names were the most common in the Middle East. As regards slogans, only one-tenth of all airports used these, and usage was most common in North America.

There are many other ways an airport can develop its brand in addition to using names and slogans. It can adopt an eye-catching logo such as using the shape of the 'H' as a runway configuration for Hannover Airport. A popular theme here is stars, planets, clouds, birds, flowers or feathers to depict the idea of flight, as well as local attributes. For example, a peacock feather is used in the logo of Chhatrapati Shivaji International Airport to represent the country's heritage

Table 6.2 Proportion of airports in each region that use each name category

Category	Region						
	Africa	Asia-Pacific	Europe	Latin America/ Caribbean	Middle East	North America	Total
Place	*84.9*	*77.5*	*89.8*	*57.1*	*78.3*	*76.0*	*80.0*
Country	1.1	2.4	0.9	0.7	3.3	0.0	1.0
Region	3.0	4.0	3.3	3.3	1.7	10.9	5.2
City, town, village	81.4	71.9	88.9	53.9	73.3	66.7	75.4
Multiple places (2 or more)	11.4	12.5	27.3	3.9	1.7	9.4	14.5
Attraction	*3.8*	*11.2*	*14.0*	*8.4*	*6.6*	*7.3*	*9.3*
Natural attraction	2.3	10.4	13.1	5.8	3.3	5.2	7.8
Man-made attraction	1.5	0.8	0.9	2.6	3.3	2.1	1.5
Services	*40.5*	*47.4*	*16.8*	*63.6*	*85.0*	*59.4*	*43.4*
International	39.4	47.4	12.2	63.0	53.3	44.8	37.0
National	1.1	0.0	4.0	0.0	0.0	3.7	2.2
Regional	0.0	0.0	0.0	0.6	8.3	7.0	2.1
Domestic	0.0	0.0	0.0	0.0	21.7	0.0	0.8
Executive	0.0	0.0	0.0	0.0	1.7	1.6	0.5
Other	0.0	0.0	0.6	0.0	0.0	2.3	0.8
Famous person	*14.8*	*13.3*	*10.4*	*42.2*	*16.7*	*27.9*	*19.3*
Royalty	1.9	4.4	0.9	2.0	10.0	0.0	1.9
Political leader/ revolutionary	9.5	4.0	3.5	23.4	5.0	14.0	9.2
Other	3.4	4.8	6.0	16.9	1.7	13.8	8.2
Other	*0.7*	*0.8*	*0.0*	*1.3*	*0.0*	*1.0*	*0.7*
Number of airports	264	249	451	154	60	384	1562

Source: adapted from Halpern and Regmi (2011)

and value and to reflect India's vibrant and colourful city. Birmingham Airport has a global graphic design made up of four circles, which is intended to match the City of Birmingham's vision of 'Global City: Local Heart' (Allett, 2010).

As in other industries, airports can have branded give-aways to reinforce their image and identity, such as badges, key rings, mouse mats, t-shirts, and stationery items. Another way an airport can create distinctiveness inside the terminal is by having a distinctive style of signposting, colour scheme and interior design. If the airport operator owns more than one airport it can use the same style in each airport, as with former BAA airports in the UK that had the distinctive black on yellow signposting. After BAA sold London Gatwick Airport in 2009, the new owner changed the signage from yellow to black as part of the airport's new branding strategy and because of copyright law associated with BAA's signs.

One of the problems in trying to achieve a distinctive airport brand within the passenger terminal is that its effectiveness may be affected by the presence of brands belonging to retailers, airlines and alliance groups. Brand effects may also be diluted as many airports will sell empty and blank wall space to advertisers, since this can be a very lucrative source of revenue. Care therefore needs to be taken to ensure that passengers are not exposed to too many brands, as this is likely to convey mixed messages and could have a negative impact on creating the airport's image and distinctiveness. Too much brand information can also cause visual pollution and give a cluttered feel to the airport, and may inhibit passengers' progress to their departure gate.

Rather than identifying a unique brand for the airport, the branding can instead be linked to the character and culture of the city or country the airport serves. The aim will be to create a sense of place and community and to contribute to the travel experience of passengers. It can be argued that the airport product is in fact just an element of the overall tourism product, which in turn can influence a destination's brand or appeal (Martin-Cejas, 2006; Vujicic and Wickelgren, 2011). In this case, by branding itself as a destination gateway, the airport will be using the brand extension rather than its own brand to market itself. It can do this by replicating a destination's traits such as the scenery, history, adventure and culture, and thus convey the same image and message as the destination. For example, the distinctive peaked roof architecture at Denver International Airport was designed to represent the nearby Rocky Mountains and native American teepees. Vancouver International Airport is themed to represent the physical characteristics and cultural heritage of British Columbia through its architecture (depicting, for example, the northwest coast with a sandy beach, an indoor creek showing the nature of the west coast and a large collection of native art including wooden sculptures and totem poles). Copenhagen Airport has a Tivoli Bar representing the Tivoli Gardens leisure park in the city. McCarran International Airport in Las Vegas has a number of outlets themed after hotels and entertainment in the city, and there are slot machines located throughout the terminal. Memphis International Airport is themed around blues, rock and roll and Elvis Presley, and at Orlando International Airport there are shops representing the major theme parks in the area. Employees can also contribute to this image. For example, at Halifax Stanfield International Airport 'The Tartan Team', who are mostly retired volunteers, give a welcome to passengers and visitors and wear tartan to reflect the area's Scottish heritage.

Giving at least some of the commercial facilities a local identity may help to reduce retail brand fatigue, which occurs when passengers find airport shopping dull and boring because of the widespread existence of common brands. Airport operators need to find the correct mix of famous brand outlets, which give some familiarity, with local outlets, which can give the airport some kind of identity and sense of place. The actual goods sold can also reflect the character and culture of the destination by using local merchandise, handcrafted goods or gourmet products such as maple syrup from Canada, cheese from Switzerland, salmon from Norway, or rum from Jamaica. By successfully engaging the passenger in the airport brand it is likely that this will enhance the amount of commercial sales made.

6.4 Evaluating the product on offer

Once an airport operator has identified the target markets it wants to attract and serve, it needs to ensure that it is providing the appropriate product and branding to meet the needs and expectations of these market segments. To achieve this, the airport operator needs to fully evaluate its product and brand attributes, as well as the product benefits, and to have a detailed appreciation of how the interaction and combination of all the product features can satisfy customer needs.

At the actual product level such evaluation is a relatively straightforward process, and in many cases will be related to ensuring that all the physical facilities and processes these customers need are provided. Such product features (e.g. number, length and configuration of runways and navigational aids; slot allocation status; opening hours; check-in desks; passenger gates; parking stands; terminal capacity; turnaround time and MCTs) can easily be supplied to airlines and appear on marketing sites such as anna.aero (see Chapter 8). However, the airport operator needs to focus most of its attention at the augmented level, where it can determine the extent to which customers are satisfied with the product it is offering and the degree to which its services provide it with a competitive edge.

For airlines, one of the most crucial elements of the augmented product will be the level of overall flight delays. This is a very difficult area for the airport operator to assess because there will be many factors (such as bad weather, air traffic control problems or airline technical problems) that are beyond its direct control. Nevertheless, it needs to ensure that when delays occur, for whatever reason, they are dealt with in a timely and appropriate manner (e.g. efficient snow clearance of the runway after a snow storm). Other key areas of concern to airlines relate to the availability of gates, stands, airbridges and operational equipment (e.g. electrical ground power, baggage carousels), and the reliability and degree of delays related to these specific features of the product.

For passengers (and again the airlines, as they too will naturally pay attention to the overall experience in the terminal for their passengers), there will be a vast range of tangible and intangible elements to be considered at the augmented level. This will include physical aspects such as queue lengths and waiting times at the key processes, walking distances and baggage delivery times. Then there will be more intangible features such as the clarity of wayfinding and flight information systems; the ambience, lighting, colour and cleanliness of the terminal; the helpfulness and attitudes of the staff; and value for money and choice of commercial facilities.

Airport operators need to understand the influence of such multiple factors and identify which are the key drivers of customer satisfaction. In a passenger survey at the six major airports of Abu Dhabi, Atlanta, Beijing, Frankfurt, Mumbai and Sao Paulo it was concluded that the most important factors contributing to a pleasant flight were the check-in processes, punctuality of the flight, and ease of access through the terminal and moving through security (SITA/Air Transport World, 2011). The least important features were access to club/VIP lounge and shopping facilities. Other insights can be gained from the ACI's ASQ data (see Chapter 4). In 2008, the highest scores for the top 10 airports in the ASQ overall satisfaction table were for cleanliness of terminal, helpfulness of staff, ambience of airport, availability of toilets, efficiency of check-in staff, feeling safe and secure and wayfinding. By contrast, the lowest scores were for shopping facilities, catering facilities, banking facilities, IT facilities, value for money with commercial facilities and opening hours of commercial facilities (UK CAA, 2009). While these two studies have some common and not unexpected findings (such as the fact that commercial facilities do not appear to have a major impact on overall passenger satisfaction rates), for each individual airport the most important factors influencing overall satisfaction will clearly vary. A case in point is at Lisbon Airport, where the critical factors appear to be ambience, cleanliness of airport, availability of washrooms, helpfulness of staff, thoroughness of security, comfortable waiting/gate areas, business lounges and arrivals passport inspection, while much lower importance is given to walking distances, parking and internet access (Madeira, 2011).

It is therefore important to recognise when considering airport product planning that improving areas of lowest satisfaction may not necessarily improve overall satisfaction and meet customers' needs. The best way to achieve this is to focus on areas regarded as less than satisfactory but

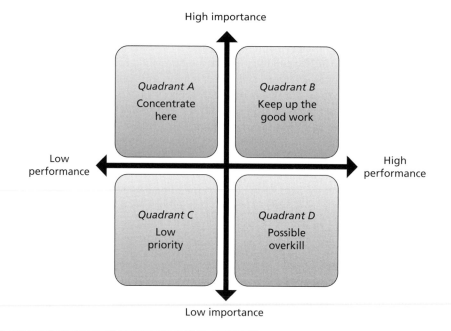

Figure 6.6 Importance–performance grid
Source: adapted from Martilla and James (1977)

important to the customer. Importance–performance analysis, originally suggested by Martilla and James (1977), is a simple way to achieve this (Figure 6.6). By plotting importance against performance (or satisfaction rates) on the grid, four different situations can be identified in the four quadrants. Quadrant A (typically labelled 'concentrate here') has features perceived as important but with poor performance scores, whereas quadrant B ('keep up the good work') requires less attention as both importance and performance scores are high. For quadrant C, where importance and performance are both low, it is acceptable to give this 'low priority', whereas if the performance scores are high but importance scores low, as in quadrant D, it might be a 'possible overkill'. This is a common way to assess a product with multiple features: ACI/DKMA use a similar approach in their priority analysis of the ASQ data, with the four quadrants respectively labelled 'primary concerns', 'key selling points', 'lower priority' and 'review commitments'.

ORC International (2009) applied a similar concept with their key drivers of satisfaction analysis for a number of UK airports: London Heathrow, London Gatwick, London Stansted and Manchester. With the pre-departure experience, the key drivers or areas of greatest importance were the ease and time getting from the boarding gate onto the plane, the information provided on flight times and departure gates, cleanliness and maintenance of airport facilities, and ease of getting around the airport. Satisfaction in these areas was generally relatively good, and most could fit into quadrant B ('keep up the good work'). Areas with lower levels of satisfaction – for example, the amount of seating and availability and helpfulness of staff – were considered not to be so important and could therefore fit into quadrant C ('low priority') or 'no change required', as defined by ORC International.

The key to fully evaluating the product being offered from a passenger viewpoint must be to focus on the total passenger experience, including transport to/from the airport (see Figure 6.7).

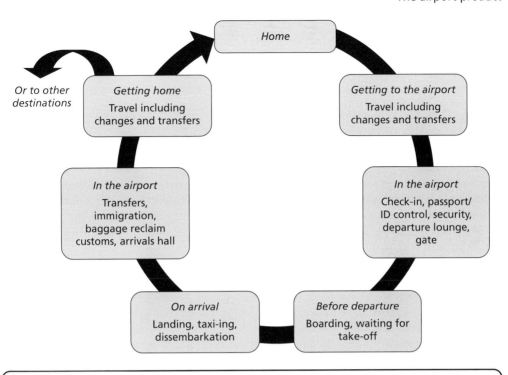

Figure 6.7 The passenger experience at the airport
Source: adapted from Department for Transport (2007)

All too often, because of the limited control and involvement the airport operator has with certain features of the product, some parts of product provision may be overlooked. However, from a passenger perspective they all contribute to their end-to-end journey experience and should be considered. This ideally involves a more holistic approach to provision of the product, including greater collaboration with other providers and greater transparency of data (Department for Transport, 2007; UK CAA, 2009).

6.5 Planning airport products

The previous sections have discussed the nature of the product and brand, and how it can be evaluated. This now needs to be considered within the context of how an airport operator can design and deliver its product to ensure that it is appropriately attracting and serving its target markets. Clearly, this needs to fit in with the overall positioning strategy discussed in Chapter 5. How the product can be developed to differentiate the airport from its competitors in order to gain a competitive advantage and create superior customer value is likely to be of major consideration. Differentiation policies with service industries including airports can be very varied, as they can relate to the physical product (such as features and design), the image, personnel differences (e.g. related to courtesy and communication) and service (such as speed and accuracy) (Hoffman *et al.*, 2009).

Historically, the airport industry tended to offer a fairly common set of services and facilities, or a rather generic product to serve all their airlines, passengers and other customers, regardless of the specific needs of the different market segments within these customer groups. Focus tended to be at the core and actual product level rather than at the augmented level. The key differentiation that did occur was separate check-in for economy and business class passengers (which was actually an airline product feature) and remote stands rather than airbridges for passengers travelling on charter or leisure airlines. Differentiation was achieved at a general rather than market segment level: for example, by having quicker processes than other airports, greater ambience in the terminal building or particularly helpful staff.

However, within the modern airport world this focus on a predominantly 'one size fits all' product for customers is no longer appropriate. Stronger competitive forces have meant that airports have had to give far greater attention to differentiating their product to meet the requirements and expectations of different market segments, while at the same time the range of different airline segments has become more varied (e.g. LCCs, alliance groups, cargo specialists). In addition, unbundling of the product – a trend observed in the airline industry for a number of years – is now occurring at airports, with airlines and passengers only paying (or paying more) for the parts of the overall package of services and facilities they want.

6.5.1 Airline customers

A key area where airports have tried to gain a competitive edge with their airline customers is in increasing the efficiency of the essential processes. In particular, if an airport wants to attract airlines that plan to use it as a hub for processing transfer traffic, it must offer an attractive MCT. This is the minimum interval that must elapse between a scheduled arrival and a scheduled departure for two services to be bookable as a connection. Some airports have one MCT that applies to all services, while in other cases a range of different MCTs may be in operation depending on the airline, terminal, type of passenger and route. Terminal design is important when considering how to minimise connection times: multiple terminals that are set some distance apart are not well suited to connecting traffic. Segregating international and domestic traffic, although efficient because of the different processes involved, also hinders the speed of domestic–international transfers. Table 6.3 shows the variety of MCTs at a number of different airports.

Likewise, there will be special attributes an airport has to have in order to appeal to specialist cargo operators and integrators. Certain airports such as Leipzig/Halle Airport, East Midlands Airport, Paris Vatry and Liege Airport have targeted such market segments by having a product that offers reliable and secure connecting processes plus other appealing features such as good connections to motorways and no night curfews.

Traffic of the global alliances of oneworld, Star and SkyTeam is also reliant on achieving good transfers between alliance members. Again, if international and domestic traffic services are not closely linked an airport would be at a considerable competitive disadvantage. In addition, if the airport is really keen to attract airlines from the global alliances, it needs to demonstrate that its design and facilities allow the alliance members to get the cost economies and brand benefits from operating joint facilities such as check-in desks and airline lounges. Such design may be difficult to achieve with established facilities but is easier with new terminals. An example is London Heathrow Airport, where the completion of Terminal 5 made it easier to allocate British Airways and oneworld traffic to Terminals 3 and 5, SkyTeam to Terminal 4 and Star to a new terminal that will replace the old Terminals 1 and 2. A potential problem is that alliance membership may change, a point illustrated by the case of Manchester Airport. In 1996 Swissair, Singapore and Delta were part of the Global Excellence alliance and were grouped together in T2. By 2012, however, Singapore was with the Star alliance in T2, Delta with SkyTeam in T2 and Swiss with Star in T1.

Certain airports also have the option to design their entire product to appeal to airlines serving premium passengers. This is comparatively rare, but London City Airport is a good example of

Table 6.3 Example MCTs at airports, September 2012

Airport	MCT (mins)	Route	MCT (mins)	Route
Amsterdam	40	Europe–Europe	50	Europe–International
Atlanta	55	Domestic–Domestic	60	Domestic–International
Bangkok	75	All routes		
Brussels	50	All routes		
Chicago O'Hare	50	Domestic–Domestic	75	Domestic–International
Delhi	90	Domestic–Domestic	180	Domestic–International
Dubai	75	All routes		
Frankfurt	45	All routes		
London Heathrow	60	T5–T5	90	T3–T5
Istanbul	30	Domestic–Domestic	90	Domestic–International
Seoul Incheon	40	Domestic–Domestic	100	Domestic–International
Singapore	60	All routes		
Sydney	30	Domestic–Domestic	60	Domestic–International
Vienna	30	All routes		

Data source: OAG (2012)

an airport whose focus is on premium – and in particular, business – traffic. Process times are kept to a minimum and there are focused services for business travellers such as shoe shine, fast upmarket food, and retail outlets offering merchandise such as shirts, ties and business books. In addition, fast and easy surface access is provided, with a chauffeur service or alternatively a car parking scheme that allows for unlimited parking and access to the short stay car park for 12 months. There are also private jet facilities. Overall there is a ten minute check-in policy, with a goal of five minutes from plane to taxi on arrival (Gooding, 2006). This product was appealing enough, combined with an ideal location near the business and financial centre of London, to attract British Airways to launch its business-only flights from this airport to New York.

By contrast, some other airports have developed their product to satisfy the needs of LCCs (Barrett, 2004; Njoya and Niemeier, 2011). LCCs are attracted to airports with simple terminals and processes such as no transfer facilities, no airline lounges, no airbridges and no passenger buses so that costs can be reduced and a short turnaround time maintained (see Figure 6.8). These needs led Amsterdam Schiphol Airport to build Pier H and M, which has a simple design with no airbridges and functions with a 20-minute turnaround. The passengers use the normal departure lounge with all the commercial facilities before proceeding to the pier. Similarly, a new low cost pier facility called CPH Go, which has some more basic facilities for LCCs, was opened at Copenhagen Airport in 2010. In order for this to work, the airport required its airline customers

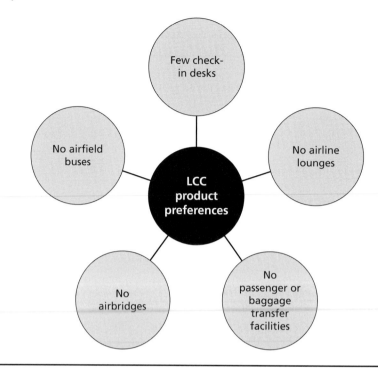

Figure 6.8 LCC product preferences
Source: compiled by the authors

to have 30-minute turnarounds, no baggage transfers, and 90 per cent of passengers checking in online, via mobile phones or using the airport self-service machines to limit the number of check-in desks needed. The airlines also have to accept that the check-in area is CPH Go branded, with no individual airline brands, to achieve better utilisation of the desks (Akerman, 2010).

Elsewhere, new low cost terminals have been built, as in Singapore and Kuala Lumpur, or converted from old facilities such as a cargo facility in Marseilles or a charter facility in Lyon. Other dedicated facilities are operating in such diverse areas as Milan, Bordeaux, New York and Zhengzhou. These terminals have a simple design with lower service standards than expected in conventional terminals. Certain costs – for example, those associated with the runway, navigational equipment, fire/rescue and security – will be no different for airlines using the low cost terminals, so landing and security charges tend to be the same for all. However, within the terminal the simpler design and lack of sophisticated equipment and facilities such as airbridges, escalators, complex baggage systems and airline lounges usually results in the airlines that use the terminal being charged a lower amount per passenger. This is an option if the airport wants to appeal to both LCCs and other airlines. If the airport operator only wants to focus on LCCs, or sees them as its only viable airline customer, it can design all its facilities around such operations, as at Frankfurt Hahn Airport (Schumacher, 2007).

An alternative approach to the airport operator managing all terminals is to get different companies to run the terminals, while still maintaining control over the airfield activities and gaining financially from property rents and fees from the other companies. This could introduce more competition and allow each terminal to be more focused on the needs of different market segments. However, problems may also arise in terms of coordinating operations and long-term planning at the airport. There has been little experience of this practice to date, the most notable exception being in the US, such as at John F. Kennedy International Airport, where airlines have their own terminals. Similarly, at a few Australian airports, including Sydney Airport, there are domestic terminals that are run by the airlines. This option has also been considered for other airports – for example, at London Stansted Airport and for a second terminal at Dublin Airport – but has not yet been adopted.

6.5.2 Passenger customers

As discussed in Chapter 3, there are many ways to segment the passenger market, but a key distinction normally has to be made between the business and leisure markets. Generally, business travellers want to get through airports as efficiently as possible with a degree of comfort. While the same can hold true for certain groups of leisure passengers, others may look at the airport in a different way as being part of their leisure experience.

Business travellers tend to have a greater need to get through the processes quickly. For example, a survey of passengers at London Heathrow Airport, London Gatwick Airport, London Stansted Airport and Manchester Airport found that 84 per cent of business passengers (compared with 63 per cent of leisure passengers) expected to wait only ten minutes or less at passport control, with comparable figures of 57 per cent versus 38 per cent and 58 per cent versus 30 per cent for security and check-in/fast bag drop respectively (ORC International, 2009). For this reason, dedicated security (and sometimes immigration and customs) processes or fast-track lanes are often available for premium passengers. If an airport is confident of delivering a fast service, it can enhance the product by adding a guarantee: for example, Copenhagen Airport's fast-track system CPH Express guarantees that 99 per cent of passengers will get through the security process in less than five minutes. Another area where processes can be speeded up is car parking. For this reason, many airports have dedicated spaces that can be reserved in advance close to the terminal, and provide additional services such as valet parking and fuelling for premium passengers.

It is common at some airports, particularly in the Middle East, to have a totally segregated area for check-in, security, immigration and other processes for premium passengers. One example is Bahrain International Airport, which has designed its premium check-in lounge to be more like a hotel-style foyer, with armchair seating and sofas that eliminate any requirement to stand and queue. There is also the option of offering a whole dedicated terminal for premium traffic, as at Doha International Airport. Frankfurt Airport was one of the first to provide such a terminal, which as well as providing dedicated processes offers a valet service, personal assistants, upper range catering, and bathroom, sleeping, entertainment and business facilities (Sobie, 2007).

At an increasing number of airports it has been recognised that there are passengers who are not travelling business class or first class who would welcome the opportunity of paying extra to have some of these product enhancements. At some airports there is an opportunity to pay for the use of a lounge. For example, at KLIA the Plaza Premium Lounge has facilities such as high speed workstations, showers and a variety of refreshments on offer. This can be used for three-, six- or twelve-hour periods. There is also the option of offering a special lounge for a certain type of customer. For example, at Amsterdam Schiphol Airport the babycare lounge, aimed at passengers with babies and children, has seven semi-transparent cubicles, each with a little bed where the baby can sleep, seating for the rest of the family and baby baths, baby changing tables, play areas and microwaves. At London Heathrow Airport, there are other product features for families such as family lanes at security, play areas, children's entertainers and free-for-kids offers at selected restaurants (see Figure 6.9). There may also be the choice of paying to go through a fast-track security queue, which is becoming increasingly popular, for instance, at UK regional airports such as Manchester, Newcastle, London Luton and Bristol, at a cost of around EUR 4.

Families get a smoother take-off at Heathrow.

With family lanes at Security, play areas, children's entertainers and free-for-kids offers at selected restaurants, Heathrow is first for families.

Go to heathrow.com/holiday

Heathrow
Making every journey better.

Figure 6.9 Advert for family-orientated product features at London Heathrow Airport
Source: courtesy of London Heathrow Airport

In some cases, payment for such enhanced services may not even be necessary, as with the Hong Kong International Airport Frequent Visitor Card; this can be provided for free to any visitor who has travelled through the airport three or more times in the last month, and allows them to experience quicker immigration clearance (see Chapter 9 for further discussion on regular traveller initiatives).

Apart from the essential services and processes, the airport operator with its concessionaire partners needs to ensure that its commercial offer also meets the needs of its target markets. For example, London Stansted Airport – which serves predominantly LCC demand – has much 'grab and go' F&B, whereas London Heathrow Airport's Terminal 5 – which has a substantial amount of long-haul and transfer traffic – has many designer retail stores and sit-down restaurants. Leisure passengers in particular will have a need for welcome desks with tourist information and other travel organisations. Airports have also found many other ways to differentiate their commercial services: for example, by having pre-ordering internet services and collection on arrival services. Many airports as diverse as Melbourne, Prague, Pittsburgh International, Hong Kong International and London Heathrow now offer price and quality guarantees.

At airports with long-stay transfer passengers a growing number have introduced innovative ways to keep these passengers occupied. For example, Singapore Changi Airport has a swimming pool, a sauna, a gym and a cinema, and both this airport and Hong Kong International Airport offer a bus tour downtown if transfer passengers are staying over a certain period of time. Amsterdam Schiphol Airport has an art gallery, library and casino. In addition to offering enhanced products for traditional transfer passengers, a number of others, such as Malaysia Airports, have recognised that they are serving more passengers who choose to self-connect and subsequently have no airline support with this. Dublin Airport, for instance, has a Genie Connect service, which provides – for the price of EUR 35 – an escort to accompany the passenger through all the processes and also to access the fast-track boarding pass channel.

6.5.3 Other customers

While airlines and passengers are usually the two key customers airports have to take account of when developing the product, there are others. These may be very specific: for example, the maritime cruise ship operators, which choose their embarkation city partly depending on factors such as how well integrated the airport is with the cruise port. This has resulted in some airports, most notably Vancouver International Airport, developing enhanced cruise passenger processing systems in collaboration with other relevant service providers (Tretheway and Kincaid, 2010).

Normally, an airport plays the role of facilitating access to a city or tourist resort. However, it is possible, by adding certain facilities to the product, for the airport actually to take on the role of the final destination. Such a practice may increase the attractiveness of the airport, as well as potentially providing an additional source of non-aeronautical revenue. Two notable examples here include Frankfurt Airport, which provides a medical clinic for 36,000 patients annually, and the chapel at Stockholm Arlanda Airport, where almost 500 marriage ceremonies took place in 2009.

If land is available outside the terminal, there may be the option of expanding beyond the boundaries of the traditional airport product in the terminal and diversifying, developing facilities such as office complexes, business parks and free trade zones; distribution and logistics centres; sport, cultural and entertainment amenities; shopping centres; and medical services (Kasarda, 2009). The aim of such product development would primarily be to exploit the commercial opportunities of the land and to target some of the additional groups of customers such as residents, visitors, airport employees and companies from the region (as discussed in Chapter 3). As a result of this product expansion and diversification, airports can potentially become multi-modal and multifunctional businesses; these are often called airport cities. These can act as regional and national competitive tools for economic development.

If the airport city continues to develop outwards, the boundaries between the airport and its surrounding urban area may become increasingly blurred and a new urban form, known as an aerotropolis, can emerge. This development, similar to a traditional metropolis, consists of a central city core (the airport city) surrounded by rings or clusters of business and residential suburbs extending as far as 30 kilometres outwards from the airport, connected with corridors of transport links and efficient communications systems. Airport cities and aerotropoli now exist in many parts of the world. They are particularly popular in Asia and the Middle East, where there tend to be newer airports surrounded by a large amount of open land. Notable examples are Hong Kong's 'SkyCity', Incheon's 'Air City' and Kuala Lumpur's 'Gateway Park'; many others are currently under development, such as Beijing's 'World City' and Dubai's 'Dubai World Central'. However, these concepts are not just confined to the large global hubs of the world, as an increasing number of airports of a smaller scale such as Dublin, Manchester, Dulles International, Vancouver International, Helsinki-Vantaa and Zurich have also given priority to this type of commercial development (Kasarda and Appold, 2010).

An airport city or aerotropolis is such a vast and complex product that it goes beyond the current consideration of the airport product because of the substantial number of different organisations and services that will each play important roles in providing the product. Nevertheless, the relevance of such developments in terms of airport marketing cannot be overlooked because of their role in increasing the attraction of the airport and bringing customers to the airport who might otherwise not have visited.

References

ACI/DMKA (2009) *ASQ Best Practice Report: Internet Access*, Montreal: ACI.

ACI/DMKA (2011) *ASQ Best Practice Report: Airport Wayfinding*, Montreal: ACI.

Akerman, A. (2010) 'Copenhagen Airport adapts to low cost market with new pier', *Communique Airport Business*, Winter; 18–20.

Allett, T. (2010) 'Hello world', *Airports International*, November; 21–5.

Barrett, S.D. (2004) 'How do the demands for airport services differ between full-service carriers and low cost carriers?', *Journal of Air Transport Management*, 5(5); 193–201.

Department for Transport (2007) *Improving the Air Passenger Experience*, London: Department for Transport.

Dibb, S., Simkin, L., Pride, W. and Ferrell, O. (2006) *Marketing: Concepts and Strategies*, 5th European edn, Boston: Houghton Mifflin.

Gooding, R. (2006) 'Surviving the low cost carrier challenge: London City Airport's business model', *Journal of Airport Management*, 1(1); 6–8.

Halpern, N. and Regmi, U. (2011) 'What's in a name? Analysis of airport brand names and slogans', *Journal of Airport Management*, 6(1); 63–79.

Halpern, N., Graham, A. and Davidson, R. (2011) 'Meeting facilities at airports', *Journal of Air Transport Management*, 18(1); 54–8.

Hoffman, D., Bateson, J., Wood, E. and Kenyon, A. (2009) *Services Marketing: Concepts, Strategies and Cases*, London: Centage Learning.

Jarach, D. (2005) *Airport Marketing: Strategies to Cope with the New Millennium Environment*, Farnham: Ashgate.

Kasarda, J. (2009) 'Airport cities', *Urban Land*, 68(4); 56–60.

Kasarda, J. and Appold, S. (2010) 'The pioneers' in J. Kasarda (ed.) *Global Airport Cities*, Twickenham: Insight Media.

Kotler, P., Armstrong, G., Wong, V. and Saunders, J. (2008) *Principles of Marketing*, 5th European edn, Harlow: Prentice Hall-Pearson Education.

Madeira, C. (2011) 'Building retail practices for the New Lisbon Airport', *Journal of Airport Management*, 6(1); 40–50.

Martilla, J. and James, J. (1977) 'Importance–performance analysis', *Journal of Marketing*, 41(1); 13–17.

Martin-Cejas, R. (2006) 'Tourism service quality begins at the airport', *Tourism Management*, 27(5); 874–7.

Njoya, E. and Niemeier, H-M. (2011) 'Do dedicated low cost passenger terminals create competitive advantages for airports?', *Research in Transportation Business and Management*, 1(1); 55–61.

OAG (2012) *OAG Flight Guide Worldwide*, Luton: OAG.

ORC International (2009) *Research on the Air-Passenger Experience at Heathrow, Gatwick, Stansted and Manchester Airports*, London: ORC International.

Paternoster, J. (2008) 'Excellent airport customer service meets successful branding strategy', *Journal of Airport Management*, 2(3); 218–26.

Schumacher, J. (2007) 'The latest business model for low cost airports: the case of Frankfurt-Hahn airport', *Journal of Airport Management*, 1(2); 121–4.

SITA/Air Transport World (2011) *Passenger Self-Service Survey Highlights*, Geneva: SITA.

Sobie, B. (2007) 'Stress free', *Airline Business*, December; 47.

Tretheway, M. and Kincaid, I. (2010) 'Competition between airports: occurrence and strategy' in P. Forsyth, D. Gillen, J. Muller and H-M. Niemeier (eds) *Airport Competition: The European Experience*, Farnham: Ashgate.

UK CAA (2009) *The Through Airport Passenger Experience*, London: CAA.

UK CC (2008) *Stansted Quinquennial Review: Assessment of Competition at Stansted Airport*, London: UK CC.

Urfer, B. and Weinert, R. (2011) 'Managing airport infrastructure' in A. Wittmer, T. Bieger and R. Muller (eds), *Aviation Systems: Management of the Integrated Aviation Value Chain*, Heidelberg: Springer.

Vujicic, S. and Wickelgren, M. (2011) 'Destination branding in relation to airports: the case of the City of Valencia', *European Journal of Transport and Infrastructure Research*, 11(3); 334–45.

Chapter 7

Airport pricing

This chapter looks at airport pricing. It introduces factors that can affect airport pricing decisions before considering the cost and revenue structure of airports, types of airport user charge, economic regulation of airport charges and incentive mechanisms used by airports.

7.1 Factors that can affect airport pricing decisions

As shown in Chapter 3, the overall cost of using an airport is not always the main determinant for customer choice; however, price does play an important role in airport marketing. It is the only element of the marketing mix that contributes revenue (product, promotion and distribution represent costs) and can therefore influence the overall success and financial viability of an airport.

Airport pricing decisions are often guided by the need to cover costs and raise money for investment, especially at airports where cost-based principles are used to set and/or regulate aeronautical charges. Nevertheless, pricing should also be customer-value orientated because the perceived value of a product or service is arguably more important to customers than price (Kotler et al., 2008). Perceived value is particularly important for service companies such as airports because of the intangible nature of what is being sold. It is difficult for customers to see and feel airport products or services or to compare the value of one airport product or service to another, unlike with a physical product that can be felt, tested and in some cases tasted by the consumer.

Price is the easiest element of the marketing mix to change quickly. It is not so easy to make quick changes to products or services, or to channels used to promote and distribute the product or service (Kotler et al., 2008). Airports should therefore monitor the effect of pricing decisions and make changes where necessary (e.g. in response to changes in demand, emerging trends or changes they make to other elements of the marketing mix). Airports should also vary prices to reflect the value and needs of different products or services and market segments.

As with any business, airport pricing decisions are affected by a range of factors. Some are internal to the airport such as its cost and revenue structure, the way it is owned and operated, its marketing objectives, and the decisions it makes relating to its marketing mix. Other factors are external to the airport such as the market and nature of demand, and the competitive and business environment within which it operates (see Figure 7.1).

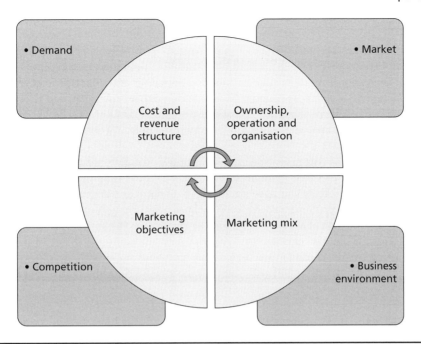

Figure 7.1 Factors affecting airport pricing decisions
Source: compiled by the authors

7.1.1 Internal factors

The cost of operating the airport is likely to impact on price because revenue generated from pricing will determine the net benefit to the airport. Airports tend to have high fixed costs (e.g. in terms of labour, maintenance and utilities) and for airports with spare capacity, the marginal cost of accommodating additional business such as new air services or concessionaires is likely to be low, while the revenue gained from increased passenger throughput and spending (e.g. on car parking, retail and catering) can be significant.

Marketing objectives affect pricing decisions because they determine whether an airport is seeking to expand or simply to be better at what it does. For instance, marketing objectives for airports with low traffic volume may be focused on developing air services, while busy, capacity-constrained airports may be more focused on retaining existing customers, generating added value (e.g. from an improved retail offer) or concentrating on public relations.

Airport pricing decisions cannot be taken in isolation. They need to fit in with the overall marketing mix strategy of the airport, including decisions about airport products and services and the channels used to promote and distribute them. Similarly, airport pricing decisions are likely to involve input from the full range of departments within an airport's organisational structure such as marketing, finance and corporate strategy. In addition, airports operated as part of a group may lack the autonomy to make decisions on pricing that reflect their own market, and privately owned or operated airports may have different marketing objectives from those that are publicly owned or operated, which subsequently affect the pricing decisions they make.

7.1.2 External factors

The nature of the market and demand for air services will affect airport pricing decisions. For instance, airports that serve a small market with relatively low traffic volume represent a fairly high degree of risk to any airline considering operating at the airport, especially airlines seeking to operate a frequent year-round service as opposed to an infrequent and seasonal service. In such circumstances, there is an incentive for airports to adopt a pricing policy that shares in the risk. The same principle applies to any commercial, non-aviation-related activities at an airport.

Competition affects airport pricing decisions. Competition may be particularly high at airports seeking to compete for LCCs or inbound services such as those supporting the development of tourism because these airlines will have a number of airports and destinations to choose from; unlike some scheduled mainline and regional airlines, they are generally more footloose and less obliged to serve particular airports because of public service obligations or network considerations. Airports are also exposed to competition on the commercial side of their business (e.g. from off-site car parks, downtown or internet shopping and other providers of real estate or airport consulting services), and will need to take into account the nature and intensity of competition when making decisions about pricing.

Issues relating to the wider business environment also influence airport pricing decisions. Fuel prices and the state of the economy tend to have a significant impact on airport customers, especially airlines that are under increased pressure to reduce or contain costs, and may be inclined to reduce capacity or drop routes at certain airports during times of hardship, moving their assets to airports in regions that are performing better. Airports are less able to move their assets and may therefore need to respond to changes taking place in their wider business environment by altering their prices.

One of the main factors affecting airport pricing decisions, especially on the aeronautical side of their business, is the extent to which they have control over pricing. Aeronautical charges are set and controlled at many airports, especially those that are owned and operated by governments and/or are part of a national or regional airport system where charges may be the same for all airports. Specific forms of economic regulation may be imposed on airports, especially larger and main airports that have the potential to abuse their market power and charge airlines high prices unless controls over pricing are in place.

Finally, airports are not always responsible for the services provided at their airport, which can also affect their ability to control and compete on price. This is often the case with ground handling services or any government taxes or en-route charges that might be levied for flying to and from their airport.

7.2 Sources of airport cost and revenue

Airports provide essential infrastructure for the movement of aircraft, passengers and cargo, and in order to facilitate continued long-term growth in demand, they need to invest vast amounts of capital. USD 26 billion in capital expenditure was invested by airports worldwide in 2010 on upgrades or expansions of existing infrastructure alone. This figure does not include expenditure on new airports or on airports in the Middle East and China, where capital investment is high (ACI, 2011).

Operating airport infrastructure also comes at a cost. Worldwide, airports incurred operating expenses of USD 56 billion (ACI, 2011). The two main cost items are personnel (36 per cent of total operating cost) and contracted services, which include outsourcing costs to third parties

Table 7.1 Worldwide airport operating costs by item (2010) and area (2009)

Item, 2010*	%	Area, 2009**	%
Personnel	36.0	Terminal and landside operations	28.0
Contracted services	19.0	Administration	19.0
Communication, energy, waste	8.0	Airside operations	18.0
Maintenance	8.0	Airport security	14.5
Materials, equipment, supplies	6.0	Sales and marketing	4.5
General administration	6.0	Other	16.0
Lease, rent, concession fees	6.0		
Insurance, claims, settlements	2.0		
Other	9.0		

Data source: *ACI (2011); **ACI (2010)

Note: ACI stopped reporting operating costs by area after ACI (2010)

(19 per cent). By functional area, the two main costs are on terminal and landside operations (28 per cent) and administration (19 per cent) (see Table 7.1).

Airports need to generate revenue to cover their costs and contribute to future investment. Worldwide, airports generated a total income of USD 102 billion in 2010 (ACI, 2011). There are two main sources of airport income: aeronautical revenue directly related to the processing of aircraft, passengers and cargo, and non-aeronautical revenue from commercial facilities and services.

Historically, airport income has been derived largely from aeronautical activities. By 1990, non-aeronautical revenue contributed about 30 per cent of total airport income (ACI, 2007) while in 2010, its contribution had increased to 46.5 per cent (ACI, 2011). Non-aeronautical revenue has therefore become a vital part of the airport business; however, it is becoming increasingly difficult for airports to generate additional revenue on the non-aeronautical side, and growth in the proportion of non-aeronautical to total revenue has stagnated at many airports in recent years, remaining at around 46.5 per cent since 2005 (e.g. see ACI, 2006). Differences exist between world regions (see Figure 7.2): 51 per cent of total revenue is non-aeronautical at airports in Asia-Pacific, 49 per cent in North America, 45 per cent in Europe, 40 per cent in Africa and 36 per cent in Latin America/Caribbean.

Airport revenue by item is shown in Figure 7.3. The darkest shaded segments represent aeronautical sources of revenue, while the grey represent non-aeronautical sources. The two largest sources of revenue are from passenger- and aircraft-related charges. Traditionally, aircraft-related charges were the main source of revenue, but there has been a trend in recent years for airports to place more emphasis on passenger-related charges – except in North America, where terminal rental fees contribute a high proportion of revenue and passenger-related charges (as discussed later in this chapter) are capped. The rationale behind focusing more on charging per passenger is that airports and airlines share the risk in changes to volume, which does not necessarily happen when charging according to aircraft movements or size. The change in focus is also reflected to some extent by changes to airline business models, especially those of LCCs, which seek to reduce aircraft-related charges to a minimum and shift responsibility for charges to the passenger (ACI, 2011).

Airport pricing

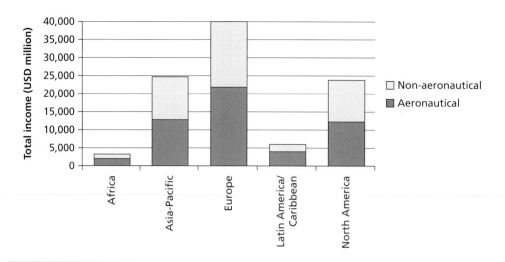

Figure 7.2 Total airport revenue by region and source, 2010
Data source: ACI (2011)

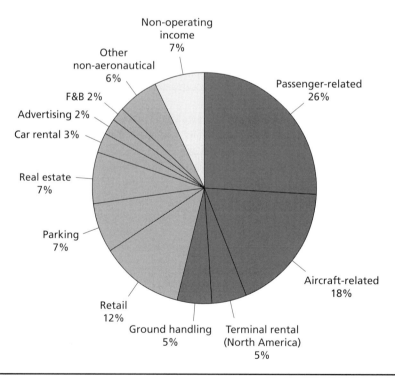

Figure 7.3 Worldwide airport revenue by item, 2010
Data source: ACI (2011)

> **Table 7.2** Proportion of non-aeronautical revenue at airports worldwide by source (%), 2010

Region	Retail concession	Car parking	Rental car concession	Property income/rent	Advertising	F&B	Other
Africa	31	17	7	23	9	1	12
Asia-Pacific	45	5	1	26	3	5	15
Europe	35	14	3	12	2	4	30
Latin America/ Caribbean	39	6	4	12	5	4	30
North America	8	38	18	14	5	7	10
Worldwide	28	18	7	19	3	5	20

Data source: ACI (2011)

The aeronautical side of the airport business is often a zero-sum game, meaning that losses are finely balanced by gains. The non-aeronautical side has therefore become particularly important for airports. It often generates higher profit margins than aeronautical activities, and allows airports to develop a diversified business. It has also helped airports to keep their charges down, remaining at about 4 per cent of airline operating cost since the 1970s (ACI, 2007), although this varies by airline and is likely to be much higher for many LCCs. A successful non-aeronautical business can allow airports to generate higher profits, meaning that they will be a more attractive option for investment, and may result in a better credit rating for the airport that subsequently enables them to achieve a lower cost of borrowing (ACI, 2007).

Retail concessions are the main source of non-aeronautical revenue at airports, contributing 28 per cent of non-aeronautical revenue worldwide in 2010. Property income/rent and car parking are also important sources. Differences exist between world regions, especially North America, where retail concessions only contribute 8 per cent of non-aeronautical revenue, while car parking contributes 38 per cent and rental car concessions contribute 18 per cent (see Table 7.2).

7.3 Types of airport user charge

Income, whether aeronautical or non-aeronautical, comes from charges levied to users of airport facilities and services. Global cost-based principles for determining standards for airport charges are recommended by ICAO (see Table 7.3). Further guidance is provided by ICAO (2012) on how individual charges should be determined, and a summary of the ICAO guidelines is provided in this chapter, along with examples from airports. Some of the examples reflect ICAO guidance; others do not. This is because individual states are not required to comply with the standards and tend to have their own guidance and regulations regarding the setting of airport charges. For instance, in Europe, individual states and their airports should comply with the EC directive on airport charges (see EC, 2009).

> ### Table 7.3 Cost-based principles for determining airport charges

---

Principles

The cost to be allocated is the full cost of providing the airport and its essential services, including appropriate cost of capital and asset depreciation, maintenance, operation, management and administration. These costs may be offset by non-aeronautical revenues.

Aircraft operators and other airport users, including end-users, should not be charged for facilities and services they do not use, other than those provided under the regional air navigation plan.

Only the cost of facilities and services in general use by international air services should be included, not the cost of those that are exclusively leased or occupied and charged separately.

Airports should maintain cost data to facilitate consultation, transparency and economic oversight.

An allocation of costs should be considered for space or facilities used by government authorities.

Proportionate allocation of costs to various categories of users should be determined equitably.

Costs related to the provision of approach and aerodrome control should be separately identified.

Airports may produce sufficient revenues to exceed all direct and indirect operating costs, provide a reasonable return on assets, and where relevant, remunerate adequately holders of airport equity.

Capacity of users to pay should not be taken into account until all costs are fully assessed and distributed on an objective basis. At that stage the contributing capability of states and communities concerned should be taken into consideration.

Costs directly related to oversight functions (safety, security and economic oversight) for airport services may be included in the airport's cost basis, at the state's discretion.

Source: adapted from ICAO (2012)

7.3.1 Passenger service charge

Airports charge passengers to use their facilities and services through what is generally known as a passenger service charge (PSC). The PSC should be collected on behalf of the airport by aircraft operators (e.g. at the point of sale for a flight ticket) because collection directly from passengers at an airport may be problematic and result in queues and delays at the airport. Airports should normally levy a charge per departing passenger. Many airports vary the PSC according to whether the passenger is taking a domestic or international flight: the charge is likely

Table 7.4 Malaysia Airports PSC, 2012

Departing	To	PSC (MYR)
Rural airports	To all destinations	0
KLIA main terminal building and regional airports	All international destinations	65
KLIA main terminal building and other airports	All domestic destinations	9
LCCT-KLIA and T2 Kota Kinabalu	All international destinations	32
LCCT-KLIA	All domestic destinations	6
Secondary airports: Alor Setar, Bintulu, Ipoh, Kuala Terengganu, Kota Bharu, Kuantan, Labuan, Lahad Datu, Limbang, Melaka, Miri, Mulu, Pangkor, Redang, Sandakan, Sibu, Tawau and Tioman	All direct ASEAN destinations	26
Kota Kinabalu, Kuching, Labuan and Miri	Brunei, Balik Papan, Manado, Santos, Puerto Princesa and Zamboanga	26
Penang, Langkawi, Alor Setar, Kota Bharu and Ipoh	Medan, Banda Aceh, Padang, Nias, Hat Yai, Narathiwat, Trang, Nikhon Thammarat and Patani	26

Source: adapted from Malaysia Airports (2012)

to be higher for international than domestic passengers due to the additional facilities and services needed to process international passengers. Charges may be the same across all airports belonging to an airport group (e.g. Avinor charges NOK 46 per departing domestic passenger and NOK 60 per departing international passenger at its 46 airports in Norway). This is not always the case. Malaysia Airports charges different rates depending on the destination (domestic, ASEAN, international), the airport, and also the terminal (see Table 7.4): passengers using the LCCT at KLIA pay about half as much as passengers using KLIA's main terminal building or other airports operated by Malaysia Airports. It is interesting to note that Malaysia Airports has a message on its corporate website reminding passengers that the PSC collected by airlines is only paid to Malaysia Airports on completion of the flight, and that passengers are therefore eligible for a full refund of the PSC from their airline if they do not travel on the flight for which they have purchased the ticket.

US airports are not legally permitted to charge for passenger services, largely because of fears that such revenues will be used by airports for non-aeronautical activities (Graham, 2008). Instead, the US has a passenger facility charge (PFC) programme, which allows commercial airports controlled by public agencies to collect a fee of up to USD 4.50 for every boarded passenger. Money earned from the fee must be used by airports to fund FAA-approved projects such as those that enhance safety, security or capacity; reduce noise; or increase air carrier competition (FAA, 2012).

7.3.2 Landing charges

Landing charges should be calculated according to the certified maximum take-off weight (MTOW) of the aircraft, or the maximum authorised weight. Flight stage length should not be used. At congested airports – or during peak periods – a fixed charge per aircraft, a variable charge related to aircraft weight or a combination of the two can be used. Charges for approach and aerodrome control may be levied by airports as part of the landing charge or as a separate charge. The charge should be consistent with policies on charges for air navigation services.

At US airports, landing charges are normally based on a fixed rate per aircraft take-off weight, although so-called signatory airlines (see Chapter 9) may pay less. Outside the US, a range of different methods are used. For example, Nairobi Jomo Kenyatta International Airport uses a variable charge related to the MTOW of the aircraft, with different rates for night and day landings, and an additional charge for night take-off (see Table 7.5).

BSCA, an airport popular with LCCs, has a landing charge per passenger instead of by aircraft weight, which reflects the trend towards passenger-related charges mentioned earlier in this chapter. The airport charges EUR 2.20 per departing passenger, but there is also a discount for airlines according to the number of departing passengers (see Table 7.6). No additional PSC is levied by the airport.

7.3.3 Parking and hangar charges

Parking and hangar charges should be levied according to the MTOW of the aircraft, and should take into account the aircraft's dimensions and length of stay. Airports should offer a period of

Table 7.5 Nairobi Jomo Kenyatta International Airport landing and take-off charges, 2012

MTOW (kgs)	Day landing (USD)	Night landing (USD)	Night take-off (USD)
0–1,500	10.00	12.00	2.00
1,501–2,500	20.00	24.00	4.00
2,501–5,000	25.00	30.00	5.00
5,001–10,000	40.00	48.00	8.00
10,001–20,000	65.00	78.00	13.00
20,001–40,000	102.00	122.40	20.40
40,001–80,000	223.00	267.60	44.60
80,001–120,000	585.00	702.00	117.00
120,001–180,000	820.00	984.00	164.00
180,001–300,000	1345.00	1,614.00	269.00
300,001+	1750.00	2,100.00	350.00

Source: adapted from Kenya Airports Authority (2012)

Note: airport operates 24 hours. Night time is between 15:31 and 02:59

Table 7.6 BSCA landing charge discounts (scheduled or charter flights), 2012

Annual discount	Annual number of departing passengers
0%	0–15,000
5%	15,001–35,000
10%	35,001–50,000
25%	50,001–100,000
35%	100,001–200,000
50%	200,001+

Source: adapted from BSCA (2012)

Table 7.7 Macau International Airport aircraft parking fees, 2012

Aircraft MTOW (tonnes)	Landings per month per airline	
	Up to 60 landings	Over 60 landings
	Charge (MOP) per hour	Charge (MOP) per hour
Up to 9	51	41
10–50	129	103
51–150	180	144
151–250	232	185
More than 250	283	227

Source: adapted from Macau International Airport (2012)

free parking for aircraft after landing, which should be determined according to factors such as aircraft scheduling and space availability at the airport. For example, BSCA levies an aircraft parking fee of EUR 1.98 per 24-hour day and per tonne, but the first 12 hours of parking are free. Massport charges per 24-hour day according to aircraft wing span. Macau International Airport charges according to the MTOW of the aircraft and the number of times the airline lands at the airport per month (see Table 7.7). Other airports such as Miami International Airport have a separate parking fee structure for cargo aircraft, which is dependent on landed weight of the aircraft and duration of stay.

7.3.4 Security charges

Airports charge for the provision of security functions. This does not include general security functions performed by states such as policing, intelligence gathering and national security, although some airports do include such charges (e.g. for policing) in the PSC. Responsibility for airport security will be delegated by individual states (e.g. to the airport, the aircraft operator, a private company, the military or the police). The cost may then be met by the state or the organisation responsible. The charge is discretionary and should be levied per passenger and/or be related to aircraft weight. Airport tenants may also be required to pay security charges and these should be recovered through rentals or other charges. Airports should identify and cost security charges separately, even though they may be levied in addition to other charges such as the landing charge. As with PSCs, security charges should be collected by airlines (at the point of sale for a flight ticket) and passed on to the airport operator for re-distribution to the relevant provider of airport security, if it is not themselves.

Riga International Airport provides an interesting case study. Historically, security functions at the airport have been financed by the state through taxpayers' money. A government regulation was introduced recently, which stipulated that the security charge would be collected from passengers departing Riga International Airport as of 1 January 2012. The airlines were asked to collect the charge when selling flight tickets. LCC Ryanair did not agree to do so; as a result, Riga International Airport collects the charge from Ryanair passengers instead of the airline. Owing to the inconvenience caused, the security charge is EUR 7 for Ryanair passengers compared to EUR 6.5 for passengers paying via their airline. Ryanair passengers can pay the charge before departure at check-in, at the airline ticket office, at the airport services office, by mobile phone, or via the internet (Riga International Airport, 2012).

7.3.5 Noise and emissions charges

Noise-related charges may be levied at airports that experience noise problems. Similarly, states that experience local air quality problems at or around airports may apply an emissions charge to address such problems. Both noise and emissions charges should only seek to recover the cost of alleviating or preventing the problem, and should normally consist of a surcharge or rebate associated with the landing fee.

Zurich Airport has a noise charge per landing and assigns each aircraft to a noise category. The airport also has an emissions charge per landing, which varies according to the absolute amount of nitrogen oxide emitted by the engine of the aircraft.

7.3.6 Fuel and oil charges

Unless an airport buys fuel and oil itself to sell to its airlines, it will typically offer concessions to private companies to supply fuel and oil. Concessionaires will normally pay a fee to the airport and/or a proportion of turnover. ICAO guidance on charges for the supply of fuel and oil is limited, recommending that charges – either direct or indirect – for both suppliers (i.e. concessionaires) and aircraft operators should not discriminate or become an obstacle to the progress of civil aviation.

7.3.7 Ground handling charges

Ground handling services may be provided by airports, independent handlers or airlines (some airlines self-handle). Charges will obviously vary according to the method used. Charges levied for ground handling by airports are complex because there is a wide range of services that can be provided. In addition, the size and scale of the airline's operation will play a major role in determining the charges to be levied (see Table 7.8).

Airport operators that allow self-handling or offer a licence to one or more independent handlers by concession will typically charge a fee for access to airport installations. This is in

Table 7.8 Tallinn Airport ground handling charges, 2012

Service	Category	Unit	EUR
Basic ground	Up to 10 MTOW	Each MTOW tonne	9.59
handling service	Over 10–20 MTOW	Each MTOW tonne	8.31
	Over 20–40 MTOW	Each MTOW tonne	6.39
	Over 40–70 MTOW	Each MTOW tonne	5.11
	Over 70–100 MTOW	Each MTOW tonne	3.83
	Over 100 MTOW	Each MTOW tonne	3.20
Weight and balance calculation		Per turnaround	57.52
Passenger and baggage service	Departing/arriving	Each passenger	3.20/2.56
Man power		Hour/call	19.17
Meeting and positioning aircraft		Each MTOW tonne	0.51
Aircraft interior/	Up to 50 seats	Call	30.00/50.00
night stop cleaning	Up to 100 seats	Call	35.00/56.00
	Up to 150 seats	Call	45.00/65.00
	Up to 200 seats	Call	55.00/75.00
	Up to 300 seats	Call	80.00/100.00
	Up to 360 seats	Call	100.00/120.00
	Up to 440 seats	Call	110.00/130.00
	Up to 500 seats	Call	120.00/140.00
Litter disposal		Each MTOW tonne	0.38
Power/GPU/Mobile GPU		Hour/call	3.20/51.13/63.9
Push-back		Call	82.45
Passenger stairs/ airbridge		Hour/call	51.13
Toilet service	Truck call/each tank	Call	38.35/19.17
Water supply		Call	57.52
Heater		Hour/call	38.35
ASU		Hour/call	198.13
Additional platform for CRJ		Call	40.00
Transporter/cargo highloader		Hour/call	83.09/250.00
Escort/crew transport on ramp		Hour/call	32.60/25.56
Crew city transport	Up to 18/19+ seats	Hour/call	31.96/57.52
Hotel booking		1 booking	12.78
Cargo loading		1 kg	0.07

Table 7.8 continued

Service	Category	Unit	EUR
Passenger terminal porter service	1–6/7–30/31+ passengers	Total/each/each	19.17/2.24/2.68
Equipment rent – towbar		Hour/call	22.37
Forklift/forklift slave pallet		Hour/call	31.96/19.17
LD1/2/3 container dolly		Hour/call	12.78
96′x125′ cargo pallet dolly		Hour/call	12.78
Baggage tractor/ baggage cart		Hour/call	22.37/6.39
Belt-loader		Hour/call	31.96
Hangar rent		Depends on MTOW	To be agreed
De-/anti-icing	Wing span up to 23m	Call	250.00
	Wing span 24–35m	Call	360.00
	Wing span 36–51m	Call	385.00
	Wing span 52–65m	Call	430.00
	Type 1 (mixture)	Litre	3.40
	Type 2	Litre	4.40
Manual snow removal		Call	100.00

Source: adapted from Tallinn Airport (2012)

addition to any charges for cost-related services such as issuing airside passes, or for centralised infrastructure (e.g. baggage transportation systems, fixed power installations and water). Manchester Airport charges GBP 500 for a new ground handling licence and GBP 250 for licence renewals. The fee contributes towards the costs incurred by the airport in administering the licence and monitoring the performance of ground handlers. Ground handlers also pay GBP 25 for each item of airside equipment and each vehicle permit for motorised vehicles operating airside at the airport, and GBP 1 per unit loading device per day in excess of the number agreed between the airport, airline, operator or handling agent (Manchester Airport, 2012).

In Europe, Article 16 of the directive on access to the ground handling market at community airports requires member states to determine fees for access to airport installations according to relevant, objective, transparent and non-discriminatory criteria, so self-handling airlines and independent handlers are generally treated the same way (see EC, 1996). In some countries, the directive has been implemented into state law and is overseen by a designated regulator, as is the case in Ireland, where the designated regulator is the Commission for Aviation Regulation (CAR). When an airport authority decides to charge a fee for access to airport installations, they need to submit a request for approval to CAR. As of July 2012, the following access fees were approved (CAR, 2012): annual check-in desk fee at Dublin Airport of EUR 25,194 per desk;

flexible hourly rental fee for additional check-in desk at Dublin Airport of EUR 30 per desk; annual check-in desk fee at Shannon Airport of EUR 9,215 per desk per annum, EUR 23 per hour (or part thereof); common user terminal equipment (CUTE) fees at Shannon Airport of EUR 0.30 per embarking passenger; annual check-in desk fee at Cork Airport of EUR 13,180 per desk per annum; half-hourly rental fee for additional check-in desk at Cork Airport of EUR 5.27 per desk; CUTE fees at Cork Airport of EUR 0.24 per embarking passenger.

Ground handlers also need to obtain approval from CAR before engaging in ground handling activities. Applicants must complete an application form and meet a number of requirements, including minimum levels of insurance cover. New applicants need to pay an application fee of EUR 1,797. Ground handling approvals are issued for a period of five years and are subject to meeting certain minimum requirements throughout that period. A fee of EUR 1,797 must be paid to CAR each year to cover administrative expenses. Ground handlers can apply to renew their licence after five years through a specific renewal process.

7.3.8 Other aeronautical charges

Airport users are likely to encounter other charges: one of these is government tax, such as the APD levied by the UK government. This does not go to the airport and is normally collected from passengers by airlines when they sell a flight ticket. Government tax can have a major impact on the overall cost of operating at an airport, and often causes controversy between airlines and governments around the world. Ryanair cancelled 15 routes and reduced 46 routes at Madrid Barajas and Barcelona El Prat airports in response to the Spanish government doubling airport departure taxes in 2012 (see Ryanair, 2012). Levels of government tax vary around the world, contributing 56 per cent of aeronautical charges in the US, 16 per cent in Europe, and 8 per cent in Africa, Australasia and the Middle East according to research undertaken in 2007 (see Saounatsos, 2007). The high figure for the US is largely due to the many taxes that go into the federal Airport and Airway Trust Fund, and provide finance for airport investment grants under the Airport Improvement Program (Graham, 2008).

Another important aeronautical charge to mention is the terminal rental charge (e.g. for airlines and handling companies), which contributes a significant proportion of revenue at airports in North America (see Figure 7.3). This is partly because passenger-related charges at US airports are capped, so the proportion of revenue from terminal rental is much higher at airports in North America than in other world regions. Terminal rental rates are usually based on a cost-recovery approach and calculated using a weighted rate based on the type of space that is rented. Miami International Airport calculates an average rental rate based on general terminal costs divided by the weighted average rentable area (square feet). The average rental rate is then multiplied by 0.5 for a class 5 space, rising in increments of 0.5 to 2.0 for a class 1 space (see Miami-Dade Aviation Department, 2012). Terminal rental may, of course, be considered a non-aeronautical source of revenue.

7.3.9 Non-aeronautical charges

ICAO guidelines on charges for non-aeronautical activities are fairly limited, stating that:

> Income derived from such sources as concessions, rental of premises, and 'free zones' is important to airports. It is recommended that, with the exception of concessions that are directly associated with the operation of air transport services, such as fuel, in-flight catering and ground handling, non-aeronautical revenues be fully developed, while keeping in mind the interests and needs of passengers and the public, and ensuring terminal efficiency.
>
> (ICAO, 2012: 22)

As shown in Table 7.2, retail concessions are particularly important to airports, although in North America it is revenues from car parking and rental car concessions that are most important. Charging practices for concessions vary by airport, as do approaches to concession contracting (see Chapter 9). Typically, airports charge concessionaires a fixed rent for the space provided or a variable rent that includes a minimum annual guaranteed rent and a percentage of the turnover. The percentage of turnover can vary dramatically depending on the size and scale of activity, location, products and services, and expected profit margins. It may range from as little as 5 per cent for concessions with lower profit margins to as much as 60 per cent for those with higher profit margins. A minimum level of capital investment (e.g. per square foot) may also be required from the concessionaire. In addition, charges will vary according to the type and length of concession contract, discussed in more detail in Chapter 9.

Antonio B. Won Pat International Airport launched a request for proposals (RFP) for its duty free and travel retail concession in 2012, offering a ten-year contract on 24,076 square feet of retail space, with an additional 1,719 square feet in the future. The previous concession generated sales of USD 34.8 million in 2011. The RFP stipulated the payment of a minimum annual guaranteed rent of USD 6 million and a rent rate of at least 25 per cent of gross revenue. A minimum capital investment of USD 250 per square foot was also required by the successful bidder. Other non-financial requirements were stipulated in the RFP, including five years' continuous experience within the last seven years, including operating a minimum of one single location with gross sales of USD 25 million per year for each of the five qualifying years, and experience of successful operations within a TSA or foreign equivalent environment for a minimum of five years. Specific categories of retail that had to be offered on an exclusive or non-exclusive merchandise basis were also listed in the RFP, including luggage, handbags, personal accessories, jewellery, cosmetics, skincare, fragrances, cigarettes, souvenirs and gifts, and packaged food (Moodie, 2012).

7.4 Economic regulatory environment

Airports often dominate their local geographic market, and at many of the world's larger airports demand exceeds supply, especially during peak periods. In these circumstances, airports may experience monopoly or near-monopoly conditions that allow them to set high prices for use of their facilities and services. As a result, many governments limit airports' ability to abuse their market power by restricting prices, especially for aeronautical facilities and services needed to facilitate the movement of aircraft and their passengers and cargo.

When airport charges are regulated, a decision will need to be made on how to treat the respective sources of aeronautical and non-aeronautical revenue. There are two main approaches (ACI, 2007). The 'dual till' approach splits the aeronautical and non-aeronautical sides of the airport business into two distinct parts. Revenue from the aeronautical side of the business (such as from the PSC, landing charges and security charges) is used for aeronautical expenditure (such as on runway maintenance and terminal development), and it is only the aeronautical side of the airport business that is regulated. Non-aeronautical revenue (such as from concessions) is then used for non-aeronautical expenditure (such as developing retail space or car parks) and contributes to company profits. The non-aeronautical side of the airport business is then allowed to operate under normal market conditions. The 'single till' approach does not distinguish between aeronautical and non-aeronautical revenue, meaning that all airport revenue is considered for the purpose of setting airport charges.

Under a single till, aeronautical charges are likely to be lower because non-aeronautical activities – which are often more profitable than aeronautical activities – will help to reduce the charges. That is why the single till is generally favoured by airlines. Their argument is that passenger expenditure on non-aeronautical activities is a by-product of airline operations and should therefore be considered for the purpose of setting airport charges. The dual till is likely to result in higher aeronautical charges. It is generally favoured by airports because they are able to generate and retain higher profits from their non-aeronautical activities. Airports argue for the dual till on the basis that their non-aeronautical activities are a separate part of their business and should not be used to subsidise charges for aeronautical activities. Comparative approaches to the single and dual till are known as 'residual' and 'compensatory' in the US, and are discussed later in this chapter.

The economic regulatory environment varies. Some airports are not regulated; this is often the case where governments own a national network of airports and subsequently set the charges themselves (e.g. with the 67 airports in Brazil operated by the state-owned airport operator Infraero). It is also the case in Canada, where airports are operated on a not-for-profit basis and are therefore not in a position to abuse market power. Elsewhere, regulatory mechanisms may be used, especially at main airports, and although a range of mechanisms for regulating airport charges are used worldwide, they can generally be grouped according to three broad types (see Figure 7.4).

Commercial negotiation is a largely market-based mechanism. It involves the negotiation of charges between airports and their users. Governments or regulatory bodies may play a passive role in the negotiations, monitoring or reviewing the prices set and relying on the threat of regulation as a deterrent for monopolistic pricing. This model is currently used at major airports in Australia (Sydney, Melbourne, Brisbane, Perth and Adelaide), where the Australian Competition and Consumer Commission monitors prices. It is also used in New Zealand (Auckland, Wellington and Christchurch), although the government may ask for an ad hoc review of prices by the Competition Commission.

Many publicly owned and operated airports set their charges on a cost-recovery basis. This method is common in the US, where many airports are owned and operated by local or national government. Airports set charges following consultation with airport users, and federal

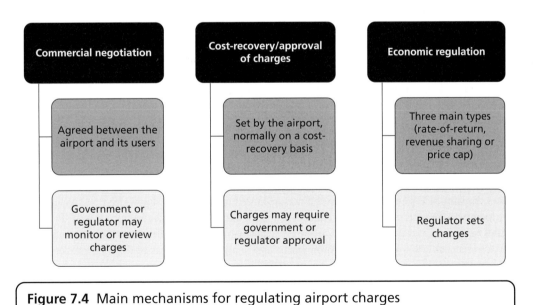

Figure 7.4 Main mechanisms for regulating airport charges
Source: compiled by the authors

government may intervene if necessary. Airports in the US may take one of two main approaches: residual (e.g. at San Francisco International, Miami International and Dallas/Fort Worth International) or compensatory (e.g. at Los Angeles International, Tampa International and Boston Logan International). With the residual approach, airlines pay charges related to the net costs of running the airport (including non-aeronautical activities). This is similar to the single till approach taken by airports outside the US, but there is one key difference: the airlines need to guarantee that the level of charges will always allow the airport to break even. The airport may levy lower charges as a result of including revenue from non-aeronautical activities but will have lower risk as it is largely passed onto the airlines. With the compensatory approach, airlines pay agreed charges related to the costs of facilities and services they use. This is similar to the dual till approach taken by airports outside the US. Airports may be able to levy higher charges but will assume a greater degree of risk. There are also a number of airports in the US that use a hybrid approach, combining elements of the residual and compensatory approaches (e.g. at Orlando International, Washington Dulles International and Reagan National).

In other countries, charges are set – or need to be approved – by the government or regulatory body. For example, charges in Japan are set by the government, which takes into consideration the overall cost of the 28 airports under its control. Other airports in Japan (Narita International, Kansai International, Central Japan International Airport Centrair and airports controlled by local governments) are also required to obtain approval from the government when setting charges. Most apply the same landing charges, except for Narita, Kansai and Centrair. These airports have traditionally experienced high levels of debt and are not supported by the same funds allocated to national or local government airports (e.g. the airport development special account that collects revenues from all airports before being re-distributed). As a result, charges levied by the three airports have traditionally been high.

Economic regulation represents the most formal and heavily regulated approach to setting airport charges. With this mechanism, the government or an independent regulator has an active role in setting airport charges. There are three broad approaches to economic regulation: rate-of-return, revenue cap or price cap.

Rate-of-return is the least heavy-handed of the three approaches. The basic principle is that airports can charge prices that will cover costs and earn a normal rate-of-return on capital. The rate-of-return method is used in the Netherlands to regulate charges at Amsterdam Schiphol Airport under a dual till approach, where the rate-of-return is determined by the regulator taking the weighted average cost of capital as the asset base. The obvious issue with this approach is that there is little incentive to reduce costs because the rate-of-return is set, irrespective of efficiency. Airports may therefore be inclined to expand their asset base (e.g. by 'gold-plating') in order to increase cost of capital, and subsequently the prices that they can charge.

Alternatively, regulators may use revenue or price caps to determine charges that can be levied by airports. A revenue cap limits the total revenue that can be earned in a given period while a price cap limits the price that can be charged within a given period. Both approaches subtract expected efficiency savings (X) from a measure of inflation such as the retail or consumer price index. Revenue caps offer airports stability in terms of total revenue. They also offer reduced risk to changes in demand because unit charges are inversely related to growth in demand. Price caps allow airports to retain profit; they offer an incentive to increase efficiency because when X is zero per cent or greater, airports can only improve financial performance through efficiency such as increased traffic or better productivity, and not through price increases. The problem with price caps is that they may also encourage cost-cutting and reduced service quality as a means of generating increased profit.

Price caps are widely used to regulate airport charges. For instance, single till price caps are used in the UK (London Heathrow, London Gatwick and London Stansted), Ireland (Dublin),

South Africa (Airports Company South Africa's nine airports) and Argentina (Airports Argentina 2000's 33 airports). India recently adopted a price cap regulation for its major airports (Bengaluru International, Cochin International, Delhi Indira Gandhi International, Hyderabad Rajiv Gandhi International and Mumbai Chhatrapati Shivaji International). The incentive-based regulation uses a single till approach and is reviewed every five years (five-year review periods are fairly standard, although some regulators review after between three and four years). The price cap takes into account the fair rate-of-return in addition to other factors such as the regulatory asset base, capital investment plans, depreciation, traffic forecasts, and expected operation and maintenance expenditure. The regulator also takes into consideration the quality of service provided by airport operators, according to specific service parameters, when determining the price cap and uses a mechanism that reduces charges for under-performance by way of rebates to airport users.

7.5 Incentive mechanisms

7.5.1 The need to share risk

As discussed earlier (e.g. Chapters 1 and 2), the airport business environment has changed dramatically in recent years. Demand for air transport has grown exponentially; air transport markets have become increasingly deregulated, meaning that airlines are freer to choose where they fly to and from; and LCCs have emerged and offer considerable opportunities to grow new and existing markets, including to and from relatively small airports. Deregulation and LCCs have also had an impact on existing airline business models, encouraging increased competition and a focus on cost-reduction.

In parallel with these changes in the airline industry, the airport business has transformed from being considered a public utility to a commercial business, sometimes with corporatised or private owners or operators that want to see growth at their airports. In addition, airports are increasingly viewed as engines for regional economic development, meaning that there is a growing level of local support and desire for airport growth. Changes in the airport business environment offer opportunities for growth, especially at uncongested regional airports; however, in order to compete, airports increasingly need to demonstrate a willingness to share in the financial risk associated with establishing new routes or growing existing services at their airport by offering incentives to airlines, especially during the early stages of establishing a new route, because the start-up cost for an airline can be particularly high.

One of the earliest and most significant examples of airport incentives was an agreement between BSCA and LCC Ryanair. BSCA is located 46 kilometres south of Brussels. It served around 50,000 passengers per year between 1990 and 1996, mainly on charter flights. Ryanair began to operate at the airport in 1997 and grew passenger demand to about 200,000 within one year. Ryanair then decided to create its first continental base at the airport in 2001 and had established 12 routes and 21 daily frequencies by 2004, serving almost 2 million passengers (Jossart, 2004). Airport incentives were central to Ryanair's expansion at the airport, and details of the financial agreement between BSCA and Ryanair became public in 2001 (see Table 7.9).

After receiving complaints about the agreement between BSCA and Ryanair, the EC launched an investigation and subsequently ruled that the airport owner – the Walloon regional government – was not behaving in the same way a private operator would have under the same circumstances. Some of the aid towards the start-up cost of the new routes was considered acceptable by the EC, but many of the payments made were not. In addition, the EC believed that the deal between BSCA and Ryanair was not conducted in a transparent and non-discriminatory manner because

Table 7.9 Agreement between Ryanair and BSCA

Annual payment	Ryanair to BSCA (EUR)	BSCA to Ryanair (EUR)	Assumptions (EUR)
Landing fees	1,000,000		1.00 p/passenger landing fee
Handling fees	1,000,000		1.00 p/passenger handling fee
Marketing fees contribution		2,000,000	2.00 p/passenger marketing
Hotel costs		250,000	250,000 p/year hotel costs
New route payment		1,920,000	160,000 p/new route payment
Recruitment payment		768,000	768,000 one-off recruitment payment
Office costs		250,000	250,000 p/year office costs
Hangar costs		250,000	250,000 p/year hangar costs
Total	2,000,000	5,438,000	
Net benefit to Ryanair		3,438,000	

Source: adapted from Aviation Strategy (2001)

Note: Traffic assumptions: Ryanair to provide 12 new routes with 1 million passengers per year

the same deal was not made available to other airlines. As a result Ryanair was ordered to repay some of the state aid it had received (see EC, 2004).

As a result of its investigation into the BSCA/Ryanair agreement, as well as EC investigations into incentives offered by other public airports to airlines, the EC issued guidelines on the financing of regional airports and state aid that can be offered to airlines (see Table 7.10). The guidelines only apply to publicly owned airports: privately owned airports are free to offer any incentives they choose. It is also worth noting that they are only guidelines, not law. There have been cases where decisions made by the EC have been overruled. For instance, the EC decision on the BSCA/Ryanair agreement was annulled by the European Court of First Instance (CFI) in 2008 (see CFI, 2008). The EC's guidelines are currently under review, but they still indicate the EC's interpretation of the law when investigating state aid cases at airports; regional airports are therefore advised to continue to follow the guidelines until the review process has been completed.

Similar issues outside Europe have resulted in states issuing their own guidance on how airport incentives can be offered. For instance, the US FAA has published an *Air Carrier Incentive Program Guidebook: A Reference for Airport Sponsors* (FAA, 2010). The guidance distinguishes between subsidies and incentives: subsidies such as direct payments of airport revenue to a carrier or to any provider of goods or services to that carrier in exchange for additional service by the carrier are not allowed; incentives such as fee reductions, fee waivers, or use of airport revenue for acceptable promotional costs where the purpose is to encourage an air carrier to increase service at the airport are allowed. In addition, the guidance distinguishes between airport and destination marketing, where airport revenue may be used to cover the full costs of activities directed at promoting competition at an airport; public and industry awareness of airport facilities and services; new air service and competition at the airport (other than direct subsidy); and a share of promotional expenses such as marketing, advertising and related activities designed to

> **Table 7.10** Summary of EC guidelines on airport start-up aid

Recommended criteria for airport start-up aid

- Regional airports with an annual passenger volume of less than five million passengers.
- Applies only to the opening of new routes or schedules.
- Not permitted when the new air route is already being operated by a high speed rail service.
- Must be strictly linked to the additional start-up costs for the new route or schedule.
- Aid must diminish over a maximum of three years (five years for disadvantaged regions).
- Must not exceed 30 per cent of total eligible costs on average, and 50 per cent in any particular year (40 per cent on average, and 50 per cent in any particular year for disadvantaged regions).
- Aid must be linked to the net development of the number of passengers transported.
- Must be non-discriminatory (made public in good time and with adequate publicity).

Source: adapted from EC (2005)

increase travel using the airport. Airport revenue may not be used to cover destination or tourism marketing; any activities, materials or expenses for general economic development and not related to the airport; or marketing or promotional activities unrelated to airports or airport systems (FAA, 2010).

The use of incentive schemes by airports has increased dramatically in recent years and they are now fairly commonplace, especially where airline competition and the concentration of LCCs is particular high. Malina *et al.* (2011) found that 63 per cent of Europe's 200 largest airports offer incentives of some kind to airlines, whether through an official incentive scheme or through airport–airline or government–airline agreements. Similarly, a survey of 52 airports in the US found that 65 per cent of airports offer incentive schemes or agreements for domestic air services and 48 per cent for international ones (Hargrove, 2010).

Objectives for incentive schemes vary, and are likely to depend on an airport's business strategy and economic situation. Fichert and Klophaus (2011) identify five main objectives: to minimise losses at underutilised airports by increasing traffic and revenues; to improve the traffic mix at capacity-constrained airports (e.g. by targeting business or long-haul passengers); to generate additional non-aeronautical revenue from increasing passenger numbers, especially at airports with regulated charges under a dual till regime; to enhance the attractiveness of the region and contribute to regional economic development; and to expand airport-based aircraft versus foot-loose services that might be easily moved to another airport. They also classify airport incentive schemes according to two main categories: those introduced within an established charging system, and separate schemes introduced in addition to an established scheme. Those set up within an established charging system focus largely on providing incentives through the way different elements of an established system are designed and weighted. For instance, a reduced PSC for transfer passengers is used at Amsterdam Schiphol Airport, Frankfurt Airport, Vienna Airport and Tallinn Airport on the basis that airports experience a lower cost of processing such passengers because there is no need for them to check in. The transfer incentive at Vienna Airport amounts to a rebate to airlines of EUR 8.21 per departing passenger. Tallinn Airport provides a 100 per cent discount of the PSC for transit and transfer passengers.

A number of airports (e.g. in the Middle East) offer a one-stop-shop approach that offers discounted charges to airlines agreeing a single contract for all ground handling services, which is possible when all the facilities and services are provided by one company. Another example mentioned earlier in this chapter is the trend to focus on passenger- versus aircraft-related charges. The main aim is to reduce risk for the airport. It may also benefit airlines with a low load factor such as those focused on providing business-orientated services (Fichert and Klophaus, 2011).

Some airports give airlines a choice in how they want to be charged. Scheduled year-round traffic at Karlsruhe/Baden-Baden Airport can chose between two alternatives: a landing charge based on aircraft MTOW and a PSC per departing passenger; or a PSC per departing passenger and aircraft seat capacity.

The main focus of this chapter is on separate incentives rather than those introduced within an established charging system. There are generally three main types: discounted user charges, risk-sharing arrangements (normally by way of guarantees from the local community to provide money or seats on a new or changed service for a limited period of time) or direct payments (e.g. to support the marketing of a new or changed route). The last of these is commonly referred to as marketing support. Airports also use RDFs (introduced in Chapter 2) and aim to develop routes that have wider economic benefits for a region.

7.5.2 Types of incentive

Discounted user charges are arguably the most common form of incentive. They typically aim to encourage new or existing airlines to enter new markets, to increase volume or value on new or existing routes (e.g. by improving frequency or capacity, the timing of flights, traffic mix or by enhanced promotional activities), or to promote greater use of airport infrastructure and services, which is sometimes encouraged using based aircraft incentives such as reduced parking charges for airlines that base their aircraft at the airport. In addition to increased use of airport facilities and services, this encourages loyalty as an airline may be more committed to develop air services at a base airport.

The level of discount typically diminishes over a set period of time and as the new route – or change to a service or base – becomes more established. The key principle behind offering a discount is that it demonstrates the airport's willingness to share in the high start-up costs and risks associated with the development of air services. Discounts are typically on aircraft-related charges (e.g. landing, parking or handling), passenger-related charges (e.g. PSC or security) or both. Duration of the discount varies, although they are normally for three to five years. The level of discount also varies, sometimes from as high as 100 per cent during the first year of the discount period to as low as 10 per cent during the last year. Discounts may also be offered as a rebate or bonus if they are focused on retrospective measures, such as with growth or increased transfer traffic relative to the previous year. Examples of airport incentive schemes offering discounted user charges are provided in Table 7.11.

Risk-sharing arrangements are also used by airports, especially in the US, where airports sometimes offer revenue guarantees (where the public and private sectors raise money to offer airlines a guarantee to cover the costs associated with starting a new or changed route) or establish so-called 'travel banks' (where the public and private sectors guarantee booking a minimum number of seats with an airline during the start-up or change to the service). Both schemes will be time-limited.

Travel banks do not have a direct cost to the airport but it will need to administer and coordinate the travel bank, including persuading organisations, companies or individuals to commit. This can be a significant drain on airport resources. It can, however, be more effective than

> **Table 7.11** Example airport incentive schemes offering discounts, as of 2012

Airport	Incentive and nature of the discount
Avinor (46 airports)	*New intercontinental routes:* 3-year discount of 100%, 75%, 50% on take-off charges and 75%, 50%, 25% on passenger charges *Other new routes:* 3-year discount of 100%, 75%, 50% on take-off charges and 40%, 30%, 20% on passenger charges *Growth:* bonus of NOK 25 (international) and NOK 12.50 (domestic) p/passenger over the previous year
Copenhagen Airport	*New routes:* Up to 5-year discount 80–100%, 70–90%, 60–80%, 20–40%, 10–20% take-off fee depending on MTOW. Up to 5-year discount 80–90%, 60–70%, 40–50%, 20–30%, 10–20% passenger fee depending on number of passengers
Dublin Airport Authority (DAA) (Dublin, Shannon, Cork)	*New long-haul year-round routes:* 5-year discount 100%, 90%, 75%, 50%, 25% on passenger, parking, airbridge and movement fees *New short-haul year-round routes:* 3-year discount 100%, 75%, 50% on passenger, parking, airbridge and movement fees *New short-haul seasonal routes:* 3-year discount 60%, 40%, 20% on passenger, parking, airbridge and movement fees *Growth:* when total traffic exceeds the previous year, airlines are rebated the PSC p/passenger in excess of that amount, according to their contribution *Transfer (Dublin only):* 5-year bonus EUR 6, EUR 6, EUR 4, EUR 4, EUR 2 p/transfer passenger *Standby aircraft:* waived parking fee p/aircraft on a standby aircraft stand
Don Mueang International Airport	*New international charter routes:* 3-year discount 95%, 95%, 95% on landing and parking fees, and a rebate of THB 120 p/passenger *Growth on existing charter routes:* bonus of THB 120 p/passenger over the previous year
Hong Kong International Airport	*New routes:* 1-year rebate on landing charges (75% months 1–6, 25% months 7–9, 25% months 10–12)
Incheon International Airport	*New route:* 3-year discount 100%, 75%, 50% on landing fees *Increased frequency:* 3-year discount 50% on landing fees *Night flight (23:00–05:00):* 3-year discount 25% on landing fees
Macau International Airport	*New long-haul routes:* 2-year discount 50%, 50% on landing and passenger fees *New regional routes:* 2-year discount 50%, 25% on landing fee and 40% passenger fee

Table 7.11 continued	

Airport	Incentive and nature of the discount
	Growth: 1-year discount 50% on passenger fees for each passenger over the previous year
Niagra Falls International Airport	*New routes:* 12–24-month waiver of landing fee depending on the destination
	New airlines: 12-month waiver of landing, terminal use and apron parking fees
Phoenix Sky Harbor International Airport	*New intercontinental routes:* 12-month waiver of landing fee
	New Americas routes: 6-month waiver of landing fee
Prague Airport	*New short-and medium-haul routes:* 4-year discount 95%, 75%, 50%, 25% on landing fee
	New long-haul routes: 5-year discount 95%, 95%, 95%, 75%, 50% on landing fee
	Increased frequency: 2-year discount 75%, 50% on landing fee
	New cargo destination: 2-year discount 50%, 25% on landing fee
	Off-peak times: discount 50% on landing fee

Source: compiled by the authors from various sources

Note: criteria for qualifying routes are not mentioned

offering discounted charges or revenue guarantees because it indicates local support through a quantified level of financial commitment. Some travel banks are binding, meaning that pledges made for a specified air service will need to be honoured if the air service is then operated. Other travel banks are non-binding and therefore offer less guarantee of local support if the air service is operated.

There are many reasons why the public and private sectors may want to support ASD at their local airport and share in the risk of developing air services. Securing connectivity for their region is likely to be the main reason, especially in less central regions where local residents, businesses and other organisations are likely to be more reliant on air transport. The airport can provide opportunities for local residents to travel for business, holiday and leisure, and to visit friends and family, as well as acting as a key location factor (e.g. for attracting and retaining skilled labour). It can also be important for businesses that rely on air transport for the movement of goods and services: airports with good air services may act as a key location factor for businesses, and may influence their decision to invest in a particular region.

Youngstown-Warren Regional Airport launched its travel bank air service initiative in 2012. Its aim is to assist the return of a regular scheduled commercial air service to a hub of a major US airline. The airport has not had such a service since 2003. The travel bank is a list of non-binding pledges made by local businesses, large employers and individuals, stating what each will spend annually on a new air service. It helps quantify local demand and sends a strong message to airlines that the community will support a daily air service. The total pledge goal is USD 3–5 million. In addition, the airport and community received a USD 780,000 grant from the US

Department of Transportation to be used as an airline revenue guarantee (Youngstown-Warren Regional Airport, 2012).

Another way airports are known to offer incentives is through providing direct payments. Market-specific advertising and promotion is central to creating awareness and generating demand for a new or changed service and, given the degree to which airlines are seeking to reduce costs, direct payments of marketing support, along with discounted user charges during the start-up phase of a new or changed route, are likely to have the greatest impact on airline decision-making.

Some airports have been known to develop advertising and promotional campaigns in collaboration with the public and private sectors in order to generate demand for services at their airport (examples are provided in Chapter 8). However, it is important to note that airports are a derived demand. This means that instead of conducting their own advertising and promotional campaigns, it may be more effective for them to offer marketing support for campaigns to be delivered by airlines and tour operators because they will have a stronger level of brand recognition among passengers and may be able to penetrate markets more effectively than airports through aggressive marketing campaigns for specific routes.

Marketing support schemes used by airports often involve providing airlines with a one-off grant to be spent on the advertising and promotion of new routes or other activities connected with route development. Some airports offer a grant that diminishes over time. The size of the grant normally depends on the pot of money the airport has available and the applications it receives for that pot; it will also depend on an assessment of the estimated impact the marketing activity will have (e.g. on airport traffic or profit). The size of the grant may also vary according to factors such as route destination and frequency, offering larger grants to activities that most support the airport's marketing objectives.

Table 7.12 Phoenix Sky Harbor International Airport marketing support, 2012

Frequency	Qualifying intercontinental routes	Qualifying Central and South American routes	Qualifying North American routes (Canada and Mexico)
3 weekly round-trips	Months 1–12: USD 600,000 Months 12–24: USD 300,000	Months 1–12: USD 500,000	Months 1–12: USD 300,000
4 weekly round-trips	Months 1–12: USD 700,000 Months 12–24: USD 400,000	Months 1–12: USD 600,000	Months 1–12: USD 400,000
5+ weekly round-trips	Months 1–12: USD 1 million Months 12–24: USD 500,000	Months 1–12: USD 700,000	Months 1–12: USD 500,000

Source: adapted from Phoenix Sky Harbor International Airport (2012)

Avinor offers marketing support in connection with new routes or other special activities. The one-time grant must not exceed 50 per cent of the direct costs of the project, and the size of the grant is assessed in relation to the estimated effect on factors such as traffic volume, profit and other types of services. Phoenix Sky Harbor International Airport offers marketing support assessed in relation to the number of weekly round-trips on the route and the destination served, for either 12 or 24 months. In the case of a 24-month period, the size of the grant diminishes over time (see Table 7.12).

7.5.3 RDFs

Most airports are focused on developing air services that generate revenue, meaning that airport-specific incentives – with the exception of risk-sharing arrangements – may not always target routes that have a wider economic benefit to the region. As a result, some airports have become involved in RDFs. These are based on a partnership approach involving the public sector (e.g. regional administrations, development agencies and tourism authorities), airlines and airports. The aim is to encourage new year-round air services that improve business connectivity and inbound tourism, thus focusing on regional economic development. The collaborative approach of RDFs allows for the pooling of resources and reduced start-up risk to an airline, but also allows the public sector to influence the type of services attracted to their region. They were initially a UK initiative, used to develop air services in Scotland and Northern Ireland.

The Scottish RDF was established in 2002 by the Scottish government through its economic development agency, Scottish Enterprise. Before this, the majority of international traffic to Scotland was routed through hub airports such as London Heathrow, and only 17 scheduled international destinations had been served from Scottish airports in any year between 1989 and 2002. After the RDF was implemented, 11 new scheduled international services were added between January 2003 and November 2004, supported by a budget of GBP 6.8 million spread over three years. By January 2008, 35 routes were supported by the Scottish RDF.

RDFs have been credited with stimulating new routes with wider economic benefits to their region (e.g. see Christodoulou *et al.*, 2009; Scott Wilson, 2009); however, their effectiveness is sometimes questioned because a number of routes end up being seasonal rather than year-round, or are discontinued after the funding period has expired (Pagliari, 2005). In addition, EC guidelines on financing of airports and start-up aid to airlines departing from regional airports (see EC, 2005) have restricted RDFs; as a result, Scottish Enterprise stopped its RDF in 2007.

RDFs are still being used at other airports. Avinor is involved in an RDF to increase visitors from abroad to regions served by any of their 46 airports in Norway, participates – together with other organisations – in setting up RDFs locally, and may provide support in planning and setting up during the establishment phase. Avinor may also offer a direct one-off grant of up to 50 per cent of the direct cost of the establishment phase.

It is important to note that incentives and other support mechanisms should have a measurable benefit for the airport and/or the region it serves. STRAIR (2005) provides useful guidance on how to plan an airport incentive strategy prior to contacting a potential airline. The starting point is to establish specific cases where the market fails by not providing adequate air services but where incentives are likely to act as a successful stimulant. An assessment of route opportunities is then needed, using both quantitative and qualitative indicators that measure the risk of the airline ceasing to operate the route (e.g. after the funding period has expired), the benefits to businesses and consumers in terms of time savings and convenience (including social impacts), the impact of additional net tourist expenditure in the region, the direct employment generated (e.g. at the airline and airport), and an evaluation of any negative environmental impacts such as noise and emissions. Airports and local stakeholders can then compare any opportunities according to their marketing objectives and underlying economic and social priorities.

References

ACI (2006) *Airport Economics Survey 2005*, Montreal: ACI.

ACI (2007) *ACI Position Brief: The Airport Business*, Montreal: ACI.

ACI (2010) *Airport Economics Survey 2010*, Montreal: ACI.

ACI (2011) *Airport Economics Survey 2011*, Montreal: ACI.

Aviation Strategy (2001) 'Ryanair, just too good a negotiator', *Aviation Strategy*, 46(July-August); 3.

BSCA (2012) *Airport Charges: Regular/Charter Flights*, Charleroi: BSCA.

CAR (2012) *Groundhandling – the Commission's role*, Dublin: CAR. Online. Available at: http://www.aviationreg.ie/licensing/groundhandling-the-commissions-role.139.html (accessed 25 September 2012).

CFI (2008) *Judgement of the Court of First Instance: State Aid – Agreements Entered into by the Walloon Region and the Brussels South Charleroi Airport with the Airline Ryanair – Existence of an Economic Advantage – Application of the Private Investor in a Market Economy Test*, Case T196/04, 17 December, Brussels: CFI.

Christodoulou, G., Smyth, A. and Dennis, N. (2009) 'The Route Development Fund (RDF) – can we sustain air transport in the regions?' in *European Transport Conference Proceedings*, London: Association for European Transport.

EC (1996) *Council Directive 96/67/EC of 15 October 1996 on Access to the Groundhandling Market at Community Airports*, Official Journal L 272, 25 October, Brussels: EC.

EC (2004) *2004/393/EC: Commission Decision of 12 February 2004 Concerning Advantages Granted by the Walloon Region and Brussels South Charleroi Airport to the Airline Ryanair in Connection with its Establishment at Charleroi*, Official Journal L 137, 30 April, Brussels: EC.

EC (2005) *Community Guidelines on Financing of Airports and Start-up Aid to Airlines Departing from Regional Airports (2005/C 312/01)*, Official Journal C 312, 9 December, Brussels: EC.

EC (2009) *Directive 2009/12/EC of the European Parliament and of the Council of 11 March 2009 on Airport Charges*, Official Journal L 070, 14 March, Brussels: EC.

FAA (2010) *Air Carrier Incentive Program Guidebook: A Reference for Airport Sponsors*, Washington, DC: FAA.

FAA (2012) *Passenger Facility Charge (PFC) Program: Airports*, Washington, DC: FAA. Online. Available at: http://www.faa.gov/airports/pfc/ (accessed 1 October 2012).

Fichert, F. and Klophaus, R. (2011) 'Incentive schemes on airport charges – theoretical analysis and empirical evidence from German airports', *Journal of Air Transport Management*, 1(1); 71–9.

Graham, A. (2008) *Managing Airports: An International Perspective*, 3rd edn, London: Butterworth-Heinemann.

Hargrove, M.R. (2010) 'Airport incentive programs: legal and regulatory considerations in structuring programs and recent survey observations', presented at *2010 ACI North America Airport Economics and Finance Conference*, Miami, May 2010.

ICAO (2012) *ICAO's Policies on Charges for Airports and Air Navigation Services – Doc 9082*, 9th edn, Quebec: ICAO.

Jossart, L. (2004) 'The airport relationship with low cost carriers', presented at *University of*

Westminster/Cranfield University Airport Economics and Finance Symposium, London, April 2004.

Kenya Airports Authority (2012) *Nairobi – Jomo Kenyatta International Airport: Aeronautical Fees*, Nairobi: Kenya Airports Authority.

Kotler, P., Wong, V., Saunders, J. and Armstrong, G. (2008) *Principles of Marketing*, 5th European edn, Harlow: Prentice Hall-Pearson Education.

Macau International Airport (2012) *Airport Charges: Aircraft Parking Fees*, Macau: Macau International Airport.

Malaysia Airports (2012) *Passenger Service Charge (PSC)*, Sepang: Malaysia Airports.

Malina, R., Albers, S. and Kroll, N. (2011) *Airport Incentive Programs: A European Perspective*, Working Paper 107 of the Department of Business Policy and Logistics, Cologne: University of Cologne.

Manchester Airport (2012) *Manchester Airport plc: Schedule of Charges and Terms and Conditions of Use, 1 April 2012 to 31 March 2013*, Manchester: Manchester Airport.

Miami-Dade Aviation Department (2012) *Fees, Rates, & Charges FY 2011–12*, Miami: Miami-Dade Aviation Department.

Moodie, M. (2012) *Four bidders line up as Guam travel retail tender is extended*, Brentford: The Moodie Report. Online. Available at: http://www.moodiereport.com/document.php?c_id=1123&doc_id=32434 (accessed 3 October 2012).

Pagliari, R. (2005) 'Developments in the supply of direct international air services from airports in Scotland', *Journal of Air Transport Management*, 11(4); 249–57.

Phoenix Sky Harbor International Airport (2012) *International Air Service Development Program: Phoenix Sky Harbor International Airport*, Phoenix: City of Phoenix.

Riga International Airport (2012) *Security charge*, Riga: Riga International Airport. Online. Available at: http://www.riga-airport.com/en/main/passengers/useful-information/aviation-security-requirements/security-charge (accessed 27 September 2012).

Ryanair (2012) *Ryanair cuts Madrid and Barcelona flights in response to Spanish Govt tax increases*, Dublin: Ryanair News. Online. Available at: http://www.ryanair.com/en/news/ryanair-cuts-madrid-and-barcelona-flights-in-response-to-spanish-govt-tax-increases (accessed 1 October 2012).

Saounatsos, G. (2007) 'Airport charges', *Airports International*, 40(8); 55–9.

Scott Wilson (2009) *Evaluation of the Scottish Air Route Development Fund*, Glasgow: Scott Wilson.

STRAIR (2005) *Air Service Development for Regional Agencies: Strategy, Best Practice and Results*, STRAIR.

Tallinn Airport (2012) *Ground Handling Fees in Tallinn Airport*, Tallinn: Tallinn Airport.

Youngstown-Warren Regional Airport (2012) *YNG will get you there*, Vienna, OH: Youngstown-Warren Regional Airport. Online. Available at: http://yngtravelbank.com/travelbank (accessed 21 September 2012).

Chapter 8

Promotion of airports

This chapter considers the promotion of airports, discussing the range of marketing communications tools used by airports (known collectively as the promotional mix) together with industry examples, and advantages and disadvantages of each tool. It also looks at the changing landscape for marketing communications, and factors that airports subsequently need to consider when developing an integrated and effective approach to marketing communications.

8.1 The promotional mix

Airports need to be effective in communicating to existing or potential customers meaningful messages that allow them to create, develop and maintain relationships, and subsequently pursue their marketing objectives. This can be achieved using a blend of tools known collectively as the promotional mix (see Figure 8.1).

8.1.1 Advertising

Advertising is used extensively by airports to create awareness and communicate certain messages to target markets. It can be carried out by producing general publicity information (e.g. advertisements, information leaflets, stickers and t-shirts) or advertising in a range of media (e.g. print, radio, television, outdoor and electronic media). Some airports use sponsorship as a means of advertising. For example, Castellón Airport adopted a policy of promoting itself and the province of Castellón through sponsoring provincial sports figures such as former motorcycle rider Álex Debón, sports infrastructure for the local community, clubs such as Villarreal Football Club (see Figure 8.2), and competitions such as the Castelló Masters Golf tournament. Castellón Airport's sponsorship has been somewhat controversial, however. The airport cost EUR 150 million to construct. It opened in 2011 as part of the grand vision of regional politicians to attract 600,000 passengers a year and turn the Costa del Azahar region of Spain into a major destination for tourism. After spending approximately EUR 30 million on promoting the airport, including EUR 2.5 million on the sponsorship of Villareal Football Club alone (Jones, 2012), the airport had not been granted permission to operate flights or found an airline that was interested in doing so by the end of 2012. This is a dramatic example of the need to target realistic and customer-orientated marketing objectives when designing the promotional strategy for an airport, let alone funding the construction of a new airport.

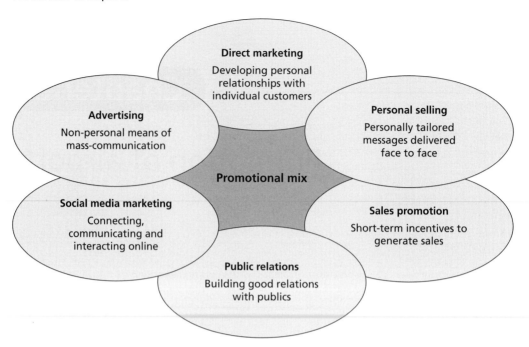

Figure 8.1 The promotional mix
Source: compiled by the authors

Figure 8.2 Castellón Airport sponsorship of Villarreal Football Club
Source: courtesy of Subside Sports

Airports are also known to sponsor local community events and the arts, although this may be viewed more as public relations than advertising. In past years, London City Airport, in association with the London Borough of Newham, has invited residents living locally to the airport to submit artwork for their annual art awards. The event has normally been based on a theme of some kind. The theme in 2009 was health, sport and fitness, which was in line with the airport's focus on promoting health and well-being in the community. Artwork has typically remained on display in the airport terminal for a set period of time so that it can be viewed by users of the airport. In 2009, the winners received cash prizes of GBP 500, 300 and 200 for first, second and third place. Three runners up were selected as 'highly commended' and were awarded signed football memorabilia courtesy of West Ham United Football Club.

As discussed in Chapter 6, airports often use catchy slogans better known as straplines in an advertising context; these aim to deliver key messages about the airport. For example, Fort Smith Regional Airport ran an advertising campaign in 2012 called 'Simply Fly Fort Smith'. The campaign focused on how easy it is to get to and through the airport without having to endure hours of driving or crowds and queues. A series of advertisements used included straplines: 'You're practically Wait-less', 'Easy Come, Easy Go', 'Leave the Navigation' and 'Leave the Road Trip' (see Figure 8.3).

Birmingham Airport launched an interesting 'David and Goliath' advertising campaign during 2012 that aimed to claw back passengers travelling from the airport's catchment area to take flights from airports outside the region, especially from London Heathrow Airport. Adverts located at key sites on motorways and at rail stations included straplines such as 'Heathrow:

Figure 8.3 Fort Smith Regional Airport 'Simply Fly Fort Smith' campaign
Source: courtesy of Fort Smith Regional Airport

congestion ahead', 'Going in the right direction?' 'Occasionally in business a U-turn is the way forward' and 'Take your business in a new direction'. Adverts also used the strapline 'Birmingham makes more sense than Heathrow'.

Advertising is an effective means of reaching a mass audience and the visual nature of advertising allows customers to compare one airport's message with that of another. It can be used in support of a range of marketing objectives with a short- or long-term focus, and advertisements can be one-off or repeated over time. Many forms of advertising are expressive, allowing airports to bring their messages to life. Companies using mass-media forms of advertising such as commercials on national television may benefit from a kind of prestige, whereby viewers feel that if the company can afford to use such media it must be a large, popular and successful company with legitimate products or services (Armstrong and Kotler, 2007). The extent to which airports derive such benefits, however, is uncertain.

There are a number of affordable approaches to advertising such as using give-aways, stickers, t-shirts and promotional literature. In addition, the cost of using mass-media forms of advertising such as print, radio and television has declined in recent years as the range of media and choice available to users has widened (e.g. with the introduction of satellite television and online media). Halpern and Niskala (2008) provide the example of Pajala-Ylläs Airport, which has developed innovative and affordable forms of advertising to target inbound tour operators. The airport has produced a range of publicity information about the infrastructure and services available and tourism activities in the region, as well as various give-aways such as airport stickers and t-shirts. It has also produced a double-sided card (see Figure 8.4), the front of which emphasises the 'Smooth and low-cost landings' available at the airport and its location in the tourist destination

Figure 8.4 Promotional leaflet used by Pajala-Ylläs Airport
Source: courtesy of Tornedalenmedia.com and Pajala-Ylläs Airport

of Lapland. The winter wonderland depicted in the picture further emphasises the tourism potential of the region. The back of the card illustrates the close proximity of the airport to the mountain resort of Ylläs in Finland and emphasises the infrastructure and services available at the airport, providing the contact details of the airport manager. The airport has also produced advertisements and an airport video, and has been represented at a number of aviation conferences and travel trade exhibitions. Advertising often uses the strapline 'Your next destination in Lapland'.

In response to concerns that government ministers are not using airports and air travel to boost the UK economy, London Heathrow Airport rolled out an advertising campaign in October 2011 both in the national press and with posters along the walls of London's Westminster underground station (to target ministers travelling to or from work). This used the slogans: 'Only Heathrow brings growth to our doorstep', 'Nothing grows without routes' and 'Right now, no island can afford to be an island' and cost an estimated GBP 100,000. Although affordable options can be used, advertising – especially when using mass-media – can be an expensive option that only larger airports can afford. Many airports advertise in trade magazines such as *Airline Business*, where a one-page colour advertisement costs EUR 11,285 (2011 display rates). This is a more affordable option than mass-media campaigns, but is still likely to exceed the budget of smaller airports.

In addition to being expensive, advertising can be impersonal, consist of one-way communication, and lack persuasiveness (Armstrong and Kotler, 2007). It only communicates general messages to a general audience, meaning that it is less effective for campaigns targeting objectives that require a more personal approach such as route development (see Chapter 4), where potential or existing customers will be interested in specific messages such as about the airport's catchment area, potential for demand, and infrastructure and services.

8.1.2 Direct marketing

Direct marketing is a form of advertising that allows airports to communicate directly with their customers in a fairly targeted, customised and interactive manner. It helps to develop personal relationships and is potentially quick to develop and deliver (Armstrong and Kotler, 2007). Traditionally, companies have used telephone marketing, mail marketing (e.g. of fliers, brochures and promotional letters) or outdoor displays as forms of direct marketing. However, companies increasingly use new technologies such as mobile messaging, e-mail, interactive consumer websites and online displays. As of 2011, 10 per cent of world airports have e-newsletters: individuals can subscribe to receive these directly via e-mail by entering their e-mail address in the relevant section of the airport website (Halpern, 2012).

Most online advertising is targeted at particular groups of customers and allows companies to trace the response of users. For instance, search engine optimisation can be used to attract users to an airport website, while paid placement gives airports the opportunity to deliver advertisements to users based on their already-indicated search criteria. Airports can also use interactive display advertisements that appear on websites as static banners, pop-ups, videos or floating units. Users can click on the advertisement to respond directly to the message or to find more detailed information.

A number of service providers are driving direct marketing opportunities for airports online. For instance, anna.aero, a website dedicated to airline network news and analysis that offers airports the opportunity to advertise on the site using static banners, pop-ups, videos or floating units (see Figure 8.5 for examples of airport 'banners' on anna.aero), was launched in July 2007. By November 2010, anna.aero had a readership exceeding 80,000 monthly visits from the worldwide network planning community and a weekly 'front page' newsletter sent directly to

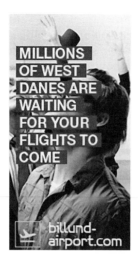

Figure 8.5 Airport banners on anna.aero, October 2012
Source: courtesy of each individual airport

the mailbox of over 35,000 subscribers (anna.aero, 2012). In addition to corporate advertising opportunities on its website, anna.aero offers airports the opportunity to advertise vacant viable air services in its online route supermarket, The Route Shop. This offers a type of paid placement: airports can place all their unserved routes and additional information (e.g. about airport infrastructure and services, catchment area or potential for demand) on The Route Shop for EUR 2,299 for six months (as of November 2012). The rationale for The Route Shop is that although airlines can find out a great deal about airports by using search engines, they are not easily able to discover which new routes airports think should be provided and, more importantly, what evidence the airport has to suggest that a particular route should be operated. Airports are able to provide such information on The Route Shop, which had over 40,000 visits and 100,000 page views in February 2010 (The Route Shop, 2012) and, as of November 2012, listed 3,381 unserved routes at airports in 51 countries worldwide.

A similar initiative to The Route Shop, called Route Exchange, was launched by Routesonline. Route Exchange is an online trading zone for new routes that provides airports with access to airline RFPs via an 'airline requirements' page on the website. Individual airlines specify criteria on how an airport should approach a new air service agreement, detail target markets, and outline essential data and support requirements. It provides airports with a secure platform to deliver their new route proposal directly to the airline network planning team who have produced the RFP. Airlines also have direct access to the profiles of airports on Route Exchange where full airport intelligence is available, new contacts can be made, and new air service dialogue can begin. As of the end of November 2012, Route Exchange had 192 listed airlines and 205 listed airports.

8.1.3 Personal selling

Methods of direct marketing can be used to target a specific audience, but are still only likely to convey fairly general messages. Personal selling offers a more effective means of communicating specific messages directly with target markets. Personal selling involves a certain degree of personal interaction; this allows marketers to read and respond to body language, and subsequently generate a better reaction from customers (Armstrong and Kotler, 2007). It can also encourage a deeper relationship between airports and their customers. Personal selling is increasingly used by airports seeking to develop new or existing routes because it is an effective means of communicating directly with operators of air services.

As mentioned in Chapter 1, ASM (2009) found that 94 per cent of airports worldwide actively market their airport to airlines, and that methods involving personal selling are those most commonly used. Attending trade shows and exhibitions is useful when targeting tour operators; however, the most effective method for airports pursuing route development as a marketing objective is likely to be the sales presentation, known in the aviation industry as the airline presentation. The airline presentation provides specific airlines with a detailed analysis of the potential for a particular route. This can then be supplemented with additional information on the catchment area, potential for demand, and infrastructure and services available at the airport and in the region in general. The analysis therefore needs to be based on sound market research in order to make a convincing case. It also needs to be realistic: exaggerated claims about route potential will only lose the trust of target markets and may affect an airport's ability to develop future air services.

Airline presentations are often delivered while meeting with airlines in their offices or at the airport. One development during the last decade or so that has experienced rapid growth in recent years and supports increased use of personal selling, however, is route development forums. They are a type of speed dating for airports and operators of air services, providing networking opportunities through one-to-one meetings. During the meetings, airports typically use market research to demonstrate opportunities for new routes or expanding services at the airport. One of the earliest examples is Routes – The World Route Development Forum, founded in 1995 and held each year, along with region-specific events such as Routes Regional Americas, Routes Regional Asia, Routes Regional Europe and Routes Regional Africa. Members of ACI North America launched a similar event called the JumpStart Air Service Development Program in 1997, which is held each year in North America. French Connect was launched in 2004 and is held each year in different locations in Europe; the Tourism and Air Services Summit was launched in 2008 and is held each year, co-located with Routes as of 2010.

Registration fees for route development forums are fairly reasonable, especially compared to the cost of advertising. To register for Routes 2012, airports were required to pay a fee relative to the size of the airport and the number of meetings the airport wanted to have. Airports with up to one million passengers per annum paid GBP 1,195 for up to eight meetings, those with one to four million passengers per annum paid GBP 2,095 for up to nine meetings, and those with four million or more passengers per annum paid GBP 2,595 for up to ten meetings. Airports were able to pay additional fees for additional meetings and separate fees were available for cargo airports, commercial suppliers, consultants, economic development agencies and tourism authorities. Airlines were not required to pay a registration fee.

Although registration fees for events such as Routes are fairly reasonable, the total cost associated with personal selling can be high due to the needs associated with using a sales force. Recruitment and training, staff travel and investment in research and development come at a cost, and while budgets for staff travel can be reduced at relatively short notice, a large proportion of the costs associated with personal selling are not escapable in the short term. Personal selling also tends to be a long-term commitment because of the time and effort that goes into each sale and any after-sales service.

Figure 8.6 Swedavia World Routes advertisement
Source: courtesy of Swedavia

Of course, airports may not only attend trade shows, exhibitions and route development forums but go for a more visible presence by being an exhibitor at such events. This offers the opportunity to showcase the airport and distribute more general publicity information in addition to conducting personal selling. General publicity information may be used before (e.g. to raise awareness for the airport and its attendance as an exhibitor at the event) or during the event (e.g. with various adverts, videos, leaflets, brochures and give-aways). Swedavia, operator of 11 airports in Sweden, actively promoted its attendance as an exhibitor at World Routes 2012 with its 'Hello, I'm Sweden' campaign. The advert in Figure 8.6 is one of a number that formed part of the campaign and could be seen in print and online versions of *Routes News: The World Air Service Development Magazine*, the *anna.aero Newsletter* and *Airlines International Magazine*. The adverts could also be seen online at routesonline.com, routes-news.com and anna.aero around the time of World Routes 2012, held in Abu Dhabi from 29 September to 2 October. The concept was launched in August 2012 and continued during 2012 after World Routes, maintaining a visible presence in more or less the same media. The 'Hello, I'm Sweden' concept was also visible on the Swedavia website, swedavia.se. As an airport group located all over Sweden, Swedavia wanted to use the perspective of Sweden rather than highlighting specific airports in the group, hence the references to Sweden in the text and the range of airports represented by hearts on the map. Adverts such as the one in Figure 8.6 draw attention to the market potential in Sweden and the strength of Sweden and Swedavia as brands. It also personalises the strong messages in a playful way.

8.1.4 Sales promotion

Sales promotion typically includes point-of-purchase displays, premiums, discounts, coupons, competitions, speciality advertising and demonstrations. It can be used to attract the attention of potential customers and provide them with information and incentives that encourage a purchase, often inviting and rewarding a fast response. It is able to dramatise product or service offers and boost sales (Armstrong and Kotler, 2007).

Sales promotion is used extensively by airports to boost sales in non-aeronautical parts of their business such as retail. Duty free shopping at airports is a type of sales promotion based on a permanent incentive because products are generally offered at lower prices than are available downtown. However, sales promotion really refers to short-term incentives designed specifically to generate sales during a limited period of time.

Singapore Changi Airport launched a '2×7%' promotional campaign recently that offered both long-term and short-term incentives to boost sales at over 40 participating retail outlets in the airport (see Figure 8.7). The airport absorbs 7 per cent goods and services tax for purchases in the airport all year round, but between August and September 2012 it offered airport users (whether flying or not) an additional 7 per cent off, with no minimum spend required. Similarly, Fraport launched a sales promotion at Frankfurt Airport in partnership with travel retailer Gebr Heinemann and airline Lufthansa that ran from July to December 2009. Lufthansa passengers received a gold coin worth two Euros when checking in or using a Lufthansa ticket counter or lounge. The coins could be used towards purchases in any of the 23 duty free stores at the airport with no minimum spend requirement. The campaign's marketing objectives were two-fold: first, to offer a shopping advantage for passengers and therefore generate more customers for the duty free shops; second, to honour and strengthen the close partnership with its largest airline customer, Lufthansa. Gebr Heinemann, which operates the duty free stores at Frankfurt Airport, absorbed the cost of the discounts.

Sales promotion is important for airports, given that airport users tend to have a much lower propensity for making impulse purchases compared to downtown shoppers, although it should be noted that this lower propensity is often debated. Dolby (2009) found that 27 per cent of

Figure 8.7 Singapore Changi Airport '2x7%' campaign
Source: courtesy of Changi Airport Group

airport purchases are made on impulse compared to 79 per cent of purchases downtown, largely because a customer's motivation for being at an airport is to travel. That traveller needs to be converted into a retail visitor and the retail visitor then needs to be converted into a retail customer: this is where sales promotion can be used to raise awareness of special offers and to stimulate a purchase. The potential value of sales promotions is significant. Topping (2010) suggests that successful promotions can generate 400 per cent growth in sales of specific products or product groups at airports, and that sales promotions can also be used across the whole retail offer of an airport or terminal building, or be activity-driven, such as in relation to major sport or cultural events.

The disadvantage of using sales promotions is that they are short lived, and therefore rarely generate long-term relationships or commitment (Armstrong and Kotler, 2007). In addition, they may not offer genuine value in the eyes of the customer, which can subsequently have a negative effect on customer trust and loyalty for the brand.

8.1.5 Public relations

The Chartered Institute of Public Relations (CIPR) defines public relations as:

> the discipline which looks after reputation, with the aim of earning understanding and support and influencing opinion and behaviour. It is the planned and sustained effort to establish and maintain goodwill and mutual understanding between an organisation and its publics.
>
> (CIPR, 2011)

Public relations is sometimes associated with the ad hoc and short-term exploitation of opportunities for free publicity. However, the CIPR definition suggests that public relations efforts should be planned and sustained, thus implying that it is a strategic, long-term commitment. This view is shared by the Aircraft Owners and Pilots Association (AOPA), which states that public relations 'is not just publicity – it involves EVERYTHING the airport is and does that addresses or affects the public interest. The best time to start a planned, positive public relations program is before you need it, probably right now' (AOPA, 2008).

Public relations should establish and maintain a mutual understanding. It is therefore dependent on dialogue that allows airports to understand both how they are perceived and what they can do to ensure that the way they are perceived matches their desired image. This is particularly important, given that many airports have significant social, economic and environmental impacts and therefore tend to provoke strong feelings – positive and negative – from a range of individuals and groups.

Most tools in the promotional mix are focused on the end-user but public relations has a much wider focus that extends to a full range of publics (publics were introduced and discussed in Chapter 2). Brassington and Pettitt (2007) identify six publics that companies may target through public relations, which are certainly relevant to airports: internal (e.g. employees, trade unions), authority (e.g. central/local government, trade associations, regulatory bodies), commercial (e.g. customers, suppliers, competitors), general (e.g. general public, community, pressure groups), financial (e.g. shareholders, investors, bankers), and the media (e.g. television and radio, national and local press, trade press).

Individuals may be a member of more than one public at a time. This means that although different messages may be used to communicate with different publics, an element of consistency should be maintained. In addition, not all publics have equal importance, and the respective levels of importance may change over time, often as a result of changes in the internal and external business environment. For instance, 'authority' publics may be most important for an airport under public ownership and control, but may be replaced by 'financial' publics if the airport changes to private ownership and control. Priorities for public relations efforts will also change over time. For instance, 'the media' may assume a greater degree of importance during times of crisis, while 'internal' publics may assume a greater degree of importance during a labour dispute. It is therefore important for airports to continually assess their public relations-related marketing objectives and the approaches they use, or intend to use, to meet those objectives.

All airports have a need for public relations. It can be used to support wider marketing objectives and promotional tools such as the launch of a new route or the introduction of a new advertising campaign. In such instances, public relations can be used to generate interest, awareness and support. It can be used to develop and maintain the image of an airport or relationships between an airport and its publics; to support customer service or staff training initiatives; and in support of crisis management, as a tactical response to unforeseen problems or incidents.

A broad range of media can be used to support public relations efforts, many of which have already been mentioned in this chapter; for instance, when discussing advertising. Airports typically use interviews or press releases (with television, radio, print or electronic media), media kits, brochures, newsletters, public speaking and announcements, featured articles and stories, awards and recognitions, events (e.g. hosting trade shows, BBQs and fundraising events such as a charity fun-run on the airport runway), sponsorship, volunteering and corporate reports (e.g. on social, environmental or financial performance). New technologies – especially social media – are being increasingly used, however, just as with other tools in the promotional mix. The medium used needs to be carefully tailored to the needs of different publics.

Public relations can be a cheap but effective means of communication. The messages can be more real and believable than those communicated using other promotional tools because they are delivered as news rather than sales-directed communication. They can be expressive, allowing companies to deliver messages that stand out and attract the attention of target markets (Armstrong and Kotler, 2007). Problems can arise, however, if any hype generated by public relations efforts is not met. A fair amount of hype surrounded London Heathrow Airport's new Terminal 5, which opened in March 2008. Public relations efforts promoted the new terminal extensively, but when the terminal opened for business problems were experienced owing to malfunctioning equipment; this resulted in overcrowding and flight delays and cancellations. The media coverage was significant and focused largely on the negative side of events that unfolded, even though the terminal became something of a success story after the initial teething problems had been resolved.

8.1.6 Social media marketing

Social media can be defined as 'the group of internet-based applications that build on the ideological and technological foundations of Web 2.0, and that allow the creation and exchange of user-generated content' (Kaplan and Haenlein, 2010: 61). This includes social and professional networking sites such as Facebook and LinkedIn, blogs such as Twitter, content communities such as YouTube and Flickr, collaborative projects such as Wikipedia, virtual social worlds such as Second Life and virtual game worlds such as World of Warcraft.

Airports have embraced social media in recent years (ACI Europe, 2011; 2012) and there are numerous examples of airports trying to attract 'fans' on Facebook, 'followers' on Twitter and LinkedIn, and 'views' on YouTube (e.g. see Figure 8.8). There is certainly a growing interest in the subject among practitioners. The role of social media was a key theme at World Routes 2011, with presentations on how social media can support airline route development at airports (Solterbeck, 2011). Nigam *et al.* (2011) discuss the role of social media in engaging customers and increasing commercial revenues at airports, and AirGate Solutions/SimpliFlying (2011) identify a number of social media initiatives used by airports to build their brands and drive customer engagement and loyalty. Passengers are typically the main focus for social media initiatives at airports, but they are also used by airports to connect, communicate, interact and share information with all publics.

Halpern (2012) investigates the use of social media at 1,559 airports worldwide. Four main categories are used by airports: social networking sites, blogs, professional business networking sites and content communities (see Table 8.1). These categories include 20 individual types of social media (see Figure 8.9), and 19 per cent of all airports use at least one type. These airports represent 52 per cent of total work load units (WLUs), which are a combined measure of passenger and cargo volume, where one passenger is equal to 100 kilogrammes of cargo. Of all airports, 13 per cent use Facebook, 12 per cent use Twitter, 7 per cent use LinkedIn and 4 per cent use YouTube. Two-thirds of airports that use social media use more than one type, and the most

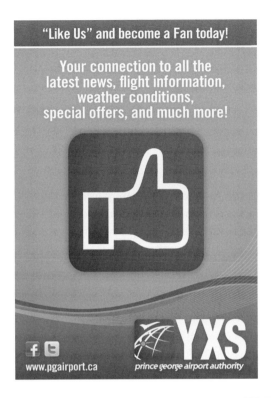

Figure 8.8 Prince George Airport advertisement for Facebook
Source: courtesy of Prince George Airport

common combination is to use both Facebook and Twitter: 75 per cent of airports that use Facebook also use Twitter. A further 9 per cent of airports, representing 13 per cent of total WLUs, belong to a group of airports that use social media even though individual airports in the group do not have their own social media networks. This includes airports operated by Avinor, AENA, Aeropuertos Argentina 2000, AdP, Infraero, Ghana Airports, and the Port Authority of New York and New Jersey. The study by Halpern (2012) is based on data collected at the end of 2010, meaning that the number of airports using social media and the range of social media they use is now likely to be much greater.

Akron-Canton Airport is one of the most active users of social media among world airports. It has direct links from its homepage to Facebook, Twitter, an airport blog, YouTube and Flickr, and then has links from Facebook to location-based social networking sites including Gowalla, Yelp, Foursquare and SCVNGR. Users of Facebook are able to view airport photos, videos and an airport route map, and can also enter competitions (e.g. win a 'Dream [shopping] spree in New York City'), book a flight and access deals such as a free airport luggage tag from the Facebook wall. The airport is also on LinkedIn. Kristie VanAuken, Senior Vice President and Chief Marketing and Communications Officer at Akron-Canton Airport blogs on a range of issues including social media. Akron-Canton Airport hosted the first ever American Association of Airport Executives (AAAE) Airport Social Media Summit on 23–25 October 2011.

Social media networking allows airports to interact with their customers and to coordinate and control various elements of the promotional mix in a traditional sense (by allowing airports

Table 8.1 Categories of social media used by airports

Categories	Brief description	Examples
Social networking	*Social networking*: online service, platform or site that allows users to develop social networks with other users who share common interests or activities	Facebook, Hyves, Google+
	Location-based networking: information or entertainment service accessed via mobile devices (e.g. to 'check in' at venues)	Yelp, Foursquare, Gowalla, SCVNGR, Qype England
Blog	*Blog*: part of a website updated with regular entries of commentary, descriptions of events, or content such as photos or video	Airport's own blog or discussion forum
	Microblog: online service, platform or site that allows users to exchange small elements of content such as short sentences or links	Twitter, Tumblr, Blip
Professional business networking	Same principle as social networking but for business-related networking	LinkedIn, XING
Content community	Online service, platform or site that allows users to share multimedia such as photos, music, videos or presentations	YouTube, Flickr, Pinterest, Instagram, Scribd, ISSUU, Podcast, Internet TV

Source: adapted from Halpern (2012)

to communicate with customers) but also in a non-traditional sense (by allowing customers to interact with the airport and with each other). In this respect, social media are a kind of hybrid element of the promotional mix (e.g. see Mangold and Foulds, 2009).

ACI Europe (2011) provides a useful classification, including examples from industry that cover most types of use by airports: customer service (as a virtual 'customer service desk'), informal relationship building (to engage directly with customers), crisis handling (to communicate quickly and directly during times of crisis), corporate communications (as a tool to raise awareness) and commercial (to promote products and services but also the catchment area and potential for demand). Halpern (2012) adds 'research and development', as airports use social media to survey customer satisfaction or opinions (e.g. about opportunities for new routes), which means that an airport's social media community can be used as an asset (e.g. when discussing route development opportunities with airlines and other stakeholders) (Scourse, 2011).

The main focus for airport social media appears to be on developing the airport's image and reputation through engaging directly and efficiently with its online community. This makes sense, given that 51 per cent of social network users are connected to brands, 36 per cent have posted content about a brand and 53 per cent would love to share their ideas with a company using

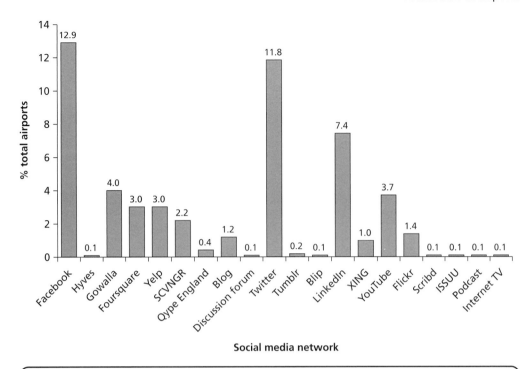

Figure 8.9 Social media used by airports worldwide, as of year-end 2010
Data source: Halpern (2012)

social media (InSites Consulting, 2011). Customer service and crisis handling are also key areas of focus. For example, London Gatwick Airport was listed as a trusted news source with Twitter's Blue Tick in April 2012. The Blue Tick is something Twitter includes on selected Twitter profiles to show that a legitimate source is authoring Tweets. London Gatwick Airport has also been given an Enhanced Profile Page on Twitter: a new profile design that improves the way important messages are conveyed to Followers. London Gatwick Airport uses Twitter extensively to keep Followers informed about flight delays, weather disruptions and daily activities at the airport, and has been particularly active on Twitter during major disruptions such as the 2010 ash cloud and UK Border Agency strike in 2011. During a severe snow fall in December 2010 the airport attracted 15,000 additional Twitter followers, and at the height of the bad weather over 300 passenger queries were fielded by the airport on Twitter every hour (London Gatwick Airport, 2012).

More recently, airports seem increasingly focused on using social media as a commercial tool, especially for the promotion of products and services. London Luton Airport often posts information on Facebook about commercial activities at the airport such as new routes or retail outlets and 'deals of the week' for flights, holidays and retail. Dallas/Fort Worth International Airport used a 'Check-In to Great Deals at DFW Airport' campaign recently. Users downloading the Foursquare application on their smartphone gained access to deals and offers at a range of shops, restaurants and services inside the airport (see Figure 8.10). The idea behind the Dallas/Fort Worth campaign was to increase passengers' knowledge of the shops and restaurants located 'right round the corner' using Foursquare, and to create a multi-retailer campaign within the airport to encourage passengers to make purchases. The campaign brought together over 200

Figure 8.10 'Check-In to Great Deals at DFW Airport' social media campaign
Source: courtesy of Moroch and Dallas/Fort Worth International Airport

retailers within the airport to develop and manage hundreds of offers, and to communicate them to passengers via Foursquare (Lopresti, 2012). The number of Foursquare check-ins went from none to 11,000 during the first three months of the campaign and the redemption of Foursquare vendor promotions increased steadily each week (Moroch, 2012). The role of social media in the distribution of airport products and services in discussed again in Chapter 9.

Of course, social media have their risks and there have been a number of high profile examples of misuse by businesses or their employees. Belkin were caught offering money to anybody who posted a 100 per cent positive review of their products on Amazon. Honda's Manager of Product Planning was caught secretly posting positive reviews about one of its new cars on Facebook, stating that he would 'Get this car in a heartbeat'. Habitat linked its online adverts to popular topics on Twitter, effectively spamming users.

Examples of misuse by airports are rare, but there are examples where airport use of social media has not been well received by everyone. Akron-Canton Airport has already been mentioned as an airport that actively uses social media. Miami Heat basketball player LeBron Raymone James took a personal flight from the airport in November 2011. Akron is his hometown and Akron-Canton Airport is his hometown airport. The airport posted a photo of him with the airport's Senior Vice President and Chief Marketing and Communications Officer on their Facebook wall with the post: 'Hometown hero LeBron James flew through CAK this morning. He was great to our employees. Thanks for flying CAK, LeBron!' Within 30 minutes, 85 posts were received on Facebook from angry fans (66 'likes' were received during the same time). LeBron's decision to leave local basketball club Cleveland Cavaliers for Miami Heat in 2010 was highly controversial. His public life had been scrutinised by the media, and in addition to being ranked in past polls as one of America's most influential athletes, he had also been ranked as one of America's most disliked athletes. The angry fans were particularly offended by the use of the word 'hero'. The airport decided to withdraw the post (see VanAuken, 2011).

Another risk for airports is that social media offer a platform for users to 'speak their mind'. This has the potential to expose the airport to negative comments from users. The comments and any responses can be viewed immediately and en masse, and may subsequently create a negative image. Nevertheless, despite the risks, a growing number of airports are embracing social media and the distribution of airports using social media has widened in recent years (see AirGate Solutions, 2011a; 2011b).

Table 8.2 Summary of promotional tools

Tool and example media	Common strengths	Common weaknesses	Common marketing objectives
Advertising: television, radio, print, outdoor, electronic media, publicity information, sponsorship	Mass audience, can repeat and compare messages, expressive, short- and long-term campaigns	Impersonal, lacks persuasiveness, one-way communication, costly	Corporate communications, promotes products and services
Direct marketing: telephone, direct mail, mobile messaging, e-mail, consumer websites, displays	Targeted, customised, quick, personal relationships, interactive	Delivers general messages	(In)formal relationship building, corporate communications, promotes products and services, market research
Personal selling: sales presentations, incentive programmes, trade shows and exhibitions	Personal contact, greater attention from customers, deeper relationships	Sales and after-sales cost and resources, a long-term commitment	Promotes products and services, especially for route development
Sales promotion: displays, premiums, discounts, coupons, competitions, speciality advertising, demonstrations	Grabs attention, stimulates (rapid) purchase	Short-lived, short-term relationships, not always genuine value	Promotes products and services, especially to boost retail revenue
Public relations: interviews, press releases, media kits, brochures, newsletters, public speaking, announcements, articles, stories, awards, recognitions, events, sponsorship, volunteering, corporate reports	Real and believable, expressive, cheap yet effective	Hype may not be met	Informal relationship building, crisis handling, corporate communications

Table 8.2 continued

Tool and example media	Common strengths	Common weaknesses	Common marketing
Social media: social and professional networks, blogs, content communities	Ability to interact and share information, engage quickly and directly, multiple interaction (B2C, B2B, C2C)	Unclear how best to manage and use it, consumes time and resources, can be misused and attract negative comments	Informal relationship building, crisis handling, corporate communications, promotes products and services, market research

Source: compiled by the authors from various sources

Table 8.2 provides a summary of each promotional tool mentioned in the first part of this chapter, including example media that can be used, common strengths and weaknesses, and example marketing objectives.

8.2 The changing communications landscape

Traditionally, marketers have focused on using mass-media communication to support mass-media marketing strategies, targeting a wide audience with general messages via advertising channels such as print, radio and television. Airport marketing only really developed as a concept after the 1980s, so few airports adopted the mass-media approach taken by companies in other industries. Besides, mass-media communication is generally very costly and has therefore been out of reach for the marketing budget of most airports.

Many larger airports use above-the-line marketing. Unlike mass-media marketing, which is all about hitting as many (mass-market) customers as possible, above-the-line marketing uses mass-media methods of communication but to target a specific market. In line with section 8.3, above-the-line marketing typically shares the content or concept across different media and is integrated with other forms of communication such as social media and public relations.

Ireland West Airport Knock, together with Tourism Ireland, launched an above-the-line campaign in the UK to promote tourism in the west of Ireland. The campaign targeted an audience of 8.4 million with the theme 'Discover the secrets of the west of Ireland' that focused on award winning golf courses, local heritage, culture and scenery. A television commercial was launched in August 2007 and shown on a wide selection of channels in the UK including Channel 4, Sky 1, Sky Sports, Sky Movies, Sky News and Fox News. Two 30-second commercials were broadcast: one at the beginning of the commercial break (featuring activities to do) and one at the end (promoting direct flights from the UK).

Above-the-line advertising is also used by airports seeking to drive growth in demand for retail and other sources of non-aeronautical revenue. Malaysia Airports launched an 'Indulge till you fly' campaign in October 2011 that promoted shopping, drinking and dining opportunities at their airports. A television commercial was launched in conjunction with the campaign to bring the message of airports as lifestyle destinations to a wider segment of Malaysians. The 30-second commercial titled 'There's always more' was shown on television channels in Malaysia including

TV3, ntv7 and 8TV. The campaign also included an 'Indulge and win contest', where travellers spending a minimum of MYR 250 could enter a prize draw. To enhance participation in the campaign, Malaysia Airports made use of a new iPhone/iPad2 application called iButterfly Asia, which uses augmented reality, global positioning system and motion sensors to enable users to receive information from the airports, retailers and F&B outlets.

London Heathrow Airport uses above-the-line advertising to drive its retail business but also passenger demand (e.g. see Figure 8.11). The airport launched its first foreign-language campaign in the UK in July 2011, encouraging overseas visitors to browse London stores but buy at the airport. The 'See it in London. Buy it at Heathrow' campaign included outdoor advertisements

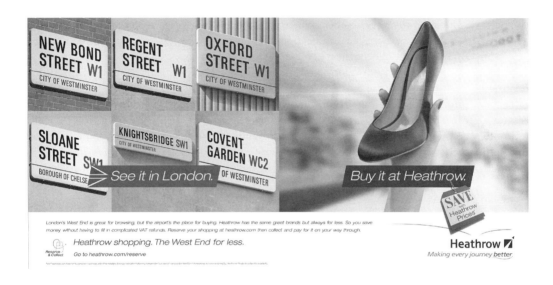

Figure 8.11 London Heathrow Airport advertising campaigns, summer 2011
Source: courtesy of London Heathrow Airport

translated into Spanish, Mandarin, Arabic, Russian and Japanese. A second phase of advertising launched shortly afterwards carried the message, 'Can't stop thinking about your holiday? Neither can we'. The campaign targeted the 9.2 million families and leisure passengers set to pass through the airport that summer, and included outdoor advertisements at the airport and around the London Underground network, supported by radio and online activity.

Two key factors are changing the marketing communications landscape, encouraging a shift away from mass-media communications (Kotler *et al.*, 2008). First, mass markets have become increasingly fragmented. This is certainly the case in the airport industry: new market segments have emerged with their own distinct needs and wants, while existing markets have become more experienced and demanding and generally have more alternative opportunities available to them. For instance, new airline business models such as LCCs have emerged; airlines are becoming more competitive, and generally have a wider choice of airports that are themselves more competitive; and airports' strategies are increasingly guided by commercial versus public service considerations. Fragmentation reduces the effectiveness of mass-media communications and erodes brand loyalty. As a result, airports need to develop marketing communications strategies that foster closer relationships with customers in more narrowly defined micromarkets.

Second, information technologies have developed at such a rate that companies can now create comprehensive information about customers and their needs, and use information technology to target more narrowly defined micromarkets with specific messages. This trend has been experienced in the airport industry, with increased use of the internet and mobile technologies for marketing communications. Marketing experts generally agree that mass-media communications will always be important but that they need to coexist with new forms of communication. As Kotler *et al.* (2005: 750) suggest, there should be 'less broadcasting, more narrowcasting'.

8.3 Integrated and effective marketing communications

The more diverse but also more fragmented and specifically targeted approach to marketing communications poses a challenge for airports. The diverse range of customers and marketing objectives at an airport means that it may be involved in communicating a range of messages using different tools and media from different sources within the company. For instance, airports typically have separate departments for marketing, media, public relations and information technology. Each department (in other words, each source) has the potential to use different tools and media to communicate its own messages, and this can subsequently send mixed messages about company image or positioning of the product. Customers generally do not distinguish between different messages and message sources in the same way that marketers do. As a result, marketing theory often calls for integrated marketing communications, which can be defined as: 'the concept under which a company carefully integrates its many communications channels to deliver a clear, consistent, and compelling message about the organisation and its products' (Armstrong and Kotler, 2007: 366).

There is no tried and tested way of integrating external communications effectively. Kotler *et al.* (2008), however, suggest that a company must begin by integrating its internal communications, and then define the roles various promotional tools will play and the extent to which they will be used, coordinate promotional activities and the timing of any campaigns, and assign overall responsibility for communication efforts to a senior manager. Many airports have a senior manager with such responsibility. For instance, Dallas/Fort Worth International Airport was advertising for the post of Director of Corporate Communications in October 2011. The post holder would assume responsibility for:

The planning, execution and success of all external and internal communications strategies and programs to help achieve the company's strategic, financial and operating objectives. The incumbent reports directly to the Chief Marketing Officer (CMO), and also advises the other members of the Executive Council and the Leadership Team. The Director ensures that the right messages are delivered to the right audiences in the right ways at the right times in order to position the company, its employees and its services and products in order to achieve sustained profitable revenue and market share growth. The incumbent is responsible for the plans, day-to-day operations and performance of all of the company's communications activities: advertising, corporate, product and services identity, media relations, public relations, employee communications and executive communications.

(SuperMedia, 2011)

In addition to being integrated, marketing communications also need to be effective. Airports need to identify the target audience and its characteristics, define the response sought (this could be awareness, knowledge, liking, preference, conviction or purchase), construct a message with an effective content and structure, select relevant media for both personal and non-personal communication, and collect feedback on market awareness, testing and satisfaction with the communication process.

Developing and implementing an effective marketing communications programme can be a costly experience and airports will always need to make trade-offs between what they would like to do and what they can afford to do. Decisions will therefore be determined, to some extent, by the budget that has been set for marketing communications. It is difficult to determine what budget airports typically set for marketing communications because it may be integrated with a budget for wider marketing activities such as branding, sales and public relations. Smaller airports may not even set a specific budget for marketing communications and instead use money from other or more general sources of finance. Examples are available for individual airports. For instance, Tampa International Airport set a budget in 2012 of USD 560,400 for travel, conferences and training expenses, including travel for marketing of USD 150,000. A budget of USD 699,300 was also set for promotional expenses (Jackovics, 2011). BAA spent GBP 6 million on retail marketing and GBP 18 million on other marketing and communications in 2011, representing 1.4 per cent of total operating costs (BAA, 2011). As shown in Table 7.1 of Chapter 7, expenditure on sales and marketing represented 4.5 per cent of total operating costs at airports worldwide in 2009, and was the fourth largest cost area for airports after terminal and landside operations, administration, airside operations and airport security (ACI, 2010). Of course, low and high spenders exist in any industry, so large variations between airports are to be expected (e.g. see Figure 1.3 in Chapter 1) and may be due to characteristics such as airport size, ownership and control, geographical location, marketing objectives and the extent to which management of the airport is market-orientated.

How to communicate effectively is also difficult to determine. Selecting the correct tool for the correct task, within the budget available, is not easy. Nor is it easy to create the correct message. Effective communications are further challenged by the need to manage the complex system of communications available to an airport. Airports communicate directly with other businesses such as retail companies, airlines and cargo operators, as well as with end-users and other publics, often as a derived demand. For instance, a passenger will rarely travel to an airport with the main objective of visiting that airport. This means that airports need to be aware of the needs and marketing objectives of various partners or stakeholders, and may benefit from entering into collaborations that enable them to pool resources and develop an integrated approach to marketing communications. Collaborations of this nature are particularly important for small regional airports targeting growth in inbound tourism as a marketing objective. Airport resources for research and promotional activities are likely to be limited, so collaboration may offer opportunities to increase resources and provide an integrated approach to tourism development in the region, providing target markets with increased support and a wider overview of the area and its potential. Small regional airports or airport groups that have been a part of a collaboration of this nature include Hemavan Airport (a member of Tärnafjällen Incoming), Lakselv Banak North Cape Airport (a member of North Cape Airport Services), and Highlands and Islands Airports Limited (a member of Highlands Loch Ness marketing group).

Fly Bergen provides a good example of a collaborative and integrated approach to marketing for inbound tourism. It was launched in September 2007 as a key component in Bergen Tourist Board's tourism development strategy for Bergen and the regions of Hordaland and Sogn and Fjordane in Norway. The three-year marketing strategy aimed to stimulate tourism by offering marketing support to airlines operating a new route to Bergen Flesland Airport or increasing the frequency of existing services at the airport. The idea of providing marketing support is to ensure that adequate marketing resources are available to share the risk of establishing a new route or frequency. Marketing support mechanisms such as this were discussed in detail in Chapter 7, but the collaborative nature of the Fly Bergen scheme is of relevance here. The scheme offered NOK 16.1 million over a period of three years to airlines. Its initiators constituted the steering committee, which included Hordaland County Council, the Municipality of Bergen, Innovation Norway (the Norwegian government's official trade representative abroad), and Sogn and Fjordane County Council. There was also an executive committee for air service tourism development, which constituted the operative unit of the Fly Bergen scheme and included Bergen Tourist Board, Avinor (operator of Bergen Flesland Airport), consultants and representatives of the steering committee. Responsibilities included managing resources, operating the Fly Bergen scheme, strategic planning, analysing priorities, producing action plans and budgets, marketing and promoting the project (to carriers, destination promoters and potential funding sources), and creating business plans for sustainable routes (including development, implementation and follow up) (see Fly Bergen, 2007).

References

ACI (2010) *Airport Economics Survey 2010*, Montreal: ACI.

ACI Europe (2011) *Airports 2.0: How European Airports are Embracing Social Media*, Brussels: ACI Europe.

ACI Europe (2012) *Digital Report 2012*, Brussels: ACI Europe.

AirGate Solutions (2011a) *Airports using Facebook*, Ontario: AirGate Solutions. Online. Available at: http://airgatesolutions.com/index.php?option=com_content&view=article&id=140&Itemid=100 (accessed 10 November 2011).

AirGate Solutions (2011b) *Airports using Twitter*, Ontario: AirGate Solutions. Online. Available at: http://airgatesolutions.com/index.php?option=com_content&view=article&id=109&Itemid=98 (accessed 10 November 2011).

AirGate Solutions/SimpliFlying (2011) *Top 10 social media initiatives by airports*, Ontario: AirGate Solutions. Online. Available at: http://www.airgatesolutions.com/index.php?option=com_content&view=article&id=189:top-10-social-media-initiatives-by-airports&catid=1:latest-news&Itemid=89 (accessed 29 November 2011).

anna.aero (2012) *About us*, Horley: PPS Publications. Online. Available at: http://www.anna.aero/about-us (accessed 22 October 2012).

AOPA (2008) *Guide to obtaining community support for your local airport: public relations plan for airports*, Maryland: AOPA. Online. Available at: http://www.aopa.org/asn/airportpr (accessed 28 September 2012).

Armstrong, G. and Kotler, P. (2007) *Marketing: An Introduction*, 8th edn, New Jersey: Pearson Education.

ASM (2009) *Industry Trends and Climate Survey: Interim Research Results*, Live Webinar, July 2009.

BAA (2011) *BAA Limited: Annual Report and Financial Statements for the Year Ended 31 December 2011*, Hounslow: BAA Airports Limited.

Brassington, F. and Pettitt, S. (2007) *Essentials of Marketing*, 2nd edn, Harlow: Pearson Education.

CIPR (2011) *What is PR?* London: CIPR. Online. Available at: http://www.cipr.co.uk/content/careers-cpd/careers-pr/what-pr (accessed 20 September 2012).

Dolby, N. (2009) *The Nigel Dolby column – 01/04/09*, Brentford: The Moodie Report. Online. Available at: http://www.moodiereport.com/document.php?c_id=1178&doc_id=20270 (accessed 29 September 2012).

Fly Bergen (2007) *Scheme Manual: September 2007*, Bergen: Fly Bergen.

Halpern, N. (2012) 'Use of social media by airports', *Journal of Airline and Airport Management*, 2(2); 67–85.

Halpern, N. and Niskala, J. (2008) 'Airport marketing and tourism in remote destinations: exploiting the potential in Europe's northern periphery' in A. Graham, A. Papatheodorou and P. Forsyth (eds) *Aviation and Tourism: Implications for Leisure Travel*, Aldershot: Ashgate.

InSites Consulting (2011) *Social Media Around the World 2012*, Ghent: InSites Consulting.

Jackovics, T. (2011) *Tampa Airport budget for 2012 would increase marketing*, Tampa: The Tampa Tribune. Online. Available at: http://www2.tbo.com/news/breaking-news/2011/aug/30/tampa-airport-budget-for-2012-would-increase-marke-ar-253807 (accessed 23 November 2011).

Jones, D. (2012) *The price of financial folly: as airports and luxury flats stand empty as monuments to Spain's overspending, miners' protest over subsidy cuts ends in bloody clashes*, *Mail Online* 12 July 2012, London: Associated Newspapers. Online. Available at: http://www.dailymail.co.uk/news/article-2172339/Airports-seen-plane-ghost-towns-luxury-flats-The-hubris-Spains-descent-anarchy.html (accessed 20 October 2012).

Kaplan, A.M. and Haenlein, M. (2010) 'Users of the world unite! The challenges and opportunities of social media', *Business Horizons*, 53(1); 59–68.

Kotler, P., Wong, V., Saunders, J. and Armstrong, G. (2005) *Principles of Marketing*, 4th European edn, Harlow: Prentice Hall-Pearson Education.

Kotler, P., Wong, V., Saunders, J. and Armstrong, G. (2008) *Principles of Marketing*, 5th European edn, Harlow: Prentice Hall-Pearson Education.

London Gatwick Airport (2012) *Gatwick is the first UK airport to be recognised by Twitter for excellent customer service support*, Gatwick: Gatwick Airport. Online. Available at: http://www.mediacentre.gatwickairport.com/News/Gatwick-is-the-first-UK-airport-to-be-recognised-by-Twitter-for-excellent-customer-service-support-74a.aspx (accessed 14 October 2012).

Lopresti, V. (2012) *DFW International Airport – foursquare campaign*, Oak Cliff: Vincent Lopresti. Online. Available at: http://cargocollective.com/vincentlopresti#vincent-lopresti-credentials-1 (accessed 28 October 2012).

Mangold, W.G. and Foulds, D.J. (2009) 'Social media: the new hybrid element of the promotion mix', *Business Horizons*, 52(4); 357–65.

Moroch (2012) *DFW Airport: an airport unstows their mobile devices in a big way*, Dallas: Moroch. Online. Available at: http://www.moroch.com/work/dfw-check-ins (accessed 28 October 2012).

Nigam, S., Cook, R. and Stark, C. (2011) 'Putting the joy back into the airport experience: can social networking platforms make a genuine contribution to increasing commercial revenues and engaging customers?', *Journal of Airport Management*, 6(1); 7–11.

Scourse, M. (2011) 'Can social media be used in route development?', presented at *17th World Route Development Forum*, Berlin, October 2011.

Solterbeck, S. (2011) *World routes 2011 social media briefings – a summary report*, Schwalbach am Taunus: Persistence. Online. Available at: http://www.solterbeck.net/blog/?p=413 (accessed 26 October 2011).

SuperMedia (2011) *Director corporate communications job*, DFW Airport: SuperMedia. Online. Available at: http://jobs.supermedia.com/job/DallasFortworth-Airport-Director-Corporate-Communications-Job-TX-75201/1407354 (accessed 25 November 2011).

The Route Shop (2012) *About The Route Shop*, Horley: PPS Publications. Online. Available at: http://www.therouteshop.com/about-therouteshop.php (accessed 20 October 2012).

Topping, P. (2010) 'Promotions and incentives in airport retailing', *Journal of Airport Management*, 4(3); 208–10.

VanAuken, K. (2011) *The 'decision' – were we right or wrong to pull the plug on a CAK FB Post*, North Canton: Akron-Canton Airport. Online. Available at: http://www.akroncantonairport.com/blog/2011/11/the-decision—were-we-right-or-wrong-to-pull-the-plug-on-a-cak-fb-post (accessed 3 September 2011).

Chapter 9

Airport distribution

This chapter introduces airport distribution, considers how it has evolved and examines approaches to airport distribution, especially in terms of the way airports conduct business with target markets. It also investigates how airports use CRM as a means of managing their interactions with customers.

9.1 Introduction to airport distribution

Distribution concerns the methods used by companies to deliver their products or services to target markets; this includes direct sales, mail order, vending machines, or selling over the telephone or internet. It also relates to the means by which companies deliver their product or service to target markets. This rarely occurs in isolation, but involves the company operating as one link in a broader supply chain otherwise known as a distribution channel (Kotler *et al.*, 2008). The simplest channel is one that links the company to its target markets by way of direct distribution. Companies using direct distribution are likely to experience relative control over the supply chain and any marketing activities; as a result, they are likely to be fairly proactive in their approach to distribution and marketing.

Manufacturing companies sometimes distribute their product via intermediaries such as wholesalers and retailers for customer-orientated channels, or business distributors for business-orientated channels. The use of wholesalers and retailers is less common for service companies because of the intangible nature of their products or services, but they may use agents or brokers to sell products or services on their behalf, or franchises to supply and market their products or services.

Intermediaries may be able to use specialist expertise and their size or scope to distribute products or services more broadly and efficiently. Companies that use intermediaries may, however, lose a certain degree of control over distribution and marketing activities, and their products or services may subsequently be perceived more as a commodity. This is significant, given the increased attention many airports are giving to branding (see Chapter 6). Another risk is that intermediaries may develop a strong bargaining position that allows them to charge excessive transaction fees or commission.

Airports use multiple distribution channels for different target markets (see Figure 9.1). An airport may have direct B2B relationships with airlines (this includes passenger and cargo operators, and airlines operated by or on behalf of tour operators), aviation service providers (e.g. ground handlers, in-flight caterers, aircraft maintenance, and services provided by government agencies such as air traffic control, customs and immigration, and in some cases fire and rescue), and non-aviation service providers such as those providing commercial passenger services (e.g. retail, F&B, car parking, car rental, catering, and the travel trade). Airports may also have B2B relationships in other commercial business areas with buyers (e.g. of airport advertising or real estate, or companies purchasing airport consultancy services) or suppliers (e.g. construction and engineering companies).

The end-user may be a passenger or item of cargo but there are other potential consumers of airport products and services that may be targeted, such as workers at an airport and visitors accompanying passengers. General aviation, especially owners of private aircraft, may also be considered to be an end-user. Airports may have direct B2C relationships with end-users or indirect relationships via intermediaries such as airlines, retail providers or estate agents. Some airports charge airlines for use of a range of airport products and services, even though these are provided by others (see Chapter 7). In this instance, the airport acts as an intermediary between airlines consuming the products and services of other service providers.

It is important for airports to understand and continually assess the respective costs and benefits of the different channels they do or do not use. In particular, airports using intermediaries should try to maintain a strong bargaining position that allows them to maximise the benefits without compromising safety, security or service quality. Airports tend to have high levels of capital expenditure, especially compared to any intermediaries they might use. They therefore need to maximise the cost–efficiency of their distribution channels while reducing exposure to risk where possible.

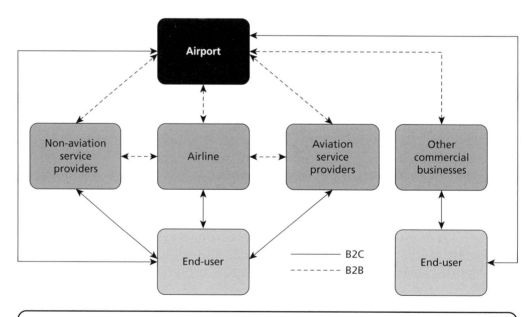

Figure 9.1 Distribution structure of an airport
Source: compiled by the authors

9.2 Evolution of airport distribution

Demand for airports, along with other forms of transport infrastructure, tends to be derived, because demand for their products or services (e.g. by end-users such as passengers) occurs largely as a result of demand for other products or services (e.g. of airlines). As a result, airport distribution has traditionally focused on B2B relationships with airlines or other service providers. Historically, airports adopted a passive approach to such relationships by simply responding to requests from airlines and other service providers as opposed to proactively seeking business, and transactions would largely be process-based. Airports also tended to adopt a passive approach to B2C relationships with the end-users generally considered to be the customers of airlines. Transactions between airports and end-users were minimal.

For some airports, especially in less developed countries, the traditional situation still exists. Changes in industry and the way airports are owned and operated, however, mean that the structure and complexity of distribution channels used by many airports have evolved. Increased deregulation in a number of areas such as the provision of air services and ground handling means that many airports now work much harder to proactively secure transactions with airlines and aviation service providers in what has become a much more competitive industry. Airports increasingly use market research and information technologies (see Chapter 4) to create comprehensive information about customers and their needs, and develop marketing communications strategies that foster closer relationships and target more narrowly defined micromarkets with specific messages. This has meant that they have more structured and proactive B2B relationships. It also means that they have a much greater knowledge about the end-user and are more involved in B2C relationships.

Change has also been encouraged by the diversification of the airport business. Airports are increasingly viewed as commercial entities and spheres of influence for commercial activity rather than simply providers of operational infrastructure for air services. In addition to the wide range of features brought together by airports to fulfil their role within the air transport industry (e.g. air traffic control, security and police, fire and rescue in the airfield, ground handling, immigration and customs services), airports offer an increasingly diverse range of commercial services (e.g. shops, restaurants, banks, foreign exchange, car parking, car rental, hotels, conference services, entertainment amenities, business parks and consultancy services).

As with most service industries, airports largely distribute directly because production and consumption of airport services occur simultaneously. Direct supply typically takes place in-house, allowing the airport to control provision and interact directly with customers, as well as receive direct and immediate feedback. Direct supply also allows airports to provide a personal service that can be differentiated to meet the needs of different market segments. Some service industries distribute supply at the customer's premises (e.g. home cleaning) or via the telephone or internet (e.g. insurance). These channels have not traditionally been used by airports, although, as will be discussed in this chapter, alternative distribution channels such as the internet are becoming more widely used.

9.3 Approaches to airport distribution

9.3.1 Airlines

Distribution of airport products and services to airlines tends to be conducted in-house. Airports increasingly have some kind of aviation marketing or development team that may have managers or specialist staff designated to different types of service (e.g. scheduled, charter, executive, cargo, general aviation), geographical coverage (e.g. domestic, international or by world region) or business area (e.g. airline affairs, market research, route development). For example, East Midlands Airport has a dedicated Aviation Development Team with separate contacts for dealing with enquiries from scheduled operators and charter/tour operators, while Zurich Airport has a dedicated Aviation Marketing Team to assist airlines in launching and promoting new services. The team includes a Manager Airline Affairs, Manager Aviation Analysis and Research and Key Account Manager. Airports increasingly use online services such as The Route Shop and Route Exchange in support of route development (see Chapter 8), but such services are largely used to promote opportunities at the airport (e.g. by advertising routes required on The Route Shop and unserved key routes on Route Exchange), as opposed to distributing the airport product. Transactions are still likely to take place directly between the airline and airport operator, unlike in the airline industry where intermediaries such as travel agents and online travel planning portals may be used to sell flight tickets on behalf of the airline.

Airlines wanting to operate at a particular airport will need to agree to the airport's conditions of use. These form the basis for a legally binding agreement between the airline and the airport. At London Heathrow Airport, this includes operational conditions, payment terms, data requirements and the schedule of charges for landing, emissions, departing passengers, parking, peak/off-peak, and noise and weight categories (London Heathrow Airport, 2011).

Airlines wanting to operate at airports in the US typically have airport use agreements in addition to conditions of use. Airport use agreements traditionally included long-term lease agreements of between 20 and 50 years, which provided airlines with effective ownership of gate and counter space, or even their own terminal. A good example of this is the development of John F. Kennedy International Airport in the 1950s. The airport master plan provided each major airline at the airport with a space to develop its own terminal; this initially resulted in five terminals for individual airlines, one to be shared between three airlines, and an international arrivals building. Some airport use agreements include a majority-in-interest (MII) clause, which means that signatory airlines with a significant share of traffic are able to influence investment decisions, and will be required to approve planned developments at the airport. The MII clause may be considered anti-competitive, especially if non-signatory airlines are not able to gain access to terminal space and gates. As a result, some airports have introduced a 'use it or lose it' clause, which returns the control of assets to the airport if an airline does not use the facilities as intended. Airports have also tried to reduce the powers of MII airlines (e.g. by requiring MII disapproval versus approval or limiting their involvement to development projects of a certain scale), or by discarding MII clauses altogether (Graham, 2008).

Recent agreements in the US between airports and their airlines suggest a move towards the model widely used outside the US, which involves joint-, multi- or non-exclusive-use gates and ticket counters (Karp, 2010). In October 2010, Dallas/Fort Worth International Airport reached a ten-year use agreement with carriers to replace a 35-year agreement that had been signed in 1974, while Indianapolis International Airport reached a new five-year deal with airlines. Both agreements emphasise a shift away from long and exclusive agreements to shorter agreements for mixed-use facilities. Recent agreements also emphasise the airports' desire to keep as much non-aeronautical revenue as possible. This is related to the discussion on single/dual till or residual/compensatory approaches to airport charges in Chapter 7.

As Starkie (2011) observes, the airport–airline relationship has evolved in recent years. Air transport markets are increasingly deregulated; as a result, airlines are less tied to particular airports. Also, new airline business models have emerged, and competition between airlines has intensified. This means that airlines increasingly have different and stronger demands from airports in terms of the facilities they provide but also their standards and service levels (e.g. for baggage and passenger handling, gate availability, and aircraft turnaround times). Such factors can have a significant impact on airline operations, and airlines are increasingly seeking to include them in their contracts with airports, alongside the standard airport charges and conditions of use. At the same time, airports are increasingly seeking commitments from airlines, especially long-term commitments that allow them to reduce their exposure to risk and make necessary investments in their facilities. This may include commitments on the number of based aircraft, guaranteed volume and plans for growth. As discussed in Chapter 7, airports may try to include different airport charges under one charge per departing passenger or per freight tonne so that the airline and airport share the impact of changes in volume. Contract duration is a challenging issue, given that airlines want the flexibility of short-term contracts (e.g. between 1 and 5 years) so that they can adapt to changes in the market, while airports want long-term contracts (e.g. between 10 and 20 years) that provide stability in a changing market. Starkie suggests that one way forward may be:

> to develop a market in contracts whereby the unexpired term of a contract can be bought and sold between airlines. The analogy here is the sale of a lease held on the assets of a residential or commercial property. And like the property market, one might expect intermediaries to facilitate the transactions as indeed, they have done in relation to the trading of slots at congested airports.
>
> (Starkie, 2011)

In addition to terms of contract, management processes are important when distributing airport products and services to airlines, especially at larger airports or airports that belong to an airport group where management decisions may be made at different levels and involve a number of departments. Some airports, such as Aberdeen Airport, have been known to use a so-called 'entry into service' process consisting of an assigned project manager who acts as a point of contact and provider of assistance to airlines establishing new routes or expanding existing services at the airport. Key account managers will assume a similar role. This might not be necessary at smaller independently owned airports, where the organisational structure may be less complicated than at larger or group-owned airports.

Part of the distribution process is the way a product or service is made available to target markets; for some airports, availability of capacity for airlines is constrained and subsequently subjected to regulatory or non-regulatory procedures for allocation. This is especially the case for allocating slots at busier airports. A slot refers to permission to land and take off at an airport at a specific date and time. As air traffic has grown, many busier airports around the world have become capacity constrained, which has resulted in a scarcity of slots.

Outside the US, the main mechanism for allocating slots is through the IATA schedule coordination conferences or committees. These are held twice a year and aim to agree on how schedules, planned in six monthly seasons, can be coordinated at airports with constrained capacity. The idea is that slots are distributed in an equitable, non-discriminatory and transparent manner. For the purposes of airport coordination, airports are categorised by the responsible authorities according to three levels of congestion (see Table 9.1).

According to IATA (2012a), there are currently 155 fully coordinated level three airports in the world. The majority of these are in Europe (98 airports) and Asia-Pacific (45 airports); the remainder are in North America, the Middle East and South Africa. Demand for runway and gate access exceeds capacity at level three airports, where slots need to be allocated through the slot coordination process. Level two airports have slot controls in place at peak times only. Slots are allocated on the principle of grandfather rights along with the 80/20 rule, meaning that airlines are entitled to slots that they operated at least 80 per cent of the time during the previous equivalent season. If new slots become available, they go into a slot pool. Half of that pool must

Table 9.1 Levels of congestion at airports

Designation	Description
Level one	Capacity of airport infrastructure is generally adequate to meet the demands of airport users at all times.
Level two	Potential for congestion during some periods of the day, week or season, which can be resolved by voluntary cooperation between airlines. A facilitator is appointed to facilitate the planned operations of airlines using or planning to use the airport.
Level three	Capacity providers have not developed sufficient infrastructure, or governments have imposed conditions that make it impossible to meet demand. A coordinator is appointed to allocate slots to airlines and other aircraft operators using or planning to use the airport as a means of managing available capacity.

Source: adapted from IATA (2012a)

be made available to new entrants currently operating less than two pairs of slots per day. Airlines can swap and exchange slots through a secondary trading process. Many actors are involved in slot allocation including airlines and other aircraft operators, air traffic control, coordinators or facilitators responsible for slot coordination at the airport, government authorities and the airport. The airport's role in the slot allocation process varies according to its level of designation (see Table 9.2).

In Europe, the EC's 1993 regulation on common rules for the allocation of slots at community airports (further amended in 2004) provides a legal basis in Europe to the voluntary IATA scheduling committee rules used in other countries (see EC, 1993). In addition, IATA's slot allocation mechanism is not used in the US, largely because it would be in conflict with antitrust laws. There may be certain operational constraints such as environmental limitations, but otherwise there is open access to airports. This sometimes results in heavy congestion during peak periods and airlines need to take this into account when designing their schedules (Graham, 2008). The exception is airports that are subject to the FAA high density traffic airports rule (HDR). Currently, the HDR applies only to Ronald Reagan Washington National Airport. The regulation limits the number of operations during certain hours of the day and requires a slot, which the FAA allocates for a specific 60-minute period for each scheduled operation (FAA, 2012).

9.3.2 Aviation service providers

In order to facilitate the safe and efficient movement of aircraft, passengers and cargo, airports offer a range of aviation services. Ground handling activities are particularly important because they impact on the operating costs and service quality of the airport's main customer: the airline (Graham, 2008). Ground handling typically includes ground administration and supervision, passenger and baggage handling, freight and mail handling, ramp handling, aircraft services, fuel and oil handling, aircraft maintenance, surface transport, and catering services.

Airports have a number of options available to them: provide all or some of the services themselves, perhaps through a subsidiary company; establish a joint venture with one or more

Table 9.2 Role of airports in slot allocation

Designation	Role of the airport
Level one	Monitor demand for airport infrastructure and develop additional capacity when required. Work with handling agents and other authorities to avoid constraints that impact on airline operations. Collect information from airlines on planned operations.
Level two	Provide support to the facilitator in seeking full airline cooperation. Provide infrastructure necessary to handle planned airline operations within agreed levels of service. Keep the facilitator and all interested parties informed about current or expected capacity limitations. After consultation with stakeholders, inform the facilitator of any capacity changes and of the coordination parameters.
Level three	Ensure that appropriate coordination parameters are agreed with stakeholders and updated twice each year. Examine capacity and implement capacity enhancements to allow for a re-designation to level two or level one at the earliest opportunity. After consultation with the coordination committee, inform the coordinator of any capacity changes and of the coordination parameters.

Source: adapted from IATA (2012a)

companies such as other airlines or handling companies; grant licences to airlines to self-handle; or grant licences to one or more handling companies in a concession agreement. Airlines and handling companies may create a subsidiary and/or enter into a joint venture to bid for a concession. For example, AI-SATs and Menzies-Bobba currently operate handling concessions at Rajiv Gandhi International Airport. AI-SATs is a consortium that includes AI (Indian Airlines and Air India) and SATs (a subsidiary of Singapore Airlines); Menzies-Bobba is a consortium that includes ground services providers Menzies Aviation and The Bobba Group.

Providing the service allows an airport to maintain full control and any profits, however, the airport is responsible for investment and any loses. Airports may lack the necessary resources, experience and expertise, and lack economies of scale that might be enjoyed by airlines or handling companies with operations at multiple airports, but may be able to exploit synergies (e.g. between ground handling and other operational functions at the airport). An advantage of offering the services themselves is that they can offer airlines a 'one-stop-shop' and a contract that includes airport charges and ground handling fees. The airport will also be able to develop a closer relationship with the airlines and passengers it handles, and have more control over service levels. The downside to this is that failure to achieve any service level agreements will place a strain on the airport's relationship with its main customers. Creating a subsidiary company may allow the airport handler to develop its own corporate identity and develop the necessary experience and expertise; however, the subsidiary will probably need to be of a certain size in order to compete with any other handling companies at the airport.

Joint ventures often allow airports to maintain a general level of influence (e.g. over service quality), although day-to-day management and operations will be through the company created by the joint venture. They can help the airport to raise funds for investment and share risks or losses, but also mean that any profit will be shared. The joint venture company can transfer its experience and expertise to other airports, allowing for expansion into new markets.

Concession agreements allow airports to devolve responsibility for management and operation of services to other companies. This makes it important for airports to include service level agreements and certain minimum standards in the contract, but reduces airport exposure to investment and risk. Specialist handling companies can operate at multiple airports, allowing them to achieve economies of size, and develop the necessary resources, experience and expertise. Airports may not share in any profits but will receive a regular income from any fees levied. Competition can be encouraged by using a tendering process for the concession as well as by allowing multiple handling companies to operate at the airport. This may result in lower prices for airlines, and act as an incentive for airlines to operate or expand at the airport.

Self-handling by airlines also offers a low-risk option for the airport and may reduce investment needs from the airport, unless the airline is dominant and uses its position to leverage lower fees and/or investment from the airport. Self-handling may also reduce competition and result in higher prices for competing airlines that have to use the services of a self-handling airline. It may also act as a barrier to entry for airlines or handling companies interested in operating at the airport.

Legal and regulatory forces are likely to play a role in how airports decide to provide ground handling services. A good example of this occurs in Europe, where in the past ground handling services were provided by the national airline or airport operator under monopoly or duopoly conditions. For example, the national airline Olympic had a monopoly over handling at airports in Greece, while Iberia had a monopoly over handling at airports in Spain. Some airport operators in Italy, Austria and Germany enjoyed near-monopoly conditions for handling at many of their airports (e.g. at Milan, Rome, Vienna and Frankfurt), and earned significant revenues from such activities (Graham, 2008). Concerns about this monopoly situation gathered pace during the 1990s as air transport markets were liberalised. In particular, airlines were concerned about the potential for high prices and reduced standards and service at airports with monopoly situations (Bass, 1994). The EC introduced a ground handling directive in 1996, which was revised in 2001 to open up competition for ground handling services at community airports. The directive (see EC, 1996), generally stipulates free access for third party suppliers of ground handling services at larger airports in Europe (with >2 million passenger movements or 50,000 tonnes of cargo annually), but states that for certain categories of services (baggage handling, ramp handling, fuel and oil handling, freight and mail handling) member states may limit the number of suppliers to no fewer than two for each category of service. At least one of these suppliers has to be independent of the airport or the dominant airline at that airport. An airline is considered dominant if it carried more than 25 per cent of the passengers or freight at the airport during the preceding year.

Airlines are entitled to self-handle, although member states may allow airports to restrict the number of handlers (e.g. when space or capacity constraints exist). For certain categories of service, member states may limit the number of self-handling airlines to no fewer than two (at airports with >1 million passenger movements or 25,000 tonnes of cargo annually) and may restrict or ban self-handling altogether (e.g. when space or capacity constraints exist). Figure 9.2 provides a summary of the directive in terms of the freedoms and restrictions it has on airports.

The directive has resulted in an increase in the proportion of independent ground handlers at airports in Europe (see Figure 9.3). In addition, prices charged for ground handling services have generally decreased, especially at airports where monopoly or duopoly situations had previously existed (SH&E, 2002). The impact on service quality is less certain, and while the benefits of competition and reduced prices have been welcomed by the industry, there are concerns that

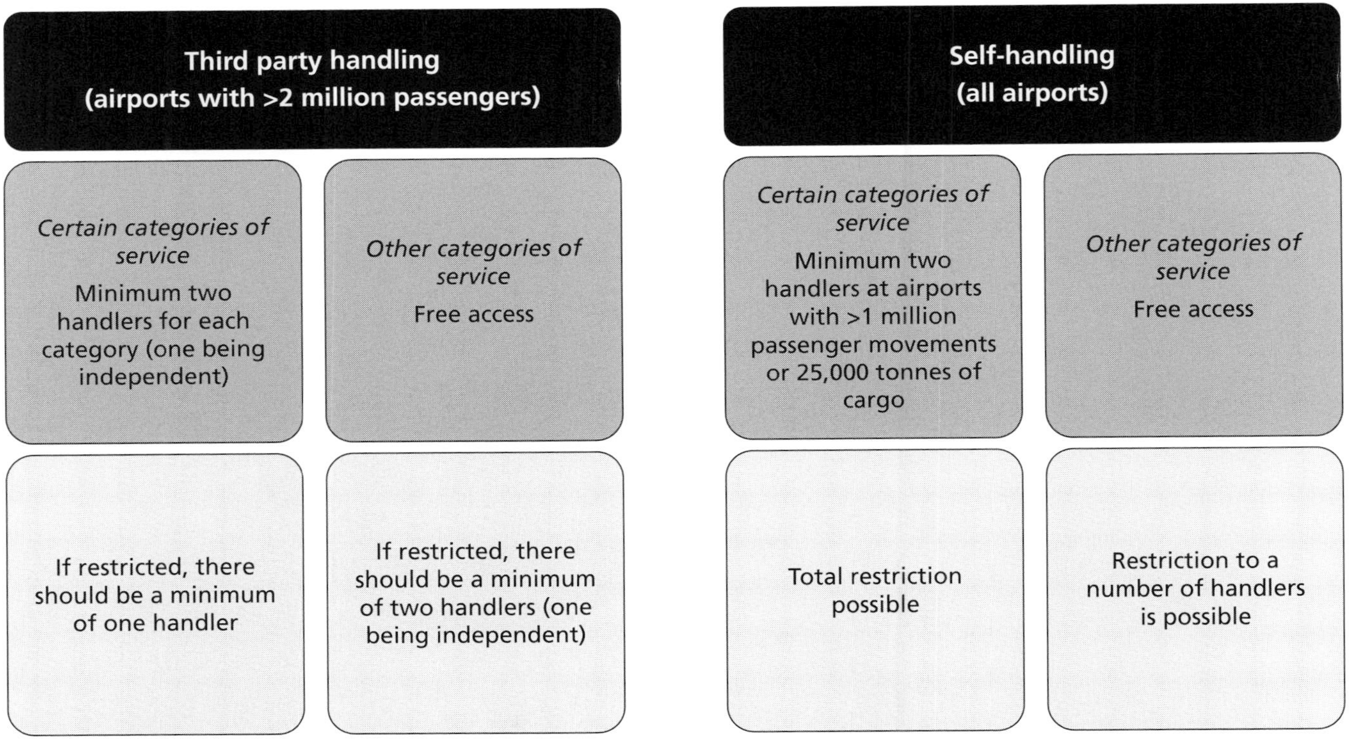

Figure 9.2 Freedoms and possible restrictions of Council Directive 96/97/EC

Source: adapted from SH&E (2002)

Note: certain categories of service include baggage handling, ramp handling, fuel and oil handling, freight and mail handling

Airport distribution

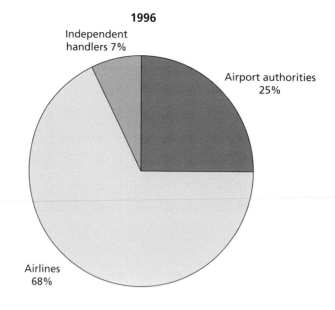

1996

Independent handlers 7%

Airport authorities 25%

Airlines 68%

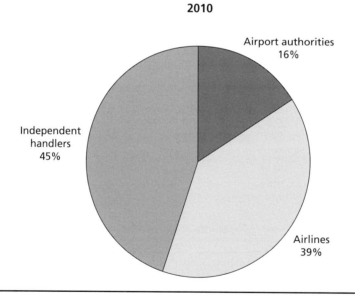

2010

Airport authorities 16%

Independent handlers 45%

Airlines 39%

Figure 9.3 Ground handling market at airports in Europe, 1996 and 2010
Data source: ACI Europe (2011)

inadequate controls over service quality can lead to inefficiencies and disruption, and subsequently impede the functioning of air transport. There are also wider concerns relating to safety and security, and the social welfare of ground handling workers who may experience reduced training, job security, and terms and conditions as a result of increased competition in the ground handling market (e.g. see ACI Europe, 2011). This has prompted many airports to introduce or strengthen standards and service level agreements with ground handling providers, and to include qualitative criteria in tenders such as staff qualifications, commitment to staff training, a social and labour policy, and availability of equipment and expertise. This is in addition to the economic criteria normally used, such as the cost and financial stability of the company.

The EC introduced new proposals in the Airport Package on 1st December 2011 and is currently considering a revision of the ground handling directive. In light of the issues discussed, a number of European social partners in the ground handling sector – ACI Europe, the European Transport Workers' Federation and the Airport Services Association – are arguing against any possible move towards uncontrolled deregulation of the market, claiming that airport managing bodies must be empowered to define and enforce minimum service levels and standards, and that social safeguards in the directive must be strengthened (ACI Europe, 2011).

9.3.3 Non-aviation service providers and other commercial businesses

At airports worldwide, 46.5 per cent of total revenue comes from non-aeronautical sources such as those related to passenger services (e.g. retail, F&B, car parking and car rental) and other commercial services (e.g. advertising and real estate) (ACI, 2011). Although non-aeronautical activities have become an important part of the airport business, it has also become more and more difficult for airports to continue generating increased income from them (Kim and Shin, 2001). Maximisation of opportunities is often determined by an airport's ability to negotiate the best contracts with the best mix of concessionaires. Many other factors play a role in determining success, including the space allocated (e.g. total space, design and layout, ambience), traffic at the airport (e.g. total traffic and composite mix of domestic versus scheduled, transit/transfer, scheduled versus charter), characteristics of airport users (e.g. demographic and socio-economic profile and behaviour, dwell time at the airport), competitive intensity (e.g. from other airports, the internet or downtown), and external forces (e.g. the political, economic, socio-cultural, technological, and legal and regulatory environment within which the airport operates). It is difficult for airports to control or even influence such factors; however, airports do have a fair amount of control over the key attributes of their concession programme (see Table 9.3) and the approach they take to concession contracting.

The approach to concession contracting determines the means by which concessions are offered by the airport. Kim and Shin (2001) identify seven main approaches to concession contracting: direct operation, wholly owned subsidiary, direct lease, joint venture, master concessionaire, developer approach and management contract. Of course, some airports – especially larger airports that have a more complex and diversified concessions programme – may use a combination of approaches. This is what LeighFisher (2011) calls a hybrid approach; it is more a strategy than a specific approach because it involves using each approach as a tool to achieve the best overall outcome for the concession programme at the airport. A summary of the main approaches to concession contracting is provided in subsequent paragraphs. Readers should refer to LeighFisher (2011) or Kim and Shin (2001) for a more detailed discussion.

Direct operation is where the airport typically operates the concession itself. This allows airports to maintain control of their concession programme and offers low commercial risk. It can be used in situations where the concession programme requires a certain level of investment that is unlikely to be undertaken by a concessionaire. The downside is that it may not offer the best means for maximising revenue, especially as the concession programme grows and becomes more diversified, because airports may lack the necessary experience and expertise. One solution to this is for airports to create a wholly owned subsidiary to operate the concession programme. For instance, Aer Rianta International (ARI) is a subsidiary of DAA. ARI is one of the world's

Table 9.3 Key attributes of successful concession programmes

Key factor	Key attributes
Aesthetics	Contemporary design, visually interesting, built with durable high quality materials, and inviting to potential customers. Complements terminal building and surroundings.
Capacity	Able to meet customer demand during seasonal and daily peaks.
Customer service	Helps to maximise sales and encourage multiple purchases.
Revenue production	The result of successfully incorporating multiple attributes into the concession programme and providing passengers with an array of choices that meets their needs.
Sense of place	Reflects unique attributes of the city and region. Local food and retail concepts and local materials and design aesthetics can also help create a sense of place.
Value	Variety of pricing policies; however, while pricing is important, it is not the only component of creating value for customers.
Variety	The broader the range of choices, the more likely it is that the customer will find something he or she wants to buy, resulting in higher sales and revenues.
The 'wow' factor	Unique, interesting and exciting concessions add to the overall passenger experience.

Source: adapted from LeighFisher (2011)

largest airport retailing companies, operating in 24 airports in 14 countries in the Middle East, Cyprus, India, Canada, Eastern Europe, Russia, Ukraine, the Caribbean and China. The company also operates downtown stores and in-flight retail. Subsidiaries such as ARI are able to develop their own corporate identity and attract the necessary experience and expertise; however, they will need to be of a certain size in order to be able to compete.

Direct leasing allows the airport to offer individual or bundled concession opportunities that can be subject to competitive tendering. This allows the airport to maintain control over its concession programme while encouraging competition between potential bidders, and can allow the airport to develop a diverse concession programme that maximises space utilisation and revenue potential. Direct leasing can also be used by airports that have contracted a master concessionaire to operate a substantial part of the overall concession programme, but seek additional smaller or more specialised concessionaires to operate remaining parts of the programme. Direct leasing is likely to be most appropriate for airports with sufficient passenger volume and an attractive business proposition that entices competitive tendering for opportunities. Otherwise, a master concessionaire approach may be more appropriate where smaller, less profitable opportunities are bundled together with larger, more profitable ones. A number of risks may arise from direct leasing. Airports may need to include a common area investment programme (e.g. for a food hall outside the individual concession areas). They may also experience low lease income and high administration costs if awarding multiple leases. Individual concessionaires may also have different aesthetic and construction needs that will need to be managed by the airport.

Airports may enter into a joint venture with one or more companies (e.g. with a specialist retailer). This can allow them to maintain some control over their concession programme while encouraging investment from its business partner, although the airport will generally lose control over the day-to-day management of concessionaires, which will be carried out by the joint venture company in which the airport has a share. Joint ventures can also be used by airport companies wishing to operate concession programmes at other airports. For example, ARI and Korean travel retailer The Shilla Duty Free formed a joint venture to bid for the duty free retail concession at Los Angeles International Airport, which closed to tenders in April 2012 (Moodie, 2012).

With the master concessionaire approach one concessionaire is contracted to develop and operate all or a substantial part of the airport's concession programme. For example, The Paradies Shops secured a ten-year master concessionaire contract in March 2012 to operate the concession programme at Long Beach Municipal Airport. As part of the agreement, The Paradies Shops has developed a number of new concepts in F&B and speciality retail stores (Knevitt, 2012). The master concessionaire will often develop and operate the concession themselves, but may sub-lease a few areas. Airports may offer categories of concession to concessionaires, such as retail or F&B. This is a type of master concession approach sometimes referred to as a prime concessionaire, or multiple primes when there is more than one (see LeighFisher, 2011). The approach will typically result in a reduced administrative burden on airports compared to direct leasing or other non-direct operation approaches because it is dealing with fewer contracts. Master concessionaires are usually large, well-established and experienced operators. They will need to have significant financial resources as they are often responsible for direct investment in individual concession spaces as well as any common areas. They often pay higher rental fees to airports because of the economies of scale they can derive. However, airports typically earn a percentage of the sales; this may be lower with a master concessionaire due to limited competition. It can also result in a less individual and diversified concession offering for customers.

The developer approach is where an airport hires a specialist company to develop and manage the concession programme. For example, as of September 2012, specialist retail developer Westfield Concession Management operates the concession programmes at Boston Logan International Airport (Terminals A and C), Chicago O'Hare International Airport (Terminal 5), George Bush Houston Intercontinental Airport (Terminals B, E and FIS), John F. Kennedy International Airport (Terminal 8), Los Angeles International Airport (Terminal 2 and Tom Bradley International Terminal), Miami International Airport (Central Terminal – retail), Newark Liberty International Airport, Orlando International Airport (Main Terminal – retail), Ronald Reagan Washington National Airport and Washington Dulles International Airport. In January 2012, Westfield Concession Management was awarded a 17-year concession at Los Angeles International Airport comprising a two-year development period and a 15-year operational period. The concession covered the development, lease and management of F&B, retail, speciality retail and other passenger services, and is expected to generate USD 331.1 million in revenue for the airport operator, Los Angeles World Airports. The agreement covers 84,261 square feet of concession area and requires Westfield Concession Management and its concessionaires to invest at least USD 81.9 million in initial improvements and USD 16.4 million in mid-term refurbishment (Welling, 2012).

While airports may reserve the right to some decisions under the developer approach, most of the decision-making and control over the concession programme and selection of individual concessionaires is likely to be delegated to the developer. Both developer and airport assume the role of landlord as they generally do not operate any of the concessions. The developer will select sub-tenants to operate individual or bundled concessions and will generally be responsible for investing in common areas while sub-tenants may be required to fund part or all of the investment needs of their own concession space, which can be too expensive for small businesses. One solution being piloted by Westfield Concession Management in their retail developer role at Orlando International Airport is the use of retail mobile units, which provide opportunities for small businesses to participate in the airport's concession programme.

The developer typically administers contracts; this reduces the administrative burden on the airport, and the fact that there is a tender process involved means that competition is encouraged. Unlike with the master concessionaire approach, there is the ability to generate higher sales and revenues due to a more competitive and diversified number of sub-tenants; however, this may be offset by the cost incurred by the airport in hiring a developer, which can be substantial. The investment expected from a developer can also be substantial, meaning that agreements will need to be long term in order to allow the developer to amortise costs and generate a return on their investment.

Airport advertising has become a big business over the years. Many of these contracts follow a developer-type approach, in which concessions may be awarded to a company responsible for both developing advertising structures and formats in or around the airport, and securing and managing contracts with advertisers. JCDecaux is one of the best-known companies that develops and manages advertising at airports worldwide. The company has an estimated 29 per cent share of the world airport advertising market and a portfolio of 184 concessions at airports in 18 countries in Europe, North America, Africa, Asia-Pacific, and the Middle East. This includes John F. Kennedy International, Los Angeles International, Miami International, London Heathrow, London Gatwick, Paris Roissy, Paris Charles de Gaulle, Paris Orly, Milan Malpensa, Frankfurt and Hong Kong International (JCDecaux, 2012).

The fee management approach entails the airport hiring one or more companies to manage concessions on a daily basis, which is typically compensated with a fixed monthly fee from the airport and sometimes a proportion of the net income from the operation. The airport will retain control over many aspects associated with the concession such as investment, facility design, space utilisation and operating standards. As a result, the airport is exposed to financial risk associated with failing to secure a profitable operation, and will also need to have a fair degree of experience and expertise in concessions planning, management and operation. This approach is often used by airports for the management of their car parks, especially given the increase in competition from off-airport parking providers. It allows airports to contract a specialist operator to maintain agreed minimum standards.

Minota San José International Airport maintains multiple parking facilities (for long-term, short-term, garage and employee parking). The airport contracted AMPCO System Parking to manage its parking facilities from November 2002, with annual options for renewal. Under the terms of the management agreement, AMPCO was required to meet certain minimum standards for customer service, custodial services and other duties. AMPCO was also responsible for charges and collected fees for the use of the parking facilities on behalf of the airport (with the exception of employee parking). In return, AMPCO received a management fee calculated as a percentage of the parking fees collected; this was 15.9 per cent in 2008–2009, amounting to USD 3.9 million (City of San José, 2010).

Airports may use a combination of channels to distribute concessions. For example, the Greater Orlando Aviation Authority awards concessions for Orlando International Airport and Orlando Executive Airport through a competitive procurement process, which involves RFPs or competitive bids. All opportunities are advertised in the legal section of the Orlando Sentinel newspaper and other Orlando-based publications. The airport also advertises opportunities on an online procurement system called Onvia DemandStar, which has a specific focus on government contracting (e.g. for suppliers to the airport). The Greater Orlando Aviation Authority also advertises opportunities, where relevant, on the airport authority website, aviation-related websites such as the AAAE, ACI and the Airport Minority Advisory Council, or in aviation-related publications. The Greater Orlando Aviation Authority uses a similar approach for commercial property (e.g. land and building opportunities for commercial developers), where they offer a brokerage commission in accordance with their broker policy.

The case of suppliers to airports is an interesting one. Airports often have huge capital expenditure programmes and often deal with a range of supplier contracts, especially for construction and engineering. A growing number of airports use intermediaries – especially those offering online services – for tendering opportunities, such as Onvia DemandStar, which is used by Greater Orlando Aviation Authority. Another intermediary used (e.g. by AdP, BAA, Birmingham International Airport, London Gatwick Airport and Manchester Airports Group) is AirportSmart, which claims:

> the world's airport industry spends on average USD 75 billion per year on acquiring, developing and maintaining its asset base; from air traffic control towers to paper clips and from baggage handling services to temporary labour. The scale and range of this expenditure is exerting pressure on both airport buyers and suppliers to transact in a way that enables the entire supply chain to maximise operating efficiencies and to reduce costs for both parties.
>
> (AirportSmart, 2012)

AirportSmart operates as a means for facilitating the contracting of suppliers with buyers across the airport sector, acting as an online marketplace. It was established as a joint venture company founded by AdP, BAA and Copenhagen Airports, which have a combined annual purchasing power of USD 3 billion (AirportSmart, 2012). However, AirportSmart operates as an independent company and is used by a number of airport operators. Buyers pay an annual fee to gain unlimited access to a supplier database, while suppliers register for free. Buyers can then use AirportSmart to manage requests for information or quotations that suppliers are invited to participate in.

9.3.4 End-users

Airports have a range of end-users including general aviation, workers at the airport, visitors accompanying passengers, local residents and passers-by, but the main focus here is on the passenger. Airports do tend to levy charges for passengers to use their facilities and services. The transaction normally occurs via airlines that act as intermediaries. Airlines include the charge in the price of the ticket they sell to passengers and pass the income on to airports (see Chapter 7). This helps to simplify the processing of passengers at airports: without it, airports would need to collect the charge from each passenger. Because of this, the passenger's contractual relationship is with their airline; this is one reason airlines feel that they, and not airports, own the passenger. However, airports can still play an important role in the distribution process and support the distribution efforts of their airline customers, especially via the internet.

At the end of 2011, the estimated number of internet users worldwide was 2.3 billion: approximately 33 per cent of the world's population. Internet penetration is particularly high in North America (79 per cent) and Europe (61 per cent) (Internet World Stats, 2012). The internet plays an increasingly important role in the way airports conduct business, allowing them to reduce costs and customise the products and services they offer to meet the specific needs of target markets (Gillen and Lall, 2002).

Nintey-four per cent of world airports now have their own website or feature on a corporate website of some kind (Halpern, 2012). Airport websites have traditionally focused on offering general information for passengers (e.g. about flight information, travel to/from the airport, and passenger services and facilities at the airport), but have more recently started to provide travel tips and information. Providing general information and travel planning support to passengers is only one of a number of benefits airports can achieve by having an online presence. Airport websites also 'offer an outstanding opportunity to sell a whole range of services directly through a fast, convenient channel' (Twentyman, 2010: 47). Halpern and Regmi (2013) find that 30 per cent of airports in Europe are already using their web presence to sell directly to passengers, including products and services such as flights, car parking, hotels, car rental, foreign currency, wi-fi access, executive lounge access and fast-track security. From a retail perspective, diversifying distribution channels via the internet is important for optimising success. Many airports now offer opportunities such as pre-order retail for collection at the airport, home delivery or collection on arrival. This can make the airport buying experience smoother and has space-saving implications as a result of reducing the need to display goods (Bamberger *et al.*, 2009). Frankfurt Airport has a 'booking' page on its website that offers opportunities to book flights worldwide, package holidays (including last minute deals), hotels in Frankfurt, car rental at the airport, sightseeing trips, day rooms and family rooms at the airport, 'park-sleep-fly' (for passengers wishing to book parking, accommodation and transfer to/from the airport), phone cards and hot spot access. It is also possible to pre-order duty free from the 'shop & enjoy' section of the website.

Airport websites have the opportunity to support the distribution of services offered by their partners (e.g. airlines, retailers and the travel trade) by providing passengers with hyperlinks from their site to the booking pages of partner websites. They may also act as a host agency and provide advertising space and hyperlinks to other websites where commission might be made from subsequent sales on those websites. Growth in the use of social media has provided airports with specific opportunities for a more targeted approach to passengers. It allows them to promote and directly or indirectly sell a range of products and services. This can take place during and outside normal trading times, and makes use of a dynamic range of distribution channels that are driven more by interaction than transaction. Airport websites can act as a platform for social media and related online initiatives.

Figure 9.4 provides an example of the website for Frankfurt Hahn Airport. In addition to providing general information and travel planning support to passengers, the website has a 'travel tips' section that provides up-to-date information on sightseeing opportunities, activities and events in Frankfurt and surrounding areas, and also in the foreign destinations served by its airlines. The website has an 'aviation' section with information for passenger airlines and cargo operators, including the schedule of airport charges and marketing support. The airport uses its web presence to sell directly to passengers, including car parking and duty free; this includes the opportunity to pre-order duty free for collection at the airport. The website supports the distribution of products and services offered by their partners including airlines, retailers and the travel trade by providing passengers with hyperlinks from their site to the booking pages of partner websites such as Ryanair, Wizz Air, Sun Express, Heinemann Duty Free, rental car companies, car and bus charter companies, hotels, travel agents, tour operators and providers of sport and leisure activities. The airport website also provides links to their social media sites on Twitter, YouTube and Facebook.

Figure 9.4 Frankfurt Hahn Airport's homepage
Source: courtesy of Frankfurt Hahn Airport

9.4 CRM

Many service industries are increasingly devoting much of their marketing effort to CRM as a means of managing their interactions with customers. CRM was traditionally viewed as a type of software, but although it is still typically underpinned by technology, it has evolved into a more customer-orientated philosophy that forms part of a company-wide strategy. The basic principle is that CRM uses people, processes and technology to understand and respond to customers in a way that encourages lasting relationships and generates added value. Dyché (2002: 4) defines CRM as 'the infrastructure that enables the delineation of and increase in customer value, and the correct means by which to motivate valuable customers to remain loyal – indeed, to buy again'. It can focus on generating and serving new customers but also on customer retention as a means to maintain long-term relationships (Hoffman *et al.*, 2009). CRM can be used to automate and enhance a range of business processes, especially those relating to sales (e.g. from cross-selling, up-selling or the use of more efficient sales processes), customer service and support (e.g. from improved service and responsiveness to customer needs and behaviour) and marketing (e.g. from improved customer profiling, identification and responsiveness to market trends, and marketing effectiveness).

CRM typically involves gathering data via a range of customer touchpoints. This is entered into what is normally a technology-based CRM system, which allows data to be stored, offers opportunities for analysis and subsequently allows companies to better target customers. Figure 9.5 provides an example of Comarch's CRM suite for airports and illustrates the way airports can gather, analyse and execute data via a range of customer touchpoints. CRM technologies are employed by airports in support of a range of initiatives such as those that enhance passenger travel, customer interactions and communications, and loyalty management.

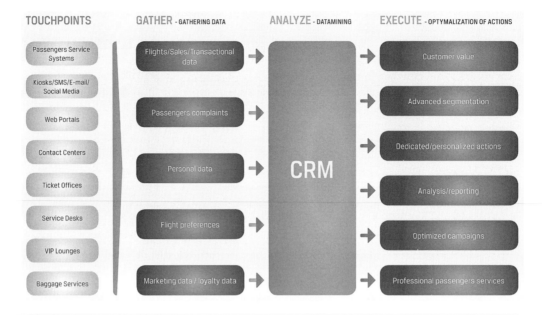

Figure 9.5 Comarch's CRM suite for airports
Source: Comarch (2012)

9.4.1 CRM for enhancing passenger travel

A number of CRM technologies are employed by airports in support of IATA's fast travel programme (IATA, 2012b), the objectives of which are two-fold: to reduce queuing time by providing passengers with more control over their journey and less time to complete airport formalities; and to reduce costs with estimated potential savings of up to USD 2.1 billion across the industry each year. The programme focuses on six key areas: check-in, bag drop, document check, flight re-booking, self-boarding, and bag recovery. By 2012, the following airline and airport pairs had achieved gold status by implementing the full suite of fast travel solutions: SAS and Copenhagen International Airport, British Airways and London Gatwick Airport, Lufthansa and Munich Airport, Air New Zealand and Auckland International Airport, Etihad Airways and Abu Dhabi International Airport, Air China and Beijing Capital International Airport, Lufthansa and Frankfurt Airport, and Iberia and Madrid Barajas Airport. The aim is that 80 per cent of global passengers will be offered a complete self-service suite based on industry standards by 2020.

Check-in has benefited from CRM technologies. For many airports, passengers can check in for their flights on the internet. Some airports offer CUSS kiosks, which can be found in different locations at the airport or even at remote locations such as transport terminals, hotels and conference centres. For example, Edmonton International Airport went live with 28 CUSS kiosks in January 2007: 26 of the kiosks are located throughout the airport terminal, while two Airport Express kiosks are located at the Downtown Visitor Information Centre, allowing passengers to check in for their flight downtown before leaving for the airport. The kiosks are owned by the airport; the vendor is ARINC (provider of communications, integration and engineering solutions). Initial airline users included Air Canada, Alaska Airlines, Northwest Airlines, United Airlines and WestJet. Passengers checking in using one of Edmonton's CUSS kiosks receive a boarding pass to take to their departure gate, either directly or after dropping off their baggage with their airline.

Some airports such as Montréal-Trudeau Airport provide self-service passengers the opportunity to use common bag drops that are assigned to the airport under shared use between airlines. Such technologies can improve capacity utilisation at airports by improving passenger-flow for airlines and passengers, enhancing efficiency and the customer experience. They can also allow airports to reduce infrastructure costs (e.g. for check-in and bag drop), free up space for commercial opportunities and exploit the extra free time passengers will have.

The first major installation of CUSS was launched at McCarran International Airport in 2003 in collaboration between the airport, ARINC and a number of airlines. CUSS was a focus area for IATA's simplifying the business programme, but the CUSS project was formally closed at the end of 2008 as over 100 airports worldwide had implemented CUSS by 2008. IATA continues to maintain the CUSS standard through their common-use working group.

Airports have also cooperated with airlines in recent years to facilitate the introduction of bar coded boarding passes that use IATA industry standard 2D bar codes. 2D bar codes feature black and white dots instead of the traditional bars and can be accessed from anywhere, such as on the internet or a mobile phone, offering increased convenience for passengers while increasing efficiency of throughput and capacity utilisation at airports.

Passenger services and information have also benefited from CRM technologies in recent years. For instance, it is increasingly common to find flight information display systems (FIDS) on screens, PDAs, mobile phones or other devices connected to the internet. Like CUSS kiosks, FIDS are increasingly found at various locations inside the airport but also at remote locations such as transport terminals, hotels and conference centres. Touch-screen technology is also increasingly used by airports. Manchester Airport has touch-screen public information kiosks in its integrated public transport hub. These provide information about onward travel and hotel options at the airport.

9.4.2 CRM for customer interactions and communications

CRM technologies are increasingly used by airports for customer interactions (e.g. to log customer information and activity) and communications (e.g. to manage and evaluate marketing campaigns, promote flights to airlines, sell retail space, manage relationships with suppliers and offer support to contacts). Some well-known examples used by airports include Maximizer, Goldmine and ACT. The focus of such technologies is not only on passengers but on the whole range of airport customers.

Airports are increasingly seeking to integrate CRM systems and data (Airport Technology, 2008). For example, Phoenix Sky Harbor International Airport integrates its FIDS with the public address system and kiosks. This means that the airport is able to page passengers visibly as well as audibly and can send messages to the public address system via its kiosks. Halifax Stanfield International Airport uses CRM software to integrate data used to manage client interactions that were traditionally stored and accessed from different locations such as lease management, billing systems, and client contact and activity reports. Similarly, DAA uses Maximizer CRM software as a reservation and booking system for VIP clients. This allows highly sensitive customer data to be stored in one secure central database instead of being shared across the company by e-mail or word of mouth. The data can be consolidated, categorised and accessed on site or remotely, but only by authorised personnel (Maximizer Software, 2011).

Manchester Airport has been running a CRM project called 'a single view of the customer'. The aim is for the airport to know as much as possible about each of its customers, such as what car park a customer is using, how a customer might respond to e-mail advertising and what a customer has complained about frequently. This can allow the airport to build a picture of the customer and tailor its service to meet their needs (see Manchester Airports Group, 2012).

9.4.3 CRM for loyalty management

A key CRM tool used by airports is a loyalty scheme involving rewards or points on loyalty cards that can then be used to gain discounts or other benefits. Such schemes help companies gain greater insight into the needs of their customers, reduce marketing costs by being more focused on familiar customers and incentivise customers to buy more products. Compared with other industries such as supermarkets, hotels or even airlines with their frequent points, the impact of these is likely to be less significant at airports because of the more limited impact the actual airport product (as opposed to the airline product) can have on passenger choice. Nevertheless it is an increasingly popular tool being used in the airport industry: a recent study showed that a quarter of all airports provided such a scheme, 16 per cent with a free loyalty programme and 10 per cent with a paid membership based on frequent flyer programmes (ACI/DMKA, 2012). A key prerequisite for such schemes to work is to have effective collaboration with the other service partners involved and to ensure that such programmes are not unpopular due to competing with other loyalty schemes, most notably offered by the airlines.

With the free schemes points are earned from travelling and spending at the airport which gives benefits such as discounts on parking and the commercial facilities, and access to fast-track systems and airline frequent flyer mileage. Milan Malpensa Airport has two linked schemes, namely ViaMilano Program and the Club SEA ViaMilano Program, with the latter being more focused towards premium travellers. Elsewhere Singapore Changi Airport has Changi Rewards, Bristol Airport has Bristol Airport Rewards, Dubuque Regional Airport has FlyDBQ Rewards Program, Venice Airport has Club il Milione, Nice Côte d'Azur Airport has Club Airport Premier, Wellington Airport has Wellington Airport VIP, and BAA has BAA World Points. Also in the US there is the loyalty card 'Thanks Again' which can be used at over 100 airports (e.g. at Cincinnati/ Northern Kentucky International Airport), and gives discounts on parking, shopping and eating as well as at local businesses and attractions. One of the main advantages of such schemes is that they encourage passengers to spend more and that they allow airport operators or their concessionaires to gather information about member's purchasing habits which helps provide customised offers.

It is worth noting that some of the free schemes are restricted to frequent flyers. For example, passengers are entitled to join Club il Milione at Venice Airport after they have collected 25 flight points (each domestic flight is worth 1.0 point while each international flight is worth 1.5 points). Passengers are entitled to join Club Airport Premier at Nice Côte d'Azur Airport if they fly out of the airport at least ten times a year.

An example membership card for the FlyDBQ Rewards programme can be seen in Figure 9.6. Dubuque Regional Airport views the scheme as being a way to thank travellers for choosing to fly from the airport, and acts as an incentive for repeat business. FlyDBQ Rewards members are able to save on Dubuque and Tri-State Area products and services. Members simply pass their card within two feet of a card reader located after passing through security, and trip points are automatically updated in a convenient and hassle-free way. The programme consists of four levels of savings determined by trip credits: green (automatically given for signing up and renews each year), yellow (after five trips from Dubuque Regional Airport per calendar year), red (after ten trips), and platinum (after 20 trips). The airport's website offers further features and savings in support of the scheme, and is currently being updated so that it is automatically synched with the card reader, allows members to print savings coupons straight from the website, and sends an e-mail to members when trips have been added to their account. The airport deposited over

480,000 American Airlines AAdvantage miles over the 2011/2012 fiscal year to FlyDBQ Rewards members in addition to purchasing several American Airlines Admirals Club memberships. The scheme is also popular with local businesses because it helps to generate interest and sales for their products and services. As a result, many are keen to provide opportunities for savings through the scheme.

Bristol Airport Rewards is another example of a free scheme (see Figure 9.7). Anyone can join the scheme by registering online. This is done by entering an e-mail address on the relevant page of the airport website. Subscribers will then receive a welcome e-mail providing access to a range of special offers online, and will start to receive e-newsletters containing the latest news and special offers from the airport. This typically includes seasonal deals on car parking, flights, holidays and travel extras such as car rental, fast track, executive lounge access, travel insurance, luggage tags and travel assistance; discount vouchers for the airport's shops and restaurants; competitions for travel prizes including flights and holidays; updates about new destinations and special offers; and the opportunity to provide feedback to the airport. Subscribers can unsubscribe anytime.

The other type of loyalty scheme involves regular passengers paying for privileges or enhanced comfort such as access to lounges, fast track and priority processes. Hence, while the free schemes tend to concentrate on incentivising passengers to spend more, these paid for schemes focus on helping passengers travel through the airport more comfortably and swiftly. The programmes can be classified as being VIP clubs or frequent flyer programmes. The former is aimed at a limited number of passengers who want VIP treatment such as personal help through the airport or access to lounges with membership fees in the range of USD 6,500 to 10,500. The latter is more aimed

Figure 9.6 FlyDBQ Rewards programme
Source: courtesy of Dubuque Regional Airport

Figure 9.7 Bristol Airport Rewards
Source: courtesy of Bristol Airport

at passengers who require speediness through airport processes (ACI/DMKA, 2012). For example, Amsterdam Schiphol Airport has its Privium scheme. This includes Privium Basic, which – as of the end of 2012 – costs EUR 121 per year and gives passengers a fast track through border control with an iris scan process, and Privium Plus, which costs EUR 199, and includes the iris scan process and other enhanced features such as nearby or valet parking, business class check-in, access to the club lounge and other discounts and special offers. There is also a partner card costing EUR 73 per year for a spouse or children under 18 of a Privium Basic or Plus member. Similarly, Riga International Airport has a RIX Club card (see Figure 9.8), which gives access to

Figure 9.8 RIX Club
Source: courtesy of Riga International Airport

the business class facilities at the airport for an annual cost of LVL 129 (approximately EUR 185). Lyon Saint Exupéry Airport has a Privilys card, which provides parking, fast track and other services. There are three different types: pass (EUR 60 per year), silver (EUR 120 per year) and gold (prices vary).

Table 9.4 Main features of Airport U

Flight information	Takes feeds from airport information systems. Data is presented in simple, clear format allowing passengers to scroll down. The passenger's own flight and status is displayed prominently on the Personal FID.
Shops and restaurants	Detailed information, maps and directions including website links, phone numbers and opening hours. Passenger profiling can be used to tailor products and promotions to target markets. Promotions and coupons can be sent. Secure payments can be made.
Campaign management	Ability to display top 600 products by brand and price. Ability to reserve and/or buy any of the 600 items via the application. Online and offline capabilities. Opportunities for integration, campaign management and electronic loyalty programmes.
Car parking	Simple, clear, key information about car parks and valet parking including location, availability, cleaning and servicing options, 'mark and find' your car, bookings and secure payments. Can include other modes of transport such as taxis, buses and trains.
Airport information	Simple, clear, key information on passenger services (e.g. airline and information desks, wellness facilities, security points, health services, prayer rooms, and foreign exchange).
Travel extras	Mobile booking, fast track, lounge and special deals. Secure payments delivered to mobile devices and tied to individual phones and/or users. Web purchases. eCommerce and mCommerce integration.
Social media integration and Uzone	Full integration with social media including Facebook and Twitter. Can use social media to drive usage. The app is environment monitored, controlled and owned by the airport. Opportunities to promote offers on social media.
Secure payments	Secure transaction platform offering a trusted relationship between airport and clients. Secure end-to-end transactions within the app. Up to four-factor authentication.

Source: adapted from Airport U (2012)

9.4.4 Social CRM

CRM has traditionally allowed companies to better target customers, largely through pushed messages. The concept of social CRM has emerged in recent years; this supports the evolution of CRM into a more customer-orientated philosophy because in addition to pushing company-driven messages, it allows companies to interact with customers and can involve everyone in the company, not just those that work with CRM. Social CRM has been encouraged initially by eCommerce or electronic commerce via the internet (although that was still largely based on pushing messages) but more recently by mCommerce or mobile commerce via mobile technologies including laptop computers, mobile devices, tablets such as the Apple iPad and mobile applications commonly referred to as 'apps'.

Airport U is a multi-channel mCommerce platform for airports released in 2011, which can be used by passengers on smartphones and tablets including iPhone, Android, iPad and Kiosk. The platform offers a number of main features (see Table 9.4). Liverpool John Lennon Airport released myLJLA in June 2012 for multiple Apple and Android devices. myLJLA was developed by Airport U using their mCommerce platform and is currently the airport's official mobile application that uses the features listed in Table 9.4. Example iPhone screenshots for myLJLA are provided in Figure 9.9. It is important to note that social CRM is not a replacement for traditional CRM, but can be integrated into existing approaches to CRM. This is illustrated in Figure 9.5 via the touchpoints such as web portals and kiosks, SMS, e-mail and social media.

Figure 9.9 iPhone screenshots for myLJLA
Source: courtesy of Airport U

References

ACI (2011) *ACI Airport Economics Survey 2011*, Montreal: ACI.

ACI Europe (2011) *ACI Europe Position on Requirements for a Performing Ground Handling Market*, Brussels: ACI Europe.

ACI/DMKA (2012) *ASQ Best Practice Report: Airport Loyalty Programmes*, Montreal: ACI.

Airport Technology (2008) *Relating to the customer*, London: Airport Technology. Online. Available at: http://www.airport-technology.com/features/feature43397/ (accessed 5 April 2012).

Airport U (2012) *Airport U*, Wicklow: Airport U. Online. Available at: http://www.airportu.co.uk (accessed 20 October 2012).

AirportSmart (2012) *Welcome to AirportSmart*, Birmingham: AirportSmart Limited. Online. Available at: http://www.airportsmart.com/en/home.asp (accessed 15 October 2012).

Bamberger, V., Bettati, A., Hoeffinger, S., Kuruvilla, T. and Wille, V. (2009) *Mastering Airport Retail: Roadmap to New Industry Standards*, Paris: Arthur D. Little.

Bass, T. (1994) 'Infrastructure constraints and the EU', *Journal of Air Transport Management* 1(3); 145–50.

City of San José (2010) *Audit of the Airport's Parking Management Agreement*, San José: City of San José.

Comarch (2012) *Comarch Travel CRM: Airport Suite*, Krakow: Comarch.

Dyché, J. (2002) *The CRM Handbook: A Business Guide to Customer Relationship Management*, Boston: Addison-Wesley Professional.

EC (1993) *Council Regulation (EEC) No 95/93 of 18 January 1993 on Common Rules for the Allocation of Slots at Community Airports*, Official Journal L14, 22 January, Brussels: EC.

EC (1996) *Council Directive 96/67/EC of 15 October 1996 on Access to the Groundhandling Market at Community Airports*, Official Journal L272, 25 October, Brussels: EC.

FAA (2012) 'High density traffic airports; notice of determination regarding low demand periods at Ronald Reagan Washington National Airport', *Federal Register: Rules and Regulations*, 77(62); 19076–7.

Gillen, D. and Lall, A. (2002) 'The economics of the Internet, the new economy and opportunities for airports', *Journal of Air Transport Management*, 8(1); 49–62.

Graham, A. (2008) *Managing Airports: An International Perspective*, 3rd edn, London: Butterworth-Heinemann.

Halpern, N. (2012) 'Use of social media by airports', *Journal of Airline and Airport Management*, 2(2); 66–84.

Halpern, N. and Regmi, U.K. (2013) 'Content analysis of European airport websites', *Journal of Air Transport Management*, 26(1); 8–13.

Hoffman, D., Bateson, J., Wood, E. and Kenyon, A. (2009) *Services Marketing: Concepts, Strategies and Cases*, London: Centage Learning.

IATA (2012a) *Worldwide Slot Guidelines: Effective January 2012*, Montreal: IATA.

IATA (2012b) *Fast Travel Program*, Montreal: IATA.

Internet World Stats (2012) *Internet usage statistics*, Bogota: Miniwatts Marketing Group. Online. Available at: http://www.internetworldstats.com/stats.htm (accessed 20 September 2012).

JCDecaux (2012) *Airport advertising*, New York: JCDecaux. Online. Available at: http://www.jcdecauxna.com/airport/airport-advertising (accessed 5 October 2012).

Karp, A. (2010) *DFW, IND use agreements differ from traditional airport-airline accords*, Silver Spring: ATWOnline. Online. Available at: http://atwonline.com/airports-routes/article/dfw-ind-use-agreements-differ-traditional-airport-airline-accords-1206 (accessed 12 August 2012).

Kim, H-B. and Shin, J-H. (2001) 'A contextual investigation of the operation and management of airport concessions', *Tourism Management*, 22(2); 149–55.

Knevitt, G. (2012) *Paradies secures 10-year master concession at Long Beach Airport*, Brentford: The Moodie Report. Online. Available at: http://www.moodiereport.com/document.php?c_id=1124&doc_id=30329 (accessed 12 September 2012).

Kotler, P., Wong, V., Saunders, J. and Armstrong, G. (2008) *Principles of Marketing*, 5th European edn, Harlow: Prentice Hall-Pearson Education.

LeighFisher (2011) *ARCP Report 54: Resource Manual for Airport In-Terminal Concessions*, Washington, DC: Transportation Research Board.

London Heathrow Airport (2011) *Heathrow Airport Limited Conditions of Use Including Airport Charges from 1 April 2011*, Hounslow: Heathrow Airport Limited.

Manchester Airports Group (2012) *A single view of the customer*, Manchester: The Manchester Airports Group. Online. Available at: http://www.ieltd.co.uk/customerservice/single_view.html (accessed 10 August 2012).

Maximizer Software (2011) *DAA flies high with Maximizer CRM*, Vancouver: Maximizer Software. Online. Available at: http://www.max.co.uk/case-studies/daa (accessed 15 September 2012).

Moodie, M. (2012) *Aer Rianta International and Shilla partner in LAX duty free bid*, Brentford: The Moodie Report. Online. Available at: http://www.moodiereport.com/document.php?c_id=6&doc_id=30586 (accessed 10 August 2012).

SH&E (2002) *Study on the Quality and Efficiency of Ground Handling Services at EU Airports as a Result of the Implementation of Council Directive 96/97/EC*, London: SH&E Limited.

Starkie, D. (2011) *Airport-airline relationships and contracts: A proposal*, Amsterdam: The Airneth Column. Online. Available at: http://www.airneth.nl./news/details/article/airport-airline-relationships-and-contracts-a-proposal (accessed 15 September 2012).

Twentyman, J. (2010) 'Web wonders', *Airport World*, 15(5); 47–50.

Welling, D. (2012) *Westfield wins LAX concession*, Twickenham: Aviation Media. Online. Available at: http://airport-world.com/news-articles/item/1321-westfield-wins-lax-concession (accessed 25 September 2012).

Index

Aberdeen Airport 197
academic study of airport marketing 5–7
accessibility of an airport 122
advertising 169–73, 206; mass-media forms of 172–3; online 173; strengths and weaknesses of 173, 185
Aer Rianta International (ARI) 203–5
Aéroports de Montréal 127
Aéroports de Paris 21
aerotropoli 139
agreements made between airports in 2012 103–4
air fares 34–5
Air France 54, 103
air passenger duty (APD) 35, 155, 164
air service development (ASD) process 66–71; *see also* route development
air traffic control 96
air traffic management (ATM) 37–8
air transport, demand for 1, 32
Airbus A380 37, 120
Aircraft Owners and Pilots Association (AOPA) 179
aircraft parking 150–1
aircraft types 37, 39, 120
Airline Business (magazine) 173
airline developments 29–31
airline presentations 175
airlines: airports' relationships with 195–8; dominant 200
airport cities 139
airport-collaborative decision-making (A-CDM) 37–8
airport development groups 108–9
airport distribution 193–216; approaches to 195–209; definition of 193; evolution of 195
airport marketing: concept and definition of 7–8, 186; evolution of 1–7; growth of 4–5; levels of 13
airport 'product' 117–39; *augmented* and *core* elements of 118–19, 131, 134; definition of 117–20; features of 120–4; holistic approach to 133; levels of value proposition for 119;

planning of 133–9; *tangible* and *intangible* components of 117–20, 131
airport service quality (ASQ) data 78, 131–2
Airport U platform 215–16
airport use agreements 196
Airports Council International (ACI) 71, 78, 131, 175, 182, 203
Airports of Thailand 103
AirportSmart 207
AI-SATs consortium 199
Akron-Canton Airport 181, 184
American Marketing Association 7–8
AMPCO System Parking 206
Amsterdam Schiphol Airport 22–4, 56, 65, 103, 135–8, 158, 214
Anchorage International Airport 37
anna.aero website 173–4
Ansoff, Igor (and Ansoff growth matrix) 101–5
Antonio B. Won Pat International Airport 156
Arab Spring (2011) 24
Armstrong, G. 8, 188
Association of Southeast Asian Nations (ASEAN) 2, 29
Athens International Airport 56, 58, 83, 103–4
Australia 85, 94, 157
aviation service providers 198–203
Avinor 163, 166

bag drops 211
baggage processing 39
Bahrain International Airport 37, 137
Baker, M. 4, 101
Bali bombing (2002) 24
Barcelona El Prat Airport 155
bargaining positions 193–4
Barkley Regional Airport 127
Basel-Mulhouse Airport 125
Belfast International Airport 35
Belkin (company) 184
Bergen Tourist Board and Flesland Airport 190
Best, George 126
Birmingham Airport 78, 127, 129, 171–2

booking data 72
Boston Consulting Group (BCG) matrix 91–3, 102
branding of airports 8, 125–30
Brassington, F. 90–2, 114, 179
Brazil 157
'BRIC' countries 33
Brisbane Airport 127
Bristol Airport 212–14
British Airports Authority (BAA) 3, 21, 26, 189, 212
British Airways 54, 135
British Columbia 100
Brussels Airport 68
Brussels South Charleroi Aiport (BSCA) 69, 125, 150–1, 159–60
budget airlines see low-cost carriers
budgeting by airports 109, 114–15, 189
build–operate–transfer (BOT) projects 26–7
business-only flights 53–4
business-to-business (B2B) transactions 118, 193–5
business-to-consumer (B2C) transactions 118, 195
business travel 36, 56, 134–7

Cambridge Airport 84
Canberra Airport 96
car parking 137, 206
carbon-neutral airports 41
Cardiff International Airport 99
cargo transport 1, 22, 32, 46–50, 55, 85–6, 120–1
Castellón Airport 169–70
catchment areas of airports 48, 67–70, 85
cause-and-effect relationships, testing of 64
'challengers' 105
Changi Airport see Singapore Changi Airport
charter airlines 55, 61, 96, 99
Chartered Institute of Marketing (CIM) 7–8
Chartered Institute of Public Relations (CIPR) 179
check-in facilities 38, 210
Cheddi Jagan International Airport 127
Chhatrapati Shivaji International Airport 128–9
Chicago Convention (1944) 24
Chicago Rockford Airport 125
choice of airport: for airlines 54, 122; for cargo 49–50; for passengers 48–51, 120
Christchurch International Airport 107, 127
'churn' on air routes 2
Civil Aviation Authority (CAA) 68–9
climate change 39–40
collaboration between airports and their partners or stakeholders 189–90
Comarch 209–10
commercial facilities at airports 2, 32, 46–8, 57–8, 66, 96, 117, 122, 124, 131, 138–9, 144, 195, 203–7
common-use self-service (CUSS) 38; CUSS kiosks 210–11

community relations 121
'compensatory' and 'residual' approaches to regulation of airport charges 157–8
competition: between airlines 188, 196; between airports 1, 21–2, 29, 65, 68–9, 93–7, 103, 118, 134, 144, 188; for ground handling services 200; within airports 136–7
competitive tendering 204, 206
concession management 26–7, 156, 200, 203–6
Concorde 37
congestion at airports, levels of 197–8
consolidation of airlines 30–1
Continental Airlines 35
contracts, short-term and long-term 197
Cooper, C. 13
Copenhagen Airport 15, 83, 130, 135–7, 163
Cork Airport 155, 163
corporate intentions of airports 89–91
'cost leadership' strategy 106
cost-recovery through airport charges 148, 157
Court of First Instance, European 160
crisis events 36
cruise ship passengers 139
CUSS see common-use self-service
customer markets for airports 20
customer relationship management (CRM) 209–16; definition of 209; for enhancing passenger travel 210–11; for interaction and communication with customers 211–12; for loyalty management 212–15; social 216
customer satisfaction 66, 78–9, 131–2
customers: of airlines 134–7; of airports 45–52, 65; see also end-users of airports

Dallas Executive Airport 97–8
Dallas/Fort Worth International Airport 15–16, 59, 105, 124, 183–4, 188–9, 196
Dallas Love Field 105
Darwin Airport 4, 96
Daytona Beach International Airport 84
decision-making on marketing 101–7
delays to flights 131
Denver International Airport 130
deregulation 2, 29–30, 34, 65, 159, 185, 196, 203
derived demand 165, 195
Desai, P. 50
descriptive research 64
destination surveys 84
Dibb, S. 52, 60
differentiation strategy 106–7, 133–4
direct distribution 193, 195
direct leasing 204–5
direct marketing 173–5; strengths and weaknesses of 185
direct operation of services by airports 203

discounted user charges 162
distribution channels *see* airport distribution
distribution structure of an airport 193–4
diversification by airports 103
Doha International Airport 137
Dolby, N. 177–8
dominant airlines 200
Don Mueang International Airport 163
Doran, G.T. 101
Dubai Airport 17, 21, 37, 57, 107, 122
Dublin Airport 68, 81, 121, 137–8, 154–5, 163
Dubuque Regional Airport 212–13
duty-free shopping 52, 177
Dyché, J. 209

East Midlands Airport 19, 125, 196
economic influences on airports 32–5
Edmonton International Airport 210–11
'80/20 rule' on use of slots 197
e-marketing 4
emissions 39–41
emissions charges 152
emissions trading 41
employee numbers at airports in relation to
    passengers 46
employee surveys 84
end-users of airports 207–8
'entry into service' process 197
environmental influences on airports 28, 39–41
European Union (EU) 2, 24, 28–9, 96, 122, 147,
    159–60, 166, 198–203
evaluation of marketing programmes 114–15
expenditure on airport marketing 5–7
experiential research 64
explanatory research 64

Facebook 180–1
family-oriented airport products 137–8
family size and structure, trends in 36
Federal Aviation Authority (FAA) 160–1, 198
Federal Express 55
Ferrell, O. 52, 63
financial intermediaries 19–20
FIschert, F. 161
fixed costs of airports 143
flag carriers 53
flight information display systems (FIDS) 211
FlyDBQ Rewards programme 212–13
focus groups 86
'followers' 105–6
forecasts of air travel 33–4, 69, 97
Fort Smith Regional Airport 171
'four Ps' of airport marketing 10–11
Francis, G. 54
Frankfurt Airport 51, 56–7, 83, 103, 137, 139,
    177, 208

Frankfurt Hahn Airport 105, 125, 136, 208–9
Freathy, P. 45–6, 56
freight forwarding companies 22, 118
frequent flyer programmes 212–14
fuel, charges for supply of 152
future prospects for aviation 41–2; *see also*
    forecasts of air travel

Gardiner, J. 49
Gatwick Airport *see* London Gatwick Airport
Gebr Heinemann 177
generic strategy framework (Porter) 106
Geneva Airport 83
Glasgow Prestwick Airport 127
global alliances of airlines 30, 53, 134
Global Infrastructure Partners (GFP) 28
global warming *see* climate change
goals as distinct from objectives 101
Gold Coast Airport 123–4
Graham, A. 46, 56, 94, 106
'grandfather rights' to slots 29, 53, 121
Greece 200
greenhouse gases 40
'grey' market 36
ground handling services 28, 96, 121–2, 144, 162,
    195, 198–203; charges for 152–5, 200
groups of airports 143, 197
growth strategy based on market dominance 105–6

Habitat 184
Haikou Meilan International Airport 68
Halifax Stanfield International Airport 127, 130,
    211
Halpern, N. 172, 180–2, 208
hanger charges 150
Hanover Airport 128
'harvesting' 101
Hazel, B. 46
Heathrow Airport *see* London Heathrow Airport
Heathrow Express link 122
Helsinki-Vantaa Airport 127
Hermann, N. 46
Herzog, Harry 4
holiday traffic 94, 99
Honda 184
Hong Kong Airlines 54
Hong Kong International Airport 138, 163
hub airports 21, 96
Humberside Airport 19
Humphreys, J. 4

immigration procedures 25
implementation of marketing programmes 108–15
'importance–performance' analysis of customer
    satisfaction 132
impulse purchases 177–8

incentive mechanisms 159–67
Incheon International Airport 163
income of airports *see* revenues
India 29, 159
Indianapolis International Airport 196
industrial marketing 4
information technology, use of 188
infrastructure of an airport 48, 120
Institute of Civil Engineers (ICE) 41–2
integrated marketing communications, definition of 188
intermediaries used by airports 193–4, 207
International Air Transport Association (IATA) 25, 29, 71–2, 121, 197–8, 210–11
International Civil Aviation Organisation (ICAO) 24, 28, 71–2, 147, 152, 155
internet use 38, 122, 207–8
investment by airports 144
Ireland West Airport Knock 125, 186
isochrones 67–8
Istanbul Ataturk Airport 21

James, J. 132
James, LeBron 184
Japan 158
Jarach, D. 6, 22, 60, 119
JCDecaux 206
John F. Kennedy International Airport 107, 137, 196
John Lennon Airport *see* Liverpool John Lennon Airport
joint ventures 198–200, 205, 207
Jones, D. 3

Kansai International Airport 15
Karlsruhe/Baden-Baden Airport 162
Kim, H.-B. 203
King County International Airport 99
Klophaus, R. 161
Kotler, P. 8, 52, 60, 188
Kramer, L. 5–6
Kuala Lumpur International Airport (KLIA) 103, 127, 137, 149

landing charges 150–1
Lauterborn, B. 10
'leakage' of traffic between airports 69, 72–3, 78
legal influences on the airport industry 24, 200
LeighFisher 203
leisure travel 56, 138
liberalisation of air travel 29–30, 34, 200
Liege Airport 105, 107
Lisbon Airport 131
Liverpool John Lennon Airport 127, 216
local businesses, airports' surveys of 85
local residents, airports' surveys of 85

location of airports, importance of 120
logos of airports 128
London Biggin Hill Airport 68
London City Airport 22, 54, 61, 83–4, 105, 107, 134–5, 171
London Gatwick Airport 29, 68, 127–30, 183
London Heathrow Airport 20, 22–4, 37, 50, 56, 68, 80, 83, 122, 127, 134, 137–8, 171–3, 180, 187, 196
London Luton Airport 50, 122–3, 183
London Stansted Airport 50, 68, 84, 127, 137–8
Long Beach Municipal Airport 205
long-haul services 37, 47
long-term contracts 197
Los Angeles International Airport 47, 105, 205
low-cost carriers (LCCs) 2, 22, 30–1, 36, 46, 50, 54–6, 61, 69, 94, 96, 99, 107, 121, 125, 135–6, 144–5, 150, 159, 188; groups of 54; types of 56
low-cost terminals 136
loyalty schemes 102, 119, 212–15
Lufthansa 53–4, 177
Luton Airport *see* London Luton Airport
Luxor Temple attack (1997) 24
Lyon Saint Exupéry Airport 127, 215

Macau International Airport 127, 151, 163–4
McCarran International Airport, Las Vegas 124, 130, 211
McCarthy, J. 10
McDonald, M. 88, 91
McKinsey/General Electric (GE) matrix 91, 93
macroenvironment of an airport 13–14, 24–42, 93
Madrid Barajas airport 155
majority-in-interest (MII) clauses 196
Malaysia Airports 127, 138, 149, 186–7
Malina, R. 161
Manchester Airport 50, 80, 122–3, 134, 154, 211–12
market for airport services 45–61
market development 103
market leaders 105
market penetration 102–3
market research 195; as distinct from marketing research 63
marketing: definition of 7–8, 186; in service industries 8–10; *see also* direct marketing
marketing audit: external 93–8; internal 91–3
marketing communications: budgeting for 189; effectiveness of 189–90; strategies for 195; *see also* integrated marketing communications
marketing control 114
marketing intelligence 63
marketing intermediaries 19–20
marketing mix 9–10, 45, 66, 142–3
marketing objectives 101–2, 109, 143

'marketing-oriented era' of airport development 3–4

marketing planning, definition of 88; *see also* planning of airport marketing

marketing programmes for airports 108–15

marketing research: categories of 66; definition of 63

marketing strategies 101

'marketing support' for new or changed routes 162, 165–6

Martilla, J. 132

Martinez-Garcia, E. 56

mass-media communications 172–3, 186–8; shift away from 188

Memphis International Airport 130

Menzies-Bobba consortium 199

Miami International Airport 151, 155

microenvironment of an airport 13–24, 94

micromarkets 188

Milan Malpensa Airport 212

minimum connect time (MCT) 134–5

Minota San José International Airport 206

mission statements 89

mixed messages 188

monopoly situations 156, 200

Montréal-Trudeau Airport 211

Moscow Domodedovo Airport 127

Munich Airport 50–1, 127

Muskoka Airport 98–9

'mystery shoppers' 86

Nairobi Jomo Kenyatta International Airport 150

names of airports 125–9

'narrowcasting' 188

network carriers 53

New York City and Port Authority 4, 21

New Zealand 157

NextGen project 38

Niagara Falls International Airport 164

Nice Côte d'Azur Airport 72–3, 212

niche strategies 105, 107

Nigam, S. 180

night flying restrictions 39

Niskala, J. 172

noise levels and related charges 39, 152

Northolt airport 68

Norwegian (airline) 37

objectives as distinct from goals 101

observational research 64, 86

O'Connell, F. 45–6, 56

Official Airline Guide (OAG) 71–2

oil, charges for supply of 152

Ontario Airport 105

'open market' agreements 2

'open skes' agreements 2, 29

operating costs: of airlines 34–5; of airports 5, 109, 143–5

operational control 114

ORC International 132

organisational structures of airports 15–17

origin/destination (O–D) data 72

Orlando International Airport and Orlando Executive Airport 99–100, 130, 206–7

outsourcing 17–19

package tours 36

Pajala-Ylläs Airport 172–3

Pantares agreement (1999) 103

The Paradies Shops 205

Paris Charles de Gaulle Airport 37

parking *see* car parking; aircraft parking

partnerships entered into by airports 65

passenger experience at an airport 132–3

passenger facility charges (PFCs) 149–50

passenger service charges (PSCs) 148–50, 161–2

passenger surveys 66, 73–8, 80–4

passive approach to marketing 1, 195

Paternoster, J. 125

penetration rates of airports 52

perceived value of a product or service 142

performance indicators 78

permission to land and take off *see* slot allocations

personal selling 175–7; strengths and weaknesses of 185

PESTE *see* political and legal, economic, technological and environmental

Pettitt, S. 90–2, 114, 179

Phoenix Sky Harbor International Airport 164–6, 211

planning: of airport marketing 88–115; of airport products 133–9

political influences on the airport industry 24–6

political and legal, economic, technological and environmental (PESTE) analysis 14, 41–2

Porter, Michael E. 55, 94, 106–7

portfolio analysis 91–3

Portuguese airports 127

positioning strategies 60–1, 133

Prague Airport 164

premium passengers 137

'price cap' approach to airport regulation 158–9

pricing decisions faced by airports 142–67; control over 144; influences on 142–4

Pride, W. 52, 63

primary customers of airports 45–6

primary research 64–5, 79–86

Prince George Airport 181

Privatair 53–4

privatisation 3, 26–30

process metrics 114

product development by airports 103

product metrics 114
promotion of airports 169–90
promotional mix 169–70, 181–2
promotional tools, strengths and weaknesses of 185–6
public–private partnerships (PPPs) 26
public relations 171, 179–80; definition of 179; media used in support of 180; publics targeted by means of 179; strengths and weaknesses of 185
publicity information about airports 169, 172
publicly-owned airports 3

qualitative research 64–5
quality of service 28
quality service index (QSI) 70
quantitative research 64–5
questionnaires, use of 80

rail services, high-speed 94
Rajiv Gandhi International Airport 199
Rankin, W. 99
rate-of-return approach to airport regulation 158
re-branding 127
Regmi, U.K. 208
regulation of air transport 24, 28–9, 96, 144, 156–9, 200
relationship marketing 4; see also customer relationship management
requests for proposals (RFPs) 110, 156, 175
research on airport marketing 63–86
resources for marketing programmes 108–14
'revenue cap' approach to airport regulation 158
revenue guarantees 162
revenues of airports 145–7
Riga International Airport 152, 214–15
risk-sharing arrangements 144, 159–66
RIX Club 214–15
Robin Hood Airport 126
route development 173, 175, 196; see also air service development (ASD)
route development forums 175–6
route development funds 27, 162, 166
Route Exchange website 175, 196
The Route Shop website 48–9, 68, 70, 174, 196
Routes Online website 48–9
Royo-Vela, M. 56
Ryanair 38, 69, 152, 155, 159–60

sales promotion 177–8; strengths and weaknesses of 185
Salzburg Airport 61
Scottish Enterprises 166
search engine optimisation 173
secondary airports 22, 125
secondary customers of airports 45–6

secondary research 64, 71–9
security at airports 65; levels of 25–6
security charges at airports 151–2
segmentation of airport markets 52–61; appropriate variables for 52–3; for cargo 52; for passengers 52, 56
self-handling by airlines 200
self-service kiosks 38
September 11th 2001 attacks 24–5
service charges see passenger service charges
service level agreements 119, 199–203
service quality 66, 78
service targets 28
services, characteristics of 9–10
Shannon Airport 29, 121, 155, 163
Shaw, S. 14, 55
Shell directional policy matrix 91
Shin, J.-H. 203
shopping behaviour at airports 57–9
short-term contracts 197
Singapore Airlines 54
Singapore Changi Airport 15–17, 33, 37, 57, 103, 107, 122, 127, 138, 177–8, 212
'single till' and dual till' approaches to regulation of airport charges 156–9
'sister agreements' 103–4
situation analysis 91–100
Skytrax 78
slogans adopted by airports 127–8, 171
slot allocations 29, 48, 53, 121, 197–9; airports' role in 199
smaller airports 50, 93, 99, 108, 122
'SMART' objectives 101
social attitudes to air travel 40–1
social customer relationship management (social CRM) 216
social marketing 4
social media 208; definition of 180; strengths and weaknesses of 185
social media marketing 4, 180–6
socio-cultural influences on airports 36–7
socio-cultural trends 93
Southampton Airport 84
Southwest (airline) 50
Spain 3, 155, 169, 200
'speak your mind' platforms 184
specialist retailers 52
sponsorship 169–71
stakeholders 22–4
Stansted Airport see London Stansted Airport
Starkie, D. 196–7
state-owned airlines 29
statistics of air transport 71–3
status symbols, airports regarded as 3–4
Stewart International Airport 127
Stockholm Arlanda Airport 139

Stockholm Arlanda Airport 51–2, 125
straplines 171
strategic control 114
subsidiary companies of airport operators 199,
    203–4
subsidies for airport operations 106
substitutes for airports 94–6
suppliers to airports 17–19, 207
surveys, airports' use of 73–86
Swedavia 176–7
'SWOT' analysis 98
Sydney Airport 90, 137
Sykes, W. 50

Tallinn Airport 153–4, 161
Tampa International Airport 189
targeting strategies 60–1
taxation 35, 155
'technical stop' airports 37
technological change 93
technological influences on airports 37–9
terminal facilities 38
terminal rental charges 155
Thelle, M.H. 1, 4–5
Thomson (charter airline) 37
Topping, P. 178
touch-screen information kiosks 211
tour operators 46, 175
tracking of passengers 86
trade magazines 173
trade sales of airports 26–7
traffic data 71–3
transfer passengers 121–2, 138, 161
transport links to and from airports 39, 50, 122
Transportation Security Administration (TSA), US
    25
travel banks 162–4

travel times 67
trends in air travel 36–9
Tretheway, M. 1
Turin Airport 123
Twentyman, J. 208
Twitter 180–3

UPS 55
Urfer, B. 117
'use it or lose it' rule 29, 196
user charges 147–56; based on cost 148;
    discounted 162

value statements 89
VanAuken, Kristie 181
Vancouver International Airport 130, 139
Venice Airport 212
Vienna Airport 127, 161
VIP clubs 213
Virgin Atlantic 55
virtual assistants for passengers at airports 122–3
vision statements 89
visiting friends and relatives (VFR) traffic 36

Washington DC airports 50–1
websites of airports 123, 173, 208
Weinert, R. 117
Wellington Airport 127, 212
Westfield Concession Management 205–6
Wichita Mid-Continent Airport 127
Wilson, H. 88
World Tourism Organization 79
Wright Amendment (US) 105

Youngstown-Warren Regional Airport 164–5

Zurich Airport 5, 152, 196